DECONSTRUCTION MACHINES

Electronic Mediations

Series Editors: N. Katherine Hayles, Peter Krapp,
Rita Raley, and Samuel Weber
Founding Editor: Mark Poster

(continued on page 249)

DECONSTRUCTION MACHINES

Writing in the Age of Cyberwar

Justin Joque

Foreword by Catherine Malabou

Electronic Mediations 54

University of Minnesota Press
Minneapolis · London

Published by the University of Minnesota Press
111 Third Avenue South, Suite 290
Minneapolis, MN 55401-2520
http://www.upress.umn.edu

Printed in the United States of America on acid-free paper

The University of Minnesota is an equal-opportunity educator and employer.

Names: Joque, Justin, author.
Title: Deconstruction machines : writing in the age of cyberwar / Justin Joque ; foreword by Catherine Malabou.
Description: Minneapolis : University of Minnesota Press, 2018. | Includes bibliographical references and index.
Identifiers: LCCN 2017018694 | ISBN 978-1-5179-0251-3 (hc) | ISBN 978-1-5179-0252-0 (pb)
Subjects: LCSH: Deconstruction. | Cyberterrorism.
Classification: LCC B809.6 .J67 2018 | DDC 149/.97–dc23
LC record available at https://lccn.loc.gov/2017018694

UMP BmB 2018

Contents

Foreword

Catherine Malabou

Deconstruction Machines is a book deeply concerned with the technical issues at play in cyberwar, but its fundamental concern is a philosophical one, namely, to what extent should cyberwar be considered the military version of what philosophy has called deconstruction? This is not a question of similitude or analogical thinking; rather, it directly confronts the workings of technology, media, and philosophy today. This deconstructive force of cyberwar is not external to philosophical deconstruction. As such, it forces us to reconsider deconstruction. This militarized deconstruction attacks texts in real time and portends a quicker and more efficient advance than deconstruction itself. In this light, cyberwar appears as a deconstructive threat to deconstruction.

This argument and its implications are sophisticated and powerful. The first striking argument is that cyberwar is doomed to fail. It happens every day and everywhere, such as in the recent attacks by Russian hackers related to the U.S. election, yet it fails; it can't but fail. Its success proves its failure. The success of these attacks calls all sovereignty and any notion of decision into question. Its failure is decidedly not the guarantee of peace or the harmlessness of cyberwar. Indeed, we are told the possibility of the successful failure of cyberwar is a threat to our continued existence: "At the start of the twenty-first century, we are faced with the increasing dependence of our life support systems on global networks and the possibility of systemwide catastrophe."

It is instead the logic of cyberwar that is doomed to fail. Cyberwar, as a military and governmental strategy, aims to control situations and best opponents, but its successful operationalization demonstrates the impossibility of such control. Any logic cyberwar could claim is ultimately undermined by its success. The conditions of possibility appear as conditions of impossibility:

> Whereas cybernetics set out to define a theory of communication and control, in the end, it succeeded in the exact opposite. It ultimately effaced the possibility of control, especially over communication. Cybernetics attempted to describe systems in such a way that they could ultimately be organized and controlled. Its proponents and detractors failed in many ways to realize that while creating, designing, programming, and utilizing computational machines and models, they were at the same time helping to build the very machines that control so clearly struggles with today. Cybernetics helped to create a globally networked system so complex that no known model could ever describe it, let alone regulate it.

The failure of cyberwar, "its collapse upon itself," appears as the failure of global control. The book lists and analyzes all the reasons why what should have been built or constructed (technological sovereignty) in fact turns out to be the deconstruction of such power. The fragility of cryptography, the publicity of all secrets, leaks and their politicization, the entropy of all systems, "the ultimate inability to control and the impossibility of being controlled" to "ever fully account for the heterogeneity of system spaces and translations between them," inscribe precarity at the heart of technological, military, and economic power.

This logic of cyberwar and the insecurity it is built upon appear initially as an inescapable closure, but its ultimate failure proves the impossibility of such a closure. Joque states, "At the same time that the creation of global networks and microscopic means of fighting war seem to condemn us to an increasingly claustrophobic closure, the advent of cyberwar makes it clear that there exists an unpredictable contingency and a heterogeneity of all spaces and systems that can disrupt even the most insidious forms of control and the most ossified systems of sovereignty." Instead of closure, we are confronted with a multiplicity of spaces that escapes control. If we were to stop here, we might think that this book is proposing a kind of contemporary version of Derrida's excellent and striking text, to which Joque refers, "No Apocalypse,

Not Now," where Derrida states that total nuclear war happens in not happening. To the extent that it never has happened, it had no real referent and remains in that sense a fiction. We might initially think that this book is rewriting this text in applying the same idea to cyberwar, switching from nuclear weapons to hacking, from a nuclear apocalypse to an information "apocalyptic catastrophe."

In this regard, points throughout the text clearly return to Derrida building an argument similar to the one advanced in "No Apocalypse." We can enumerate a few examples: the multiplicity of spaces stressed in the first chapter; the affirmation that cyberwar and computation function as writing, immediately raising questions of the archive, knowledge, and information; the absence of the author; the loss of origin (the attribution problem, for example); the undermining of presence, and so on. We could, of course, list others. But all of these confirm and develop the relationship between cyberwar and deconstruction.

But, through the insistence on space and its multiplicity, the analysis here aims at reconfiguring the Derridean system to explicate a logic more threatening, and possibly more deconstructive, than the nuclear theory of "No Apocalypse." Attack and defense in cyberwar create new spatial dimensions: Joque argues, "Geography does not simply disappear. Rather, it is overrun by a variety of additional networks that define, shift, and reshape the power of geography." Though these dimensions may be characterized in terms of the Deleuzian concepts of smooth and striated space, as Joque does in places, this text remains essentially faithful to the Derridean notion of *différance* and textual economy. These spaces, and Joque's development of a theory of spacing, are primarily conceptualized as participating in the inscription and circulation of writing.

It is critical, then, that cyberwar functions not through a pure acceleration but rather through constructing multiple speeds and spaces: "Although there may be an increasing number of connections and interlinkages between and within these spaces, cyberwar does not always fight on the side of connection or disconnection, speed or slowness. Successful strategies seek out specific sites of intervention, creating connections and disconnections alike. Like Deleuzian nomads, they vary their speed: the slowness of geography and earth here and the speed of light there." Cyberwar operationalizes and attacks a textuality that consists simultaneously of marks in place and the movement of these inscriptions through networks of dissemination, networks that are always variable.

Joque argues that "we begin to enter a space of what we could call militarized deconstruction." This new logic blurs the frontiers between the inside and the outside, reminding us of the relationship between speech and writing as Derrida analyzes them, but now taken up for the purposes of global warfare. Writing is not exterior to speech; neither is it interior. Just as writing and speech are heterogeneous to each other, the multiple spatialities and purposes of deconstruction are shown to be heterogeneous to each other. This opening up of the space and purpose of deconstruction presents a dangerous and new force of deconstruction that works on technology directly.

Cyberwar, militarizing this multiplicity of spaces, replicates the logic of deconstruction. Joque notes, "These attacks, despite coming from the outside in a sense, inhabit systems and structures, turning their intended aim against itself." So, it is not a matter of deconstructing the concept of cyberwar but to see cyberwar as deconstruction. This is a very Derridean gesture, to see the movement of these technologies as a force of deconstruction, but a gesture that at the same time is depicted as a threat to the very nature of the Derridean gesture. This text requires us to reconceptualize our very understanding of deconstruction and its future.

The book shows that cyberwar is not only a military version of deconstruction but a deconstructive threat to deconstruction. Joque works on the Derridean text as a hacker, working it over and inhabiting its logic. He identifies what he calls a slippage that Derrida makes in the grammatology, a mistake in the program or the code:

> One possible candidate for the attack vector, to put it in terms of computer security, is a slippage Derrida makes in *Of Grammatology* when discussing the spacing of language. . . . In one instance, Rousseau is read as distributing language and its formation in topological space, a space without distance, and then again, Derrida suggests that Rousseau distributes language throughout topographical space. This slippage between topology and topography immediately suggests one of the central concerns of cyberwar: the movement between connected and disconnected spaces, spaces for which distance matters and spaces of nearly instantaneous movement.

This slippage occurs at a very specific place in the grammatology between topography and topology, developing the spatial logic of deconstruction:

> The replacement of topology with topography suggests a move from *topos,* meaning "place," as *logos* to *topos* as writing and grapheme. But what is at stake between topology and topography cannot simply be the difference between *logos* and writing. Both open the space of deconstruction, but if language requires localization and spacing, it is because spatiality, or spacing, as Derrida says, is a critical component of deconstruction. Thus the shift between topology and topography can never be secondary to the movement of deconstruction. . . . This slippage cannot simply be discovered or put into motion by deconstruction; rather, it defines a difference within deconstruction itself.

It is on the shifting grounds of this multiplication of spaces that we can understand the deconstruction of the opposition between text and program that Joque develops. If space is multiple and unstable, any topological cut internal to writing is always threatened by topography and the plasticity of spatiality. It becomes impossible to maintain a distinction between text and program, between a deconstructable writing and a writing so exact that it offers nothing to be deconstructed. The connections and proximities of computer code expose it to a deconstruction that cannot be held within the bounds of philosophy or literature.

This is exactly what cyberwar attempts to do: to erase the limits between topology and topography, continuity and discontinuity, text and program, militarizing their *différance* and revealing at the same time that deconstruction has not sufficiently spaced itself, conceptualized its own concept of space, thus allowing war and capitalism to destroy it. Without a spacing of deconstruction, it contains no immunity to the threat of cyberwar and its deconstructive force. It appears at first, then, that perhaps the only way to resist global power is then to maintain the difference between topography and topology. Philosophy should be able to open a topographic space within space, to let open the possibility of a recess, which also means that philosophy should vary according to the multiplicity of spaces, vary the resisting means, the concepts, the analyses. *Différance,* as it has been conceptualized to date, is not plastic enough; it attempts to function in an undifferentiated space.

As Joque argues, "in sliding so easily between topology and topography, we risk ignoring the spatial specificity of deconstruction and the other deconstructions that lie within these multiple spatialities, temporalities, and modes of writing. Cyberwar slides into this place between global deconstruction, invents a local and machinic deconstruction, and attacks not "metaphysics" but the specific metaphysics or program of a chosen system." Thus the notion of local deconstructions is very important for moving forward. If philosophy is to succeed in this age of cyberwar, it can no longer adhere to deconstruction writ large but must rather select specific deconstructions and specific localizations.

But how are we to characterize the movement between connection and writing? There is a risk that one repeats the same slippage, not ultimately differentiating connecting and writing. Although recognizing the plasticity of this differentiation is an important step, we still must specify its functioning. How are we to define the movement, the kinesis, between connection and writing? Is it not made of plurality or regimes of movement? And how are we to confront this plurality?

The difference between topology and topography is a very important point and highly contributes to the great value of this work. It is at the heart of the discussion between Derrida and Lacan in the seminar on the purloined letter, which this text takes up in the fourth chapter. In a sense, Derrida criticizes Lacan for not differentiating between topology and topography: the letter's trajectory is always continuous, and in the end, whatever the deformations of the same form, the letter always arrives at its destination. Derrida opposes to this model a discontinuous trajectory: the letter can always be disseminated in the accidents and irregularities of topography and may never arrive at its destination.

Yes, Lacan might have answered, but topology has to include topography because topography alone can never explain a shift. The space of topography offers no radical outside or cut. The topological figures Lacan used to represent Freud's description of the psychical apparatus suggest the importance of these concepts to his thought: the Möbius strip, the Klein bottle, and the cross-cap. In *Seminar XX* (1972–73), Lacan presented a figure that has now become the icon of Lacanian psychoanalysis: the Borromean knot. All of these topological structures structure the psychic topography and create the possibility of a shift, of the movement between places.

In the light of the deconstructive threat of cyberwar, we have to inquire into what this does to the relationship between the conscious and the unconscious. If human language is no longer differentiable from a program, how are we to account for the movement of language from the conscious to the unconscious?

We have to remember that Freud conceives of the ego as a surface, a space, which therefore partakes of both the outside and the inside of the psychical system. In his 1916 *Introductory Lectures on Psychoanalysis,* Freud says that an idea can have the *property* of being conscious or unconscious, stating that psychoanalysis "cannot accept the identity of the conscious and the mental. It defines what is mental as a process such as feeling, thinking and willing, and it is obliged to maintain that there is unconscious thinking and unapprehend willing."[1] In *The Interpretation of Dreams,* he explicitly describes the conscious and the unconscious as *locations* between which ideas circulate. Freud says,

> It is not clear what Fechner had in mind in speaking of this change of *location* of mental activity; nor, so far as I know, has anyone else pursued the path indicated by his words. We may, I think dismiss the possibility of giving the phrase an anatomical interpretation and supposing it to refer to physiological cerebral *localization* or even to the histological layers of the cerebral cortex. It may be, however, that the suggestion will eventually prove to be sagacious and fertile, if it can be applied to a mental apparatus built up from a number of agencies arranged in a series one behind the other.[2]

These *topoi*, these topographical places that are conceptually localizable, are topologically connected. And that is precisely the set of "properties that are preserved through deformations, twisting, and stretching of objects." The deformations of the topographical surface of the ego provided by its topological connections account for the possibility of a shift.

Topology can then account for the fact that an idea goes from one location (the conscious) to another (the unconscious). In the same way, the idea of writing can transform from *différance* to plasticity, or from inscription to connection. It is topology itself that allows the transformation of the idea of writing. It seems, then, that there is a risk in any analysis that one insists too much upon a difference between topology and topography, such as Derrida's comments on Lacan. Without topology, topography is immobilized and open only to contingency, rather than the possibility of a truly radical shift. It is unable to theorize its own plasticity. What if, in the end, Derrida, in eliding the difference between topology and topography in the grammatology, was right when he was wrong? What if topology and topography are nonseparable—and we must include each in the other to describe the kinesis between inscription and connection? We must recognize their difference but, at the same time, their codependence in the movement of thought between inscription and connection. Ultimately, language and writing, and with them the movement of ideas between conscious and unconscious thought, are localized in the connection and inscription of topology and topography.

This book makes an important contribution to the future of philosophy under the threat posed by cyberwar and calls us to reconsider and continue working on the philosophical and deconstructive notion of spatiality. Even as this cyberwar fails and advances by not happening, it threatens philosophy and what we call deconstruction. At the same time, it demonstrates the relevance of deconstruction and philosophy to the twenty-first century. It calls us to think through what role the conscious, the unconscious, and their connection and inscription are to play in the future of a philosophy besieged by a cyberwar that inevitably fails, but is no less dangerous for failing.

Acknowledgments

This book owes its existence to innumerable friends, colleagues, thinkers, writers, and computers. Elliott Mallen, Jean-Christophe Plantin, Daniel Tutt, and Aaron McCullough provided generous feedback for which I am grateful. This book also owes much to the extensive feedback provided by the reviewers at the University of Minnesota Press; their criticisms, suggestions, and careful reading have greatly helped the development of this book. I am also incredibly thankful for the feedback and support provided by Robyn Anspach (who agreed to marry me somewhere along the way of writing this book).

Furthermore, it would not have been possible to complete this work without the support and understanding of my colleagues at the University of Michigan Library. This book also owes an immeasurable debt of gratitude to Wolfgang Schirmacher, his little school in the Swiss Alps, and the many dear friends I met there; this book would not exist if not for that place and all the people who make it what it is. Finally, I would especially like to thank Catherine Malabou for her feedback, assistance, and intellectual guidance on this project.

INTRODUCTION

Root Kit

At the start of the twenty-first century, we are faced with the increasing dependence of our life support systems on global networks and the possibility of systemwide catastrophe. From energy supplies to agriculture to the global climate, these systems are now directly exposed to global fluctuations and, with them, the possibility that a local breakdown could spread globally. We seem to be learning repeatedly that the unavoidable dark side of our networks of communication, production, finance, and information is the ever-present threat of contagion and cascading system failure.

Nowhere is the logic of this threat of global system breakdown clearer than in the expanding discourse around cyberwar. Over the past decades, a growing chorus of politicians, military strategists, computer security experts, and journalists has cited the dangers and opportunities that the subversion of digital systems provides for future conflicts. Governments are investing increasing amounts of energy and money in guaranteeing that they can attack, subvert, and monitor opponents' digital networks, from command-and-control systems to banking to electric grids. The early outbreaks of cyberwar, such as a series of Russian attacks on Estonia in 2007, have resulted mainly in temporary inconveniences, but as militaries invest in being able to destroy physical infrastructure through networked attacks and governments attempt to subvert other states, future cyberwars threaten the possibility of massive destruction and destabilization.

Cyberwar seizes directly on the networked nature of twenty-first-century economic, military, and communicative power by exploiting vulnerabilities, bugs, and insecurities in the code and systems that run these networks; the more well connected and technologically advanced one is, the more one has to fear the contagious threat of both networked accidents and attacks. The military investment in cyberwar and the political, media, and economic responses to acts of cyberwar speak directly to the complicated nature of our networks and information technologies. It is here, where these technical, programmatic, and social systems begin to break down and are transformed into sites of military intervention, that we can most fully begin to elucidate what is at stake in these global networks.

DEFINING CYBERWAR

There is no easily agreed-upon definition of cyberwar. Even within closely related literatures, there exists an ongoing debate over what constitutes cyberwar. Some, such as Rid, who has written at length declaring there is no such thing as cyberwar, question whether such a concept is a helpful lens for thinking the present situation at all.[1] The term *cyberwar,* in most invocations, refers to the notion of cyberspace and the possibility of a war carried out in this global networked space, wherein computer systems are taken over to disrupt and surveil an enemy's communication and networked infrastructure either as part of a "kinetic" war or as a form of low-level conflict aimed at gaining geopolitical advantages. Though it is important to follow authors, strategists, legal scholars, and others wherever they happen to see "cyberwar" occurring, one particular etymological meaning will guide this inquiry. The prefix *cyber-* refers to the term cybernetics. *Cybernetics,* originating from the Greek *kubernētēs* ("steersman" or "governor"), is the science and study of systems, their structures, regulation, emergent properties, and possibilities, spanning disciplines from technology to biology to society. By explicitly thinking the *cyber-* in *cyberwar* as referring to systems, it will be fruitful to understand cyberwar as a war against systems: computer systems, state systems, systems of organization, and even systems of meaning.

This etymological understanding of *cyberwar* closely mirrors some of the earliest deployments of this term. One of the first unclassified uses of the term *cyberwar* comes from a 1992 publication by Arnett.[2] For him, the term means the replacement of human operators with machines that decide on targets, trajectories, movement, and so on—essentially the culmination of a long history of the insertion of "intelligent machines" into the arsenal of war fighting. That same year, Der Derian used the term "in the sense of a technologically generated, televisually linked, and strategically gamed form of violence."[3] Arquilla and Ronfeldt subsequently published a paper defining cyberwar as a tactical and strategic movement whereby communication, information, and the visibility of the battlespace become the central concern. They assert that while information technology brings cyberwar to the fore, it is not necessarily a technological phenomenon. In fact, the exemplary case of cyberwar they recount is a thirteenth-century Mongol offensive against Khwarizm, where the Mongols succeeded in defeating a significantly larger army by cutting off communications and disrupting the control of forces.

These definitions complement each other. Der Derian and Arnett's definitions focus on carrying out a kinetic war through the cybernetic organization of humans and technology, while Arquilla and Ronfeldt's definition stresses disrupting all of the enemy's cybernetic systems regardless of whether they are human, technological, or a combination. We are faced, then, with something much more expansive than war in cyberspace; rather, what these authors begin to explore in the early 1990s is an understanding of war in which one tries to construct and defend systems of communicating, knowing, controlling, and, ultimately, existing. Simultaneously, one attempts to disrupt, infiltrate, corrupt, and destroy these same systems belonging to the enemy. Arquilla and Ronfeldt state that such a strategy "may aim to confound people's fundamental beliefs about the nature of their culture, society, and government, partly to foment fear but perhaps mainly to disorient people and unhinge their perceptions."[4]

Clearly this is not completely new. Belligerents have always attempted to deceive their opponents and disrupt economies and governments. Furthermore, war has often had as a central objective the destruction of one critical system and the infiltration of another: the body and the territory of the opponent. Despite this, we can outline three critical factors that mark cyberwar as a historical shift. First, proponents of cyberwar, such as Arquilla and Ronfeldt, stress that in cyberwar, information and structures of knowing become central rather than peripheral to conflict. They say that cyberwar "means disrupting if not destroying the information and communications systems, broadly defined to include even military culture, on which an adversary relies in order to know itself."[5] Second, cyberwar attempts to disrupt not only the enemy's knowledge but also the entire structure of knowledge. In short, cyberwar invests epistemology itself as a battlespace. Third, cyberwar seeps outside of "war" proper. In calling into question modes of knowing, cyberwar breaks down the limits of the time and space of war.

Thus the term *cyberwar* describes two distinct but related phenomena. On one hand, it is a strategy for fighting war, and we will include whatever is named cyberwar by strategists, legal theorists, authors, and warriors. On the other hand, we will mean a historical shift—in a sense, a global cyberwar that marks a tendency whereby the critical element in war becomes the flow of information and the fortification and disruption of systems. In making this shift, cyberwar has opened an epistemological and cybernetic battlespace wherein notions of war, enmity, and knowing become directly contestable. While these concepts have always been unstable and problematic, cyberwar seizes them as systems of direct military intervention, turning what was once a question for philosophers into a domain of the global battlespace. In its most abstract sense, cyberwar has become an event that calls everything including itself into question at the moment it arrives. It is the historical possibility that all systems may break down—or, in their military occupation, be caused to break down—but it is also possible that cyberwar may undermine itself before anything actually "happens." Cyberwar as historical event marks a moment of radical militarized unknowability.

A COMPROMISED HISTORY

Many discussions of cyberwar, be they historical, strategic, or legal, begin not with the earliest examples or contemporary attacks but rather with a future catastrophe that demonstrates the danger of our over-reliance on vast, connected, yet vulnerable systems. These catastrophes normally start with a nonstate actor or a "rogue" state hacking into key networks, destroying critical infrastructure in the United States or multiple European countries. Airplanes crash into each other, trains derail, communication channels shut down, and electrical systems are disabled. Not only are these systems forced to shut down but they are hijacked and made to spin out of control, sometimes destroying themselves so completely that they would take months to return to normal usage. These imagined scenarios often place the reader at the time immediately following the catastrophe. At this point in time, one can survey the wreckage of our technological hubris before the aftermath begins in earnest. It is the moment when the full scale of a possible collapse is revealed but not yet realized.[6]

Where a historical account begins in the past, it often starts with a CIA attempt to secretly destroy a Soviet gas pipeline.[7] According to Thomas Reed, a National Security Council staffer, in 1982, the CIA was able to insert an intentionally faulty piece of code into a pump that the Soviet Union obtained from a Canadian company. According to Reed's account, the pump was installed in the Trans-Siberian gas pipeline; varying pump speeds and valve settings produced extreme pressures that caused an explosion large enough to be detected by U.S. satellites. The secret introduction of a so-called logic bomb—a somewhat antiquated term for a malicious piece of code inserted into software—has been touted by a number of commentators as one of the earliest examples of cyberwar.

Although Reed, who made this story public for the first time in a 2004 book, never referred to this attack as cyberwar, this story has become something of an origin myth for those who write about cyberwar more generally.[8] The event prefigures a number of issues that arise again and again in the myriad discourses surrounding cyberwar. Most important, it becomes clear how vulnerable complex systems of computation have become. These systems aggregate code written across the globe and parts manufactured outside the purview of their owners into complex networks that belie attempts to control them. Computation is exposed to the exterior places in which it is produced.

Furthermore, even if unintentionally, the use of this event as the first in a series of international cyberattacks offers an answer to a question that is often asked of theorists of cyberwar: how can such an event lay claim to being "war"? Is this merely sabotage? Placing the origin in the Cold War responds to those critics of cyberwar hype who believe it is nothing more than a collection of high-tech tools in service of the ancient techniques of spying, deception, and sabotage. For the Cold War proved that wars need not be explosive and could consist of decades of low-level conflict. As Virilio says of the threat posed by nuclear weapons, "the weapon's serious danger is not that it could explode tomorrow . . . but that for thirty years it has been destroying society."[9] The bomb's destructive power has been felt directly through its threat. Likewise, as can be seen in the futuristic scenarios described earlier, cyberwar seems always to threaten catastrophe. Placing cyberwar's origins in the Cold War suggests the possibility of a nonwar that is as destructive as a kinetic war. The second half of the twentieth century has demonstrated that even in the absence of a hot war, conflict can destroy governments and societies.

Furthermore, at least for those theorists and strategists of cyberwar in the United States, this origin story contextualizes contemporary cyberwar discourses in another way. Several military and political commentators writing about cyberwar as a strategic area of study were the same theorists who worked on nuclear deterrence strategy in the latter part of the Cold War. A number of authors—many of whom work for the RAND Corporation, a think tank that was created in 1948 to provide research and analysis to the U.S. military—even attempt to employ strategies learned from nuclear deterrence research to mitigate military hacking and offensive use of global networks.[10] Tying the origin of cyberwar to Cold War global strategic thinking offers an opportunity for those making the transition from strategizing in a bipolar world defined by nuclear weapons to a multipolar, interconnected global economy.

While the Siberian pipeline attack's similarity to contemporary issues surrounding cyberwar is noteworthy, the most striking aspect of the whole affair is that it possibly never happened. Following the release of Reed's book, an ex-KGB officer with direct knowledge of the region at the time disputes Reed's account. He acknowledged there was an explosion but claims it was at a different, smaller pipeline and was caused by specific construction mistakes, not by faulty equipment.[11] Moreover, no known media reports from the time confirm an explosion, which Reed claims was the size of a small nuclear blast. Other than Reed's account, no other documentation has been found, and the CIA has never confirmed the event.[12]

The origins of cyberwar in this event are seemingly impossible to verify. Pipeline explosions were common at the time, and there would have been no way for the CIA to know for certain if it was caused by their purposefully faulty equipment or accidently faulty Soviet equipment. Given our current evidence, the event is completely unknowable. Moreover, even if there was an explosion, it is impossible to verify if it was the logic bomb or a mechanical failure. Depending on one's perspective, either the fake event or fake refutations seep into the historical record like a computer virus corrupting the system's memory.

Thus, in a largely unrecognized way, this event is archetypal for cyberwar. Cyberwar and cybersecurity weave a complicated relationship between the knowable and the unknowable. Our networked world has become so complex in sheer technical terms that the system as a whole cannot be known from the outside. Mapping even just the public Web has become a scholarly pursuit in its own right. Computers and networks represent information as tiny bits on a magnetic disk or pulses of light across a cable that, owing to their size, speed, and complexity, are on their own essentially meaningless and impenetrable to human observers. One always interacts with abstractions and complex representations of the material reality of computing. Cyberwar, in attacking these systems, is always on the verge of being meaningless itself. Moreover, in attacking systems of knowing that guarantee information, a successful attack impairs even our ability to know if something has happened. Cyberwar is fought precisely in this space between the possible catastrophe and the possibility of nothing happening at all.

The event itself is ambiguous and our public historical record is already compromised. It could of course be argued that all history is ambiguous, constructed, and selective. What is unique in the case of cyberwar is that the whole structure of knowing and observing is opened as a site of direct military intervention. It is not only a question of interpretation and selective archives. The entire archive and our ability to comprehend the archive may be attacked at any moment. In a sense, we are dealing with a limit case of historical unknowability—not just ambiguity but a military attack on the data of history itself. Now, even if the victors write history, it may no longer be written from data they control.

Thus an effective understanding of cyberwar will only be possible by not prematurely deciding in favor of an event happening or not happening. Cyberwar operates both as a strategy and as a mediatized cultural phenomenon directly in the space between happening and not happening. It succeeds as a military strategy by never succeeding too much. It always seems to be leading us to the verge of catastrophe and at the same time to an interminable boredom where nothing will ever actually happen. Cyberwar could easily be dismissed as not really being war or violent, but what is so virulent and dangerous about cyberwar is its ability to atomize and distribute warfare into everyday life. Cyberwar succeeds so much more effectively for being either overhyped or dismissed. Ultimately, we must resist deciding in favor of catastrophe or boredom, for in doing so, the entirety of cyberwar will certainly escape us. Instead, we must attempt to interrogate the history and discourses of cyberwar by following its vacillations between these two poles as it hides in the theoretical space between war and nonwar.

WAR AGAINST MEDIA

A 2014 attack on Sony Pictures is exemplary of this militarization of networks and its ensuing ambiguities. On November 24 of that year, as Sony employees logged in to their corporate network, they were greeted with an image of a skeleton and threats to leak large amounts of stolen data if the attackers' demands were not met. All the while, the hackers deleted information on about half of the company's 6,797 personal computers and more than half of its 1,555 servers, crippling large parts of Sony's network.[13] Sony's e-mail system was disabled, leaving employees to communicate with handwritten notes. Payroll had to be done with paper checks. In the following weeks, the hackers released Sony's confidential data, including internal communications and four unreleased films. Leaked e-mails contained embarrassing accounts of internal conflicts and personal information, including employee Social Security numbers. Three days before the computers and servers were wiped of their data, executives had received e-mails requesting monetary compensation to prevent Sony from being "bombarded as a whole," but these initial demands went completely unanswered.[14]

Aside from the initial request for money, hackers made no direct demands on Sony before leaking the data. It was not until December 8, more than two weeks after the initial attack, that the hackers demanded, "Stop immediately showing the movie of terrorism which can break the regional peace and cause the War! You, SONY & FBI, cannot find us. We are perfect as much [sic]."[15] The movie at issue turned out to be *The Interview,* a comedy depicting the assassination of Kim Jong-un, leader of the Democratic People's Republic of Korea. Even before the demand that *The Interview* not be shown, suspicion fell on the North Korean regime, with Sony suggesting that they were investigating the possibility of the attack being carried out by state-sponsored hackers.[16] Furthermore, the previous June, North Korea's United Nations ambassador Ja Song Nam sent a letter to Ban Ki-moon, secretary-general of the United Nations, claiming that "to allow the production and distribution of such a film on the assassination of an incumbent head of a sovereign state should be regarded as the most undisguised sponsoring of terrorism as well as an act of war."[17]

Sony initially proceeded with plans to release the film in theaters following a December 18 premier in New York City. But, on December 16, Sony received an e-mail threatening physical attacks on any theater showing the film. After a number of theaters decided not to screen the film, the premier and the general release were both cancelled.[18] The cancellation of the release was followed by a public outcry from those in the industry who felt that giving in to the demands of hackers empowered them. Even President Obama called the cancellation a mistake, stating, "I am sympathetic to the concerns that they faced. Having said all that, yes, I think they made a mistake. . . . We cannot have a society in which some dictator someplace can start imposing censorship here in the United States."[19] The film was ultimately given a limited release on December 25, largely at art houses, and was distributed through online streaming services.

On December 19, the same day Obama called Sony's decision a mistake, the FBI announced that they had enough evidence to tie the attack to North Korea. The FBI, in addition to secret information that could not be shared, cited evidence that the malware used had been written on Korean-language computers and bore similarities to a 2013 attack on South Korean banks and television stations believed to be of North Korean origin.[20] This initial public evidence tying the attacks to North Korea was sparse, and a number of cybersecurity experts questioned the veracity of the attribution.[21] In January of the following year, the New York Times published an article revealing that the secret evidence implicating North Korea was gathered by National Security Agency (NSA) intrusions into North Korean government computers. Since 2010, the NSA had infiltrated North Korean networks to track the activities of the country's six thousand strong army of hackers. Supposedly, this source of intelligence allowed the NSA to identify the attacks retrospectively in the data they had gathered, although the attacks went unnoticed while they were occurring.[22]

Following the attribution of these attacks to North Korea, the United

States responded with sanctions targeting three North Korean businesses and barring ten government officials from utilizing the U.S. financial system.[23] In addition, North Korea subsequently experienced several Internet outages, one lasting nine hours. The North Korean government quickly blamed the United States, while Obama and other U.S. government officials refused to comment.[24] Even if the United States was responsible, both the outage and the sanctions were largely symbolic, as North Korea was already heavily sanctioned and had limited Internet connectivity. One of the noteworthy elements of cyberwar in contradistinction to traditional war is that more technologically advanced nations tend to be more vulnerable, as they rely significantly more on networked technologies. A country like North Korea that relies little on digital technologies and infrastructure is more insulated from cyberattacks than a heavily networked country like the United States.

On one hand, the entire conflict appears absurd: an overly sensitive dictator attacked an entertainment company—reducing the company to using office technology from forty years ago—for producing a satirical film. The U.S. government responded publicly by stressing this absurdity but at the same time taking the conflict seriously. Obama mocked the North Korean regime for its sensitivity, joking that "the notion that that was a threat to them I think gives you some sense of the kind of regime we're talking about here."[25] On the other hand, media can have serious geopolitical implications. The North Korean regime was not the only organization thinking the movie could be dangerous for their continued rule. Sony's CEO, Michael Lynton, concerned about the fallout from the movie, received assurances that the film was OK to release, both from RAND, where he sat on the board, and from at least two officials from the State Department who saw rough cuts of the film. A senior RAND defense analyst and North Korea specialist brought in to consult on the film recognized the implications of its release but advised against cutting an especially gruesome assassination scene, suggesting in a now leaked e-mail that "a story that talks about the removal of the Kim family regime and the creation of a new government by the North Korean people (well, at least the elites) will start some real thinking in South Korea and, I believe, in the North once the DVD leaks into the North (which it almost certainly will). So from a personal perspective, I would personally prefer to leave the ending alone."[26]

The whole affair was a strange intertwining of state and corporate power. The North Korean government understood a corporate action to be an act of war, and the Obama administration, while castigating the corporation for not protecting "society," ultimately responded to North Korea's actions. The actors in these conflicts are no longer subjects or states but rather digital systems, reliant on insecure media. Kittler goes so far as to say, "It has become clear that real wars are not fought for people or fatherlands, but take place between different media, information technologies, data flows."[27] This was never directly a conflict between the U.S. and North Korean governments; it was a conflict between different mediatized systems of power. As part of the e-mail hack fallout, Sony lashed out at the news media and social media platforms for spreading the leaked documents. Aaron Sorkin, a screenwriter who has worked with Sony, wrote an opinion piece for the *New York Times* claiming that "as demented and criminal as [leaking private documents] is, at least the hackers are doing it for a cause. The press is doing it for a nickel."[28] Sony threatened to take legal action against Twitter after a user shared images of a leaked e-mail and likewise threatened similar actions against journalists reporting on the information contained in the e-mails.[29] Even more dramatically, Sony supposedly attempted to overload servers providing access to the leaked documents to prevent the files from being downloaded.[30] The conflict was in a sense one between film, newspaper, and social media, along with the added concerns of various state-run media (e.g., press conferences, propaganda machines), more than it was a direct conflict between two states.

Individual communications also played an important role in the conflict: in addition to constituting a critical portion of the embarrassing information leaked, e-mail likely provided the initial means of intrusion into Sony's network. According to the NSA, hackers entered the network using a technique known as spear phishing, where targeted messages are sent to individuals within the organization that entice them to click on a link, enter a password, or download a file that compromises their machines. Hackers with knowledge of the organization often craft messages that appear to be legitimate personal or business requests, increasing the odds that someone in the organization will click on a malicious link. Once in control of a single machine, the attackers can then move into other parts of the network. In the case of the Sony hack, the attackers gained access to the network in this manner and then spent more than two months mapping it before destroying it.[31] These targeted e-mails constitute a type of social engineering, wherein human social relations and expectations are exploited to gain access to a system.[32] Such an attack moves fluidly between the symbolic expectations of humans and machines, exploiting the differences and misapprehensions of both.

Thus this conflict was both a war between media—entertainment media, news media, e-mail, the mediatized state, and so on—and a war carried out through and within the gaps that separate these media. It is in this symbolic space of media that war, and especially cyberwar, is now carried out. As Baudrillard reminds us, "just as wealth is no longer measured by the ostentation of wealth but by the secret circulation of speculative capital, so war is not measured by being waged but by its speculative unfolding in an abstract, electronic and informational space."[33] The very nature of war gets caught up in the conflict between media and at the same time comes to focus on one specific medium, which runs and manages these networks: computer code. This mediatic war becomes a symbolic and textual exchange. Gray, in his book on postmodern war, states, "War is a living text, after all, and we are all of us bound into it, of it, even as we tell our parts, as it writes our future."[34] On every level, the attack against Sony is an interpretive and textual affair: the plot of the movie made all the difference, e-mail messages exploited vulnerabilities in code, private e-mails were leaked, and so on. In short, the media as text has become an increasingly important element in geopolitical conflicts.

Although it is imperative to stress the development of the logic of this violence, especially in its symbolic dimensions, we must not overlook the implications this development has on the physical violence of war. Many of the conflicts detailed in this book have had little direct impact on individuals' ability to continue living, but even the indirect economic impacts created by the destruction of networked systems can cause hardship and even death.[35] Perhaps it will turn out that the advent of cyberwar will supplant kinetic violence, as physical violence is sometimes called in the cyberwar literature, and ultimately make war and international conflict less deadly. It is also possible that the militarization of networks will make it politically easier to start conflicts that cascade into full-scale kinetic violence or, even worse, that small teams of hackers will be empowered to begin conflicts that then escalate further, removing the decision to start war from visible and accountable organizations.[36] Moreover, many of the agencies carrying out these primarily digital attacks are part of larger, heavily nuclear-armed militaries that still threaten the destruction of the globe multiple times over with their arsenals.

CYBERWAR/MEDIA WAR

Through these attacks on digital systems, war becomes invested in the media and communications systems of everyday life. Like the European countryside in World War I, the media landscape is becoming disfigured by violence. Cyberwar militarizes information and information flows. As is clear in the case of the Sony attack, and as Galloway and Thacker note, the "media have now become a core component of war and political conflict."[37] In refiguring our relationship to media, the new modalities of warfare opened up by cyberwar bear directly on the state of media today and our relationship to them.

The media, and with them the war machines that developed these technologies, are now dedicated to consuming their own progeny by constantly attacking the networked infrastructure that all types of media now rely on. Kittler states, "One century was enough to transfer the age-old monopoly of writing into the omnipotence of integrated circuits."[38] Despite this omnipotence, we should be careful not to read into it a flattening of all media to a single digital idiom.[39] These networks constantly remediate and transcode other media and data.[40] Different languages, codes, and insecurities function in divergent and destabilizing ways, giving form to the multiple media that Kittler sees as at war with each other. Despite the varied cultural languages and valences of "new media," these media and the technologies that support them have turned them into both weapons of war and the space of war itself. Though the cultural expressions of these media are important to both global capital and nations, cyberwar has managed to militarize the machines, programs, and data that write and underwrite the media we consume.[41]

In 2014, EMC, a large-scale data services and storage provider, fell victim to an attack that its management believes was carried out by a state actor. The attackers compromised a Korean-language news website that an EMC engineer visited, installing malware on his computer that then infected his clients' secure data centers. EMC believed that South Korean military or government agencies may have been the ultimate target.[42] Like the Sony attack, this attack underscores the speed and ease with which attacks cross traditional media boundaries. An engineer's news media consumption habits were somehow known and exploited to gain access to the work machine he used when visiting clients. The attack weaves its way through the networks of various media and organizations, blurring the lines between their proper functioning and their exploitation. It is increasingly unclear if media affect society more by how they work or by how they malfunction.

With the growth of cyberwar, one of the essential elements of networked computers is becoming their insecurity. All of the examples of cyberwar, from the pipeline attack to the Sony attack to the other attacks described throughout this book, suggest that absolute security is functionally impossible. As Schneier, a noted cybersecurity expert, has stated, "there's no such thing as absolute security. Life entails risk, and all security involves trade-offs."[43] It is this lack of absolute security that makes cyberwar possible and also calls into question any attempt to fix the essence of computers and media. In this light, we can only fully understand what media can do when they break down and are turned against themselves.

Schneier also states, "Security is a system. People often think of security in terms of specific attacks and defenses. But it's not that simple. Security is always part of a system, and that system is always more complex than the individual components."[44] This systematic nature of digital media and networked computing means that the nature of these digital systems lies not in the media themselves but in the threat or disturbance that always risks arising from elsewhere. Parikka argues that these breakdowns and insecurity are not accidents that come to affect an otherwise healthy system; rather, they are part of any system's logic that must inform any analysis.[45] Vulnerabilities are not merely forces that alter networks ex post facto; rather, the very essence of a network is to be exposed to the mutability of its essence. For example, in the Sony attack, only one user of the corporate network had to click on a malicious link in an e-mail. The vulnerability does not lie in a specific individual but rather in the shape of the networks and the statistical aggregate in which it is highly likely that at least one person will click the link.

This mediatic breakdown and indeterminacy make it difficult to declare once and for all what constitutes the essence of digital systems.

Computers, in their programmability, are systems designed to be constantly redesigned and rewritten. In this sense, Galloway argues that computers and the code upon which they run become an antimedium: "Code is the medium that is not a medium. It is never viewed as it is, but instead is compiled, interpreted, parsed, and otherwise driven into hiding by still larger globs of code."[46] The ability of computers to automate tasks is founded on their ability both to be constantly changed and to hide large portions of their operation.

Despite the importance of this mutability, there is a tendency in discourses about media to stress the fixed mathematical nature of our digital systems and networks. Galloway argues that

> there is something that makes today's mode of production distinctive from all the others, the prevalence of software. . . . But what is software? Software consists of symbolic tokens that are combined using mathematical functions (such as addition, subtraction, and true-false logic) and logical control structures (such as "if x then y"). Simply put, software is math. Computer science is a division of mathematics.[47]

Likewise, Columbia states, "the major function that computers perform routinely in our society is calculation."[48] We will see in more depth the ways in which computers are not merely mathematical devices—and even how calculation itself is not straightforward—but for the time being it is important to note that the insecurity and vulnerability of computational systems undermine any attempt to fully situate the ontological nature of computation in mathematical rigor and fixity.[49] Galloway is correct about the overwhelming importance of software, but if software is math, it is only insomuch as math has always been writing, insecure inscription, given over to its possible subversion.

Moreover, computation differentiates itself from mathematics by offering a relatively complex control structure to iterate a relatively simple set of mathematical operations. Programs and networks are full of accidents and capable adversaries to exploit them. In this way, the complex global network of machines and code adds an insecure remainder to the calculations they were originally designed to carry out. This surplus insecurity always points to other machines, other connections, and other code that escapes control. Thus we approach something resembling

Derrida's conception of writing; it is "not a sign of a sign, except if one says it of all signs, which would be more profoundly true."[50] A single computer is not an exclusively mathematical system but rather points to the entire network of all computations and computers. Meaning is always produced by the totality of the system, but only insomuch as the system is constituted by the traces of nonpresence that arise from other parts of the system.

Components come from overseas factories, code is installed that was written elsewhere, e-mails arrive from unknown correspondents, and computers are connected across networks to millions of other computers. To compute today is always to be exposed to the other and the unknown. As Parikka suggests, these insecurities always risk rupturing the symbolic order and its logic: "A virus can accomplish a rupture in such a symbolic frame of media culture both incorporeally and in the form of the very material interruption it can achieve in the normal functioning of a society—a virus is a disruption to the everyday logic and rhythm of the social order, a catastrophe."[51] This last point is crucial; modern technology has changed the density and speed of networked connections along with a massive proliferation of programs, text, and media. While these systems have arisen out of a long history of improving the efficiency of calculations, they have become something entirely different: a complex communicative and symbolic network that everywhere explicates our being-within-writing, an insecure and malleable network of signs and symbolic logic that unceasingly points to the deferment of any fixed meaning.[52]

To understand what is at stake in cyberwar, and especially the ways in which it reconfigures our mediatic networks, a Derridean account of writing is especially fruitful. By understanding both systems and the attacks against them as a type of writing, it becomes clear the ways in which their inscription is always a trace of a nonpresence. Computation now appears as a system of writing and signification that everywhere threatens to destroy systems by way of its vulnerability. In short, it constitutes a system of inscription exposed to the constant threat of deconstruction, but a deconstruction that carries with it the risk of global catastrophe.

PROGRAM/TEXT

To advance this understanding, it is critical to explicate the ways in which programs function as a type of writing. In this way, this book is closely aligned with Galloway's claim: "I consider computers to be fundamentally a textual medium." He further claims, "The largest oversight in contemporary literary studies is the inability to place computer languages on par with natural languages."[53] Our global networks interact as texts, constantly sending and receiving symbols that always point elsewhere, every variable and program deferring their ultimate result, always awaiting input from some other place. The pipeline pump's ultimate logic only becomes visible at the moment it explodes. We only learn what a program does and means at the moment of execution.

Many commentators take issue with the textual and linguistic aspects of programming languages. Despite Galloway's call to treat computer languages on par with natural languages, he insists on their fundamental difference, claiming, "Code is the first language that actually does what it says."[54] Arguments such as this most often claim that code is directly translated into binary and hence is not communicative or expressive but instead directly acts. Likewise, Hayles argues, "nor does code allow the infinite iterability and citation that Derrida associates with inscriptions, whereby any phrase, sentence, or paragraph can be lifted from one context and embedded in another."[55]

Looking at machine code (the binary strings that ultimately tell computers how to act), it may appear that code lacks all iterability and acts directly upon the machine, but from the perspective of complex computer ecologies—especially if we admit their necessary insecurity—iterability, citation, and intertextuality become the most important components of what is called code. Programs increasingly use frameworks and libraries written by others to manage underlying and common tasks; many of these libraries contain code written years ago in earlier languages.[56] What is today called code is a vast archive of texts written by myriad programmers over the course of decades. The complex ecologies of reuse and borrowing have resulted in a situation where a bug in a single piece of important code can threaten a large portion of software and systems.

For example, in 2014, a buffer overflow bug was discovered in Open-SSL, an open source cryptography library that at the time was used on a half million websites to protect user data. The bug allowed an attacker to read encrypted data off of the Web server, including passwords and credit card numbers, of others who had visited the website.[57] The bug, now known as Heartbleed, existed as part of the program for two years prior to its discovery.[58] While writing all of one's own code, were such a feat even possible, would be no panacea—as the odds of making a mistake are high, even more so than reusing code and already existing programs that have been tested by many users—in this case, it was the iteration and reuse of the OpenSSL code that left two-thirds of Web traffic open to eavesdroppers.

Hayles recognizes that repeating the fixity and rigidity at lower levels allows higher levels of the computer to function in a more literary and human manner; in short, there is a spectrum from the fixed machine code at the bottom to more "natural languages" built on top of those.[59] Kittler makes a similar argument that all programming merely amounts to "signifiers of voltage differences" and that software, which he claims does not really exist, merely serves to obfuscate the actual machine, hiding what is going on at the level of hardware.[60] But, to attempt to think a fundamental level of computation (e.g., hardware) is to believe that at some level there can be a secure experience of computation. The insecurities of cyberwar announce that this relationship between voltage difference and the abstractions of language is not unidirectional: errors, vulnerabilities, oversights, and translation mistakes between languages all allow insecurities in high-level languages to cascade downward, affecting the fixity at lower levels. As we will see in the case of Stuxnet, vulnerabilities in code can ultimately cause damage in the physical world. Once trace, writing, and undecidability are introduced into the system at higher levels, or discovered as being always already there, they can never be excised.

In this way, the advent of cyberwar demonstrates Chun's claim that there exists a gap between code and action.[61] As she suggests, the argument that code does what it says assumes a direct and unproblematic relationship between enunciation and action, a fantasy of Western sovereignty and the logos of a full and present speech.[62] In contrast to this fantasy of code's ability to act directly, cyberwar militarizes the gap between enunciation and action, denying any ability for either enunciation or action to maintain its sovereignty and self-sameness. A successful attack, such as the claimed pipeline attack, marks the failure somewhere along the chain that runs from the programmer through code to the functioning system. A compromised system can function normally until an attacker decides to activate the vulnerability. Such an attack leaves the machine and its programs in a state where it is impossible to know if action will directly follow enunciation.

Other aspects of programming further suggest that code does not simply do what it says. Programming languages have been invented, and grown drastically in complexity, to alleviate the difficulties inherent in programming directly in machine language. Even early languages were designed largely to make programming more human understandable.[63] As Hayles notes, there are "multiple addressees of code (which include intelligent machines as well as humans)."[64] Computer languages are often designed to make coding certain tasks more manageable by making code more easily human readable so that both a programmer and her colleagues can understand what she wrote. Large distributed systems often involve multiple components written in different languages that interact, further complicating the direct relationship between saying and doing. Finally, programs act as systems that are designed to respond to a set of inputs, but for any program of even moderate complexity, anticipating the total possible set of inputs is impossible. Developing a program in a context where it is exposed to multiple users, networks and unexpected inputs often reveal bugs and insecurities.

A widespread class of vulnerabilities of which Heartbleed is a good example, known as buffer overflows, are instructive in this regard.[65] Buffer overflows occur when a program expects a variable of a certain size, only allocating that much space in memory, but a larger number or string is given as input. The program keeps writing the entire input, overflowing the intended variable and depositing data into other places in memory. When this is done accidently, it can cause programs to crash, as the computer may try to execute the accidental information, because computers store data and commands in the same place. Buffer overflows can also be used maliciously to take over a machine by getting new commands into the memory locations that will be executed. So, while Hayles is correct in her claim that "in the worldview of code, it makes no sense to talk about signifiers without signifieds. Every voltage change must have a precise meaning in order to affect the behavior of the machine;

without signifieds, code would have no efficacy,"[66] on a different level, the existence of buffer overflow errors belies any complete insistence on precise and stable signifieds. The signified is assumed to be a certain location in memory, but there are always risks that the series of voltage differences will overflow their presumed place. Code always addresses the address of an empty place, waiting to be read, a signifier more than a signified. It is the unexpected input that the programmer does not prepare for that is able to turn the program against the computer. Cox summarizes the position succinctly, stating, "Code cannot simply be reduced to its functional aspects, as it also extends the instability already inherent in the relationship of speech to writing, where it can also go out of control. Like all codes it is only interpretable within the context of the overall network of relations that make its operations inherently unstable."[67]

THE DEPTH OF CODE

In this light, Hayles argues, "code always has some layers that remain invisible and inaccessible to most users. From this we arrive at an obvious but nevertheless central maxim: print is flat, code is deep."[68] These layers and inaccessibilities guarantee an unbridgeable gap between saying and doing.[69] Although Hayles is absolutely correct in this assessment of the depth of code, as the case of Heartbleed demonstrates, it is important to note that the depth applies to print as well. Neither print nor code relates saying to doing or enunciation and meaning. Code does create a depth and complexity that resists mastery, but this is what makes of code and programs a type of text rather than what differentiates printed "natural languages" from machinic languages. All text, and with it language, is made up of deep networks of citation, reference, complex encodings, and nonpresence that both differs from and defers its own meaning—what Derrida calls *différance*. In confronting cyberwar, it is of the utmost importance to maintain the centrality of the trace, which inscribes an absence in all language, whether it is what is commonly known as code, speech, or writing.

Kittler makes a similar claim to Hayles, arguing that digital writing is different from earlier forms of writing, but as such has come to define all types of writing and media since its invention. His argument is thus one of historical difference rather than a typological difference. He claims the "last historical act of writing" was the manual design of the 4004 microprocessor in the late 1970s, which then allowed future chips to be designed directly on computers, beginning what he calls "our postmodern writing scene."[70] Kittler insists we have seen the last historical act of writing, but he recognizes that this end of historical writing does not, in fact, end writing; rather, we commence a new "postmodern" scene of writing. Kittler thus concludes that rather than the ambiguity of human languages and subjects, "computers operating on IF-THEN commands are therefore machine subjects. Electronics, a tube monster since Bletchley Park, replaces discourse, and programmability replaces free will." Thus, for Kittler, computers represent not the end of writing but the end of historical writing as the writing of enlightenment man. The postmodern writing that is instantiated is a writing with a new subject that leaves man behind, both in history and as history.[71]

Like Hayles's claim that code is deep, Kittler's claims accurately diagnose the nonpresence and vulnerabilities that plague programs, even if they flatten previous modes of writing by ignoring the insecurities and complexities that have always affected language. Most important for present purposes, this postmodern and computational writing produces traces, self-difference, and differed meaning: while writing may change media, language, and speed, we still move only from the monopoly of writing to the monopoly of writing. But Galloway explicitly warns against such a move, stating,

> To see code as subjectively performative or enunciative is to anthropomorphize it, to project it onto the rubric of psychology, rather than to understand it through its own logic of "calculation" or "command." . . . Code exists first and foremost as commands issued to a machine. Code essentially has no other reason for being than instructing some machine in how to act. One cannot say the same for the natural languages.[72]

In different ways, all three attempt to differentiate programming languages from "natural language," but to do so requires insisting that some type of language, whether code, print, or another historical era, is flat and fully present. In each case, language and the program are differentiated by arguing that one is fully understandable and directly present in both signifier and action, while the other withdraws. Cyberwar and the constantly growing list of examples of the insecurity of these systems that wind through the multiple media that constitute them, from low-level code to human users of e-mail, belie any attempt to differentiate these languages along the lines of a direct relationship between enunciation and machinic action.

In fact, with the advent of cyberwar and the militarization of the gap between enunciation and act, we are confronted with the opposite risk than the one Galloway identifies—namely, a deanthropomorphizing of the performative and the enunciative, of the human itself. What truly appears threatening today is not that computers will begin to act as humans but rather that humans appear machinic and automatic. Faced with this fear, we are constantly told that natural language must be kept apart from the cold, calculative, and masterful logic of the machine. Hayles moves code into an infinite depth that pushes it away from natural language, Kittler creates deep historical divisions, and Galloway makes of code a mere surface that links enunciation directly with action. All three try to maintain the distance between natural language and code, holding apart the programmatic and machinic from the human and the natural. We risk today the condition that Kittler describes: "Technologies that not only subvert writing, but engulf it and carry it off along with so-called Man, render their own description impossible."[73] The postmodern writing initiated with computation marks the end of man; thus, if it is enunciative or performative, it does not enunciate man but instead, as Deleuze says, constitutes "a new form that is neither God nor man and which, it is hoped, will not prove worse than its two previous forms."[74]

Kittler claims that the only thing left to write is the stories of how the end of writing came to pass; for him any description or writing after this end is impossible. While this postmodern writing may be infected by unknowability, we must insist that a description of this situation is possible for two interrelated reasons. First, the gap between coding and acting explicated under the conditions of cyberwar means that this postmodern writing shares the same ambiguities, complications, and differences that define historical writing. Second, and as a direct corollary, if description is impossible, it is because a fixed description of historical writing has always been impossible. Writing has always carried so-called man off with it. Writing always contains within it both command and data and the possibility of the subversion of the gap between the two.

To advance in such a way, it is necessary to conceptualize the sign in a way that is both Deleuzian and Derridean. For Deleuze and Guattari, language is first and foremost a force that acts. They state, "The elementary unit of language—the statement—is the order-word. . . . Language is made not to be believed but to be obeyed."[75] Furthermore, for them, language is one among things. They suggest, "An assemblage of enunciation does not speak 'of' things; it speaks *on the same level as* states of things and states of content. So that the same *x,* the same particle, may function either as a body that acts and undergoes actions or as a sign constituting an act or order-word."[76] This description is apt for computation; just as a particle can be either body or sign, within a program, the same bit can be either data or command.

We must add two additional elements to this pragmatics of the sign. First, as Deleuze and Guattari suggest, we are dealing not with a single logic of the sign but rather, as they argue, with multiple regimes of sign.[77] They contend that this pragmatics is not a logic or syntax but rather underlies the logic of the sign, which is historically mutable. The specific distribution of particles between sign and body is not fixed. So, a specific act of writing, coding, cyberwar, and so on, can redistribute and disrupt the relationship between sign and bodies. Second, a pragmatic theory of the sign should not be confused with one based on a full presence of the sign or its action. Despite this pragmatic and material conception of signs, they still point elsewhere to absences that can never be fully accounted for. The sign is always a trace in a Derridean sense. It is an order-word, but what is ordered is only realized at the moment of enunciation or execution.

This notion of pragmatics and trace can both explain and be demonstrated by computer code. Take the simple command $a = a + 1$. It adds 1 to whatever value is stored in a and then stores the result back into a. There is here pragmatics and command—the signs do something physical to the bits in the computer—but there is also trace and absence: the a points elsewhere to a location in memory that is not known until the moment of execution. In certain languages, even the + can behave differently, dependent on the type of data stored in a. One cannot know exactly what will happen until the moment of execution, just as human language is pragmatic, but under conditions of trace, absence, and vulnerability.

This is not to suggest that programming and various "natural" languages do not differ, but rather, as Raley argues, "it is not possible to locate a strict or fundamental difference in the metaphysical sense: this mode of distinction must always be fated and any binary that is constructed between the analog and digital is bound to be unraveled or dissolved."[78] Denying this metaphysical difference does not mean that writing does not change or that its logic is static. Stiegler attests, "The history of the *grammē* is that of electronic files and reading machines as well—a history of technics—which is the invention of the human."[79] Writing and with it so-called man have a history, of which cyberwar is a notable development that changes the speed, methods, and dominate character of writing. While cyberwar fixes on the structure of writing and its vulnerability, it changes that structure and partakes of its history. Cyberwar thus appears as a historical phenomenon and as a structure of vulnerability inherent to all writing. In short, it names both a historical cyberwar and also a cyberwar-in-general, which is characterized only by its constant change under conditions of unceasing insecurity.

THE UNDECIDABILITY OF WAR

The insecurity of programs and the vacillations that appear already in these instances of cyberwar are not merely an ambiguity standing in the way of full knowledge. On the contrary, this unknowability constitutes a fundamental condition of this new type of war. Even at the origins of cyberwar itself, we are faced with digital systems and their military history that integrate and express the structure of what Derrida calls the undecidable: "The undecidable is not merely the oscillation or the tension between two decisions. Undecidable—this is the experience of that which, though foreign and heterogeneous to the order of the calculable and the rule, must nonetheless—it is of *duty* that one must speak—deliver itself over to the impossible decision while taking account of law and rules."[80] The undecidable we are faced with in cyberwar is not merely an ambivalence between two equally possible scenarios: war, not war; event, non-event; state, non-state actor, and so on. It is an absolute heterogeneity that infects epistemology and renders impossible a pure decision that would not risk itself in these conflicts.

We must insist, against Derrida's position, that this force of undecidability is not foreign to calculation, nor does it come to affect computation after the fact; on the contrary, it lies at the heart of computation itself. Derrida outlines three domains affected by undecidability: law/ justice, war, and calculation. Ultimately, the undecidability of calculation underlies the others. Derrida explains that law is an element of calculation and that justice is incalculable; the undecideability between the two demands that one calculate the incalculable. For Derrida, the undecideable is not the impossibility of choosing but rather the very experience of being outside the realm of calculation. But this distinction is built upon an absolutely secure notion of calculation founded on the opposition between the (calculable) program and the (incalculable) text; it is a calculation that always arrives at the same answer rather than an exposed and vulnerable computation. Cyberwar demonstrates that every calculation is potentially already compromised, and all attacks against digital systems, from the pipeline attack to the Sony hack, bear this out. Thus cyberwar calls on us to decide on a calculation that is always already undecidable.

Moreover, computability theory directly attests to the undecidable nature of computation itself, with a whole subdiscipline dedicated to "undecidable problems." In 1936, Alan Turing proved one of the earliest and most canonical examples, the halting problem, undecidable. The halting problem consists of determining for a given program and a given input whether the program will run forever or eventually finish. Of course, for some programs, determining this is simple; for example, a program such as

```
Print 1+1;
```

will simply print 2 and complete, whereas a program such as

```
While 1==1: Print 2;
```

will run forever, printing the number 2 over and over, because 1 will always equal 1. Despite the existence of some programs for which it can be determined whether they halt, Turing proved that no algorithm exists that can determine for all programs and all inputs whether they will run forever.[81] Even the theoretically pure realm of computability theory, where rarified algorithms rarely have to deal with hardware failures or compromised systems, admits a fundamental undecidability to computation. There is no way always to know what a program will do with a given input without running it. Computation cannot be computed; it is undecideable until it is compiled and run. Although we may imagine that computation is predictable and knowable, its very conditions, exposed to cyberwar, speak to a deep undecideability and unknowability at the heart of what any given calculation will produce.

With the advent of cyberwar, this undecidability infects war itself, calling into question the nature of war as a concept. This infection of war by undecidability constitutes for Derrida a new type of violence:

> A new violence is being prepared and, in truth, has been unleashed for some time now, in a way that is more visibly suicidal or auto-immune than ever. This violence no longer has to do with *world* war or even with *war,* even less with some right to wage war. And this is hardly reassuring—indeed quite the contrary.... There is essentially no longer any such thing today that can be called in all rigor "war" or "terrorism," even if there can still be, here and there, in a secondary sense.[82]

The violence unleashed by cyberwar partakes of this autoimmune structure, as the violence turns against the coherence of the institutions that carry it out. As states risk themselves in conflicts such as the Sony attacks, the very nature of "the state" threatens to fracture. This violence is not merely a self-destruction. It is a deconstruction that calls into question the possibility of a comprehensible whole in regard to both geopolitical actors and the entire concept of war. Cyberwar, in its attack on our technology and networks, threatens to intervene directly between states—as well as nonstate actors and subjects in general—and their mediatized relation to the world. Thus systems, individuals, and nations become heterogonous to themselves and harbor an endemic gap between our understanding of the system and its actual function.[83] While this discrepancy is not a new feature of the relationship between understanding and world, it is explicitly militarized by the advent of cyberwar.

As this undecidable violence militarizes the technologies of our everyday existence, we are exposed to a war that turns both against our media and against us as the subjects of this media. Kittler argues that no subject extends itself through media but rather that a subject is produced through its mediatization. Alluding to Lacan's writing, he claims, "Both people and computers are 'subject to the appeal of the signifier'; that is, they are both run by programs."[84] These attacks infect the production and constitution of contemporary subjects. This violence is one that tears asunder the concept of war, media, the subject, and the state. But it is not simply a violence that destroys these concepts; rather, it constantly refigures them as mobile systems exposed to their own vulnerability. Cyberwar is a war fought between mediatized subjects and subjectified media, each transforming the other, themselves, and the gap that maintains any difference between the two.

WRITING CYBERWAR

In this light, cyberwar appears not only as a historical–strategic development but also as a philosophical development. This is not at all to say that the arguments put forth by the proponents and detractors of cyberwar provide a coherent whole; their texts are as ambiguous as the space and time of cyberwar itself. Still, these texts and their history work directly on philosophy. As Galloway suggests, "the computer does not remediate other physical media, it remediates metaphysics itself."[85] As warfare moves into the microscopic spaces of computing machines and the global space of networks, rewriting the texts that flow through them and reconfiguring their structure, it elucidates and reshapes what is at stake philosophically. Cyberwar, broadly construed, marks a form of war that calls all systems into question. Systems of spatiality, temporality, and textuality are all undermined as they are converted into sites of military intervention. Ultimately, cyberwar is founded on the irrepressible contingency and entropy at the heart of all systems: the instability of space, writing, and the creation of network structures. Thus cyberwar is founded on a particularly Derridean observation: no one ever writes in a language of which she is in complete control. Through the lens of cyberwar, all systems, including the states and subjects that use them, appear vulnerable as their internal tensions are converted into possible attack vectors.

The appropriation of these insights by military organizations pushes them to their philosophical limit. Ultimately, under the name of cyberwar, we enter a future that threatens a constant military intervention beyond the time and space of war into the minutiae of the everyday.

Still, despite and against this reality, it also guarantees the impossibility of any closure. Cyberwar explicates the always local and contingent nature of all systems and calls us to think this contingency as an integral part of our digital systems and our understanding of space, writing, and sovereignty in the twenty-first century.

It should be noted that this book was written, in the main, before the events of the 2016 U.S. presidential election. While the dust has yet to settle, it increasingly appears as though Russia waged a multipronged cyberwar to undermine the election process and the solidity of U.S. institutions. Although this book does not directly deal with or recount these events, the arguments and history that are laid out here provide a context and theory whose relevance are hopefully clear.

The broad aims of this book are twofold. First, through the history of cyberwar, it becomes evident that any description of programming and computation must come to terms with the insecure and vulnerable nature of code, a nature that is always deferred and subjected to a networked nonpresence. Thus computer programming appears as the clearest instantiation of Derrida's description of writing. With computer code and the increasing attacks on its security, the danger of the trace and *différance* become a daily concern for individuals, states, and corporations: "Always differing and deferring, the trace is never as it is in the presentation of itself."[86] Globally, quintillions of times a second adding 1 to 1 returns 2, which is then stored somewhere else in memory, but with the rise of networked computing, we increasingly risk that in some critical moment, either by accidental or malign intent, the calculation will go awry: an unauthorized user will be let into a network; a monitoring system will fail to take corrective action; an uncontrollable chain of system failures and catastrophes will cascade across the globe. The program and the programmer can never know with absolute certainty the underlying state of the machine or the outcome of a calculation. As more and more systems, writing, media, and information depend on networked computation, this gap between text and action, between self and self-perception, risks infection and deflagration.

This is not to suggest that such self-sameness or secure programs existed before cyberwar and only now fall into disarray. The entire history of deconstruction has read this non-self-sameness into all origins, especially that of language, writing, and speech.[87] Moreover, as Arquilla and Ronfeldt's explanation of the importance of disrupting communication and information security for the thirteenth-century invasion of Khwarzim attests, the strategic and philosophical implications of the insecurity of all systems and all language long predate the advent of modern cyberwar. Thus the second broad concern of this book is the implication the militarization of this insecurity bears on this history, especially as it has been understood under the name of deconstruction. If, under the conditions of programmatic writing, we are most directly faced with the danger wrought by the insecurity and nonpresence of language as writing, it becomes increasingly imperative to recognize a machinic force of deconstruction beyond human intentionality. This machinic and at times militarized force of deconstruction haunts deconstruction itself. The viruses, bugs, and unforeseen gaps in the security of computer networks and programs exploit the logic of the programs they afflict. The existence of these programmatic traces and vulnerabilities both opens programs to a type of deconstruction and also threatens to turn a deconstructive force against deconstruction by militarizing its functioning.

This deconstructive machine that comes into focus through cyberwar turns not against a specific metaphysics or logocentrism but rather against all metaphysics and logics and, in doing so, reshapes and remakes them in the image of the vulnerabilities discovered there. We discover not only that programming is a type of writing but also the obverse, that all writing and language is a type of programming. Thus Chun's claim that software functions as a type of ideology in that it simultaneously obfuscates hardware while appearing to make it present and understandable is particularly accurate insomuch as software and ideology function to instruct machines and to make the resulting movement understandable as language.[88] Galloway responds to Chun's claims about ideology by insisting that software is a machine and ideology a narrative.[89] Cyberwar directly requires that we abandon this distinction between machines and narratives. We must instead understand, in a sense that is Deleuzian but also Derridean, that narratives are a type of software, that both make sense out of machines while simultaneously obfuscating and ordering their actual physical function. Ultimately, to come to terms with the machinic other of deconstruction requires that we recognize both what is machinic in human language and that even the most rigorous automaticity produces traces, difference, and exposure to self-deconstruction. There is a ghost in the machine and a machine in the ghost—a *mise en abyme* of vulnerable nonpresence and machinic rigor.

While the undecidability of war and these mediatic systems threaten to undermine any accounting of essential attributes, Derrida's writings on the nonpresence of writing and deconstruction are exemplary in attempting to describe that which always already escapes description. Likewise, it is imperative to write and describe the undecidability of these systems from war to media to the subject that confronts them. In a sense, we are confronted with the Lacanian real, that which "never stops not writing itself." This real both invokes writing and always produces a nonpresent remainder that deconstructs any writing that attempts to master its presence and essence. In this sense, this book attempts to partake of the autodeconstruction of these computational and communicational systems, to write the impossibility of writing this. To engage in this deconstruction is to experience the real not writing itself, or more accurately, to write and read both with and against these systems, to witness their autodeconstruction and to write and read the non-self-identity of one's own deconstruction through them.

1

Buffer Overflow:
The Space and Time of Cyberwar

Throughout the short history of cyberwar, the vast majority of attacks have taken place outside of declared conflicts and kinetic wars. It is striking, then, that if we follow both the media and military establishments in calling these events war, war appears no longer to exist in a specific time or place. If cyberwar is taken in its broadest sense to mean a new mode of war targeted against systems, it then marks a new relationship to the space and time of war and attests to the reconfiguration of global spaces by economic, legal, social, and military forces. While many are quick to see in cyberwar an inevitable apocalyptic catastrophe, and while others dismiss these warnings as pure hype, it is most productive to set aside that particular debate and instead explore the specific logic of cyberwar. Under the logic of computer and network-based attacks, certain tendencies of military and economic thinking about the global space of the twenty-first century come to the fore regardless of the ultimate success or failure of these computerized attacks.

Cyberwar exploits security gaps in digital systems and networks and at the same time leverages the global reach of these networks. The attacks that have been organized under the name of cyberwar create nearly immediate effects at a distance, sending information and malicious code around the globe at the speed of light. Cyberwar exists intimately within what Castells calls "the rise of the network society."[1] These attacks on networked digital systems both speak to and engage with these increasingly connected global spaces. Moreover, even while these attacks exploit the vulnerabilities of programs, they are exploited by and in order to leverage spatial and temporal networks. To understand what is at stake in cyberwar, especially as it moves outside the time and space of declared war, requires us to account for these shifts in geography and for the impact of cyberwar on the continual reconfiguration of geography and networks.

This transformation of global space through networks does not mark the end of geography. Rather, geographic space is supplemented by networks of computers, trade, international law, migrations, and so on, some of which privilege flows, speed, and networked contiguity, while others privilege place, slowness, and disconnection. Cyberwar takes place across and between this entire set of geographic and networked spaces. Twenty-first-century military and political strategy does not give up on geopolitics; rather, it engages a multiplicity of spaces and domains. Within these spaces, certain nodes are selected as sites of intervention for their importance to the multitude of networks of which they are part. In a sense, though territory does not disappear, it becomes another type of node in a global set of interwoven networks. Hence warfare, and especially cyberwar, ceases to be exclusively territorial (if it ever was) and becomes primarily concerned with networks. If territory is merely another node in a variety of networks, then war and politics have always been nodal, but what arises with cyberwarfare is a purposeful attempt to explicate and strategize a nodal politics. Thus we must attempt to interrogate the logic of cyberwar as it fixes upon this networked time and space of global politics.

MOONLIGHT MAZE AND THE GHOST OF TERRITORY

One of the first serious cyberattacks against the United States, referred to as Moonlight Maze, was a multiyear operation targeting a number of governmental, industrial, and academic computers. Hackers supposedly broke into numerous systems, including those of the Department of Defense, the Department of Energy, military contractors, and leading research universities, with the likely purpose of stealing large amounts of data. Anonymous U.S. government sources claimed that the data could have included classified naval codes and information on missile guidance systems.[2] The attacks were first discovered in 1999, but it remains unclear what the ultimate motives were. Some have speculated that the most likely purpose was to steal technological secrets for economic purposes. There were even some suggestions that the intrusion may have been carried out at the behest of the French government or military.[3]

Though a full description of the event was never produced and Russia denied involvement, initial investigations traced the event back to servers near Moscow. Tracing an attack back to a server often provides little evidence toward the identity of attackers. It is common for attackers who do not want to be known to route their activities through multiple servers in multiple countries. The more uncooperative those countries and the owners of the servers are with the target, the more difficult it becomes to trace the attack back to its origins. Many cyberattacks wind their way across the globe to hide their tracks before connecting to the targeted system. Moreover, the connection between attackers and state institutions is often speculative at best. Although a growing number of countries are incorporating cyberwarfare units into their militaries, many attacks are still carried out by loosely affiliated groups, allowing easy deniability by the host nation.[4]

In the case of Moonlight Maze, which has never been officially attributed to a known organization either by the U.S. government or through public claims of responsibility, some in the U.S. government were convinced that the attacks were of Russian origin because the attacks happened exclusively on weekdays between 8:00 A.M. and 5:00 P.M. Moscow time and never occurred on Russian holidays. Other U.S. government officials were skeptical, thinking that the evidence pointed too clearly toward Russia and so must have been a carefully planned diversion. This "attribution problem," as it is often phrased, arises over and over again in both assessing prior attacks and theorizing political options around future attacks.[5]

The attribution problem is central to the theoretical shift in conflict marked by cyberwar. The ease with which attackers can masquerade as someone else and hide their tracks through a networked global underground often makes covering up an attack much easier than finding the source. Furthermore, even in cases where the server from which the attack originated is found, tying the attack to a country or group in a convincing way can be even more difficult than the forensics work. Unlike physical acts of espionage or sabotage, there is no spy to catch. If system administrators detect an intrusion and are able to stop it, attackers often simply disconnect their servers, and any forensics trail quickly goes cold.[6]

Two interrelated aspects of the global Internet increase the ease of carrying out anonymous attacks. First, the Internet significantly reduces the cost of creating effects at a distance. Even U.S. Predator drones, which have substantially lowered the cost of military operations carried out at long distances, cost multiple millions of dollars, while Internet access in some parts of the world costs pennies an hour. A laptop and an Internet connection can be cheaper than a transcontinental flight. Second, the speed at which a computer can connect, probe, and exploit vulnerabilities completely changes security equations. It is now possible to attack hundreds of systems a second. At its peak rate, one of the fastest replicating computer worms, a 2003 worm named "SQL Slammer," doubled the number of infected computers every 8.5 seconds. Less than 15 minutes after the worm was released, large portions of the global Internet shut down under the traffic from infected computers trying to find other computers to infect.[7] Physical security can be enhanced through keeping components of the security system secret. An attacker generally has one chance to try to defeat a physical security system before being stopped or apprehended. Thus secret mechanisms tend to be very efficient because they are able to surprise an adversary and ruin an intrusion attempt. While secrecy and deception play a role in computer security, they can often be overcome by the speed of computer systems. For example, a keypad to open a door with a four-digit code on a ten-digit pad produces ten thousand possible combinations. If a human intruder were to take two seconds to try each code, exhausting the entire key space would take longer than five and a half hours. Even a slow computer could easily try one hundred codes a second, exhausting the key space in less than two minutes.

The situation becomes even more complicated when an attacker is interested in cracking not a specific system but rather a class of systems or users (e.g., credit card holders, users of a specific piece of software, employees of a large office). While most users may implement security protections, an attacker merely needs to find those who have failed to implement these protections (e.g., those users who did not change the default password or upgrade to the newest version). Dealing with physical security, an attacker would be left hoping that a security measure was not installed, while with computer security, an attacker could try the whole group of users until they found those who were not secure. This was precisely how the SQL Slammer worm replicated. Microsoft was aware of the vulnerability in its SQL Server software and released a patch to fix the problem six months prior to the release of the worm. But many users had not installed the patch.[8] After infecting a machine, the worm would seek out other unpatched computers.

The combination of computing speed and the global reach of the Internet serves to radically redefine security along with space generally. In a certain sense, distance is replaced by networked connections. As Virilio argues, "continents have lost their geographical foundations and been supplanted by the tele-continents of a global communication system which has become quasi-instantaneous."[9] Still, it should be added that the shape of these telecontinents is not completely divorced from the shape of geographic continents. In the case of Moonlight Maze, the borders of the Russian territory still determine traces, such as national holidays, that seep into the global network. These telecontinents appear as ghostly reproductions of geographic continents, which do not vanish but persist in ever more minute detail, awaiting a savvy analyst to seek out and interpret these clues. Still, it is also possible that the remains of geographic space may appear too clearly and thus not convincingly enough.

Thus, while global networks and communication flows tend to be thought in their frictionless instantaneity, it is absolutely critical to assert the importance of what geography remains.[10] These networks are defined as much by their blockages and slownesses as by their speed and connection. While these networks allow individuals to overcome spatial distance, the spatial arrangement that arises is not a uniform closeness of all spaces on the earth. The crossing of border spaces in the network is full of possible diversions, perversions, recordings, and control by various juridical, security, and military regimes. Borders opened up through networks are like all borders: differential and differentiating. Some flows are allowed to move frictionlessly and unnoticed across global networks, while others are resisted and documented. This process of allowing and restricting flows then serves a differentiating function. Some information flows, such as the bank accounts of suspected terrorist organizations, are "frozen," while others are allowed to move in and out of banks completely undocumented.

Castells argues that those who exist in the "space of flows" have access to power, capital, and the globe, whereas those who exist in the "space of place" are often limited, divested, and exploited by the global network.[11] He suggests, "The global city is not a place, but a process. A process by which centers of production and consumption of advanced services, and their ancillary local societies are connected in a global network, while simultaneously downplaying the linkages with their hinterlands."[12] So not only do these telecontinents mirror geographical continents but they are also divided into territories, and the flows between and within them are regulated, watched, and diverted.

Thus Moonlight Maze suggests a way in which cyberattacks can be understood as a series of investments, divestments, and readings of place and flow. The Pentagon and other organizations attempted to limit information flows within secured networks contained within something resembling a territory in the global network of computer systems. Pentagon networks exist as an island territory within larger information territories, but with added secure connections to agents and information outside of the central network. Ultimately, attempts to constrain these flows were undermined by the attackers. On the other side, these attackers, in attempting to force information to flow outside its protected networks, were implicated by their attachment to the place of Moscow, revealed by the times during which they carried out their attacks.

Space begins, then, to take on a very different meaning in a networked world. Geographic space is supplemented by a whole collection of other spaces. Virilio suggests this proliferation of spaces when he refers to the importance of disabling radio and television signals during the NATO bombings of Serbia as a "clash in Hertzian space, which is a continuation of the clash in the air-space of the Balkans."[13] Some of these spaces, then, are organized by distance and duration, while others are organized by near-instantaneous connections. Moreover, some of these spaces are experienced as both flow and place. The global Internet often appears as pure flow concerned only with millisecond-scale lag time between servers, but, as soon as a main trunk line is disconnected, the geographic nature of the physical infrastructure comes to the fore. Bruno Latour summarizes this condition of space well:

> Out of geographers and geography, "in between" their own networks, there is no such a thing as a proximity or a distance which would not be defined by connectibility. The geographical notion is

simply another connection to a grid defining a metrics and a scale. The notion of network helps us to lift the tyranny of geographers in defining space.[14]

It should be added that while geography may be just another connection, it likely has a historical and political primacy as one of the earliest and still most important connected spaces of human existence. The difficulty of hiding the traces of Moscow and the existence of the Internet's physical infrastructure in geographic space attests to its political–historical importance. Perhaps it has always been true that geography has existed among a series of different channels that expand and minimize space. Even the creation of footpaths alters geographic space and creates new networked connections between spaces. Still, modern communication technologies rapidly create new technological spaces of both flow and place. Moreover, the growing interest in networks in fields from computer science to sociology to philosophy speaks to the ascendancy and importance of networked conceptions of space.[15]

Cyberwar develops this theorization of space in two ways. First, it exploits the reworking of distance inherent in communication technologies. As in the case of Moonlight Maze, attacks in cyberspace can happen at any distance so long as both the attacker and the target are connected in some way. As more and more critical systems and databases are networked to the global Internet, the possible impact of such attacks grows drastically. Second, most recent cyberattacks have occurred outside the space of war. Cyberwar, along with a number of other techniques, such as drone warfare, tends to take place outside of traditional conflicts with their delimited battlefields. It is not just cyberwar but a whole shift in the ways in which wars are fought in a networked globalized world that pushes war away from battlefields.

The time of war is also problematized by the rise of cyberwar. While Moonlight Maze is rarely discussed as being part of a war, John Hamre, U.S. deputy secretary of defense at the time of the attacks, declared during a congressional briefing, "We are in the middle of a cyberwar."[16] In all but a handful of instances, computer-based attacks that are often labeled as "cyberwar" have occurred without a kinetic war and in many cases between countries that are arguably allies. It seems that we may be witnessing an especially acute stage in the breakdown of the time and space of war. While some of these new wars may be slight in comparison to the bloody conflicts of the twentieth century, the way in which they rearrange the time and space of war should not be underestimated.

ESTONIA BETWEEN FLOW AND PLACE

While Moonlight Maze was declared a cyberwar by a few individuals, a row between Russia and Estonia in 2007 is often mentioned as one of the earliest all-out cyberwars.[17] On April 26 of that year, Estonia moved the *Bronze Soldier,* a memorial to Soviet soldiers killed during World War II, from the center of the Estonian capital Tallinn to a cemetery on the outskirts of town. Russians within both Estonia and Russia protested. Riots broke out in Tallinn, killing one and injuring more than a hundred people.[18] In response, the Russian parliament called for the resignation of the Estonian government and stopped rail service from St. Petersburg, train shipments of oil through Estonia, and even heavy vehicles from crossing a major bridge from Russia into Estonia.[19]

At the same time, a host of computer-based services in Estonia were hit with a distributed denial-of-service (DDoS) attack. A DDoS attack involves overwhelming a server with traffic such that it is no longer able to respond to legitimate requests. It is relatively easy to automatically block computers that are sending inordinate numbers of requests to a server, so most DDoS attacks must be distributed across a large number of machines to succeed. This is achieved either by maliciously taking over machines to create what is called a botnet, some of which have involved tens of millions of computers, or by convincing people to voluntarily lend their machines for the purpose of an attack. These voluntary or commandeered machines are then turned against servers to overrun them with requests and disable them. DDoS attacks thus do not require breaking into a machine and do not compromise private data that may reside on the server; rather, they disable the server for as long as the botnet can continue sending requests.

In Estonia, these attacks targeted government websites and critical businesses such as banks and newspapers, shutting down ATMs and some means of communication within the country. These attacks were especially symbolic because, at the time, Estonia was one of the most well-connected countries in Europe, with more than 90 percent of bank transactions completed online. The country even allowed Internet voting by this point. Seven years prior, in 2000, the Estonian parliament declared Internet access a human right.[20] Estonia was ultimately unable to counter the attacks and responded by shutting off Internet connections to other countries. This allowed services to resume within the country but prevented access to those outside the country. The attacks finally slowed down two weeks later. The Russian government denied any responsibility, and a number of security specialists have speculated that the attacks would have likely been more destructive if there had been direct government or military involvement, but there were extensive calls on Russian Internet for participation and instructions for how to join the attacks against Estonian institutions.[21]

The attacks on Estonia were carried out with a clear intent to disrupt the country in response to moving the *Bronze Soldier,* but beyond that and some technical details of the attack, little is discernable. The underlying purpose and the actors involved remain largely unknown, as Russia has refused any cooperation with Estonian law enforcement in finding and apprehending those responsible, despite a treaty guaranteeing mutual legal assistance. While it seems unlikely that the Russian government or military directly organized the specifics of the attacks, they have offered it their tacit approval by refusing to assist in any investigations. Thus the attacks against Estonia appear most likely to have been a "war" carried out by patriotic hackers not officially affiliated with the military, but perhaps with military support, and clearly outside the bounds and means of traditional kinetic warfare.[22] As much as it is possible to discuss the purpose of these attacks that were carried out by a variety of unidentified individuals, the attacks were aimed directly at disconnecting Estonia from the global Internet and economy. In addition to the DDoS attacks, the other provocations all served to disconnect Estonia. Cutting rail and heavy truck connections to Estonia act in this light as physical denial-of-service attacks. To return to Castells's point mentioned earlier, exclusion from global networks is perhaps now one of the gravest threats that could be wrought upon a nation. A denial-of-service attack, in both its digital and physical forms, relegates the target to the space of place, severing its connections to global networks. While cyberwar functions through a variety of modes, it seems one goal that is often invoked is to disconnect one's enemies from global spaces of flow.

All these attacks function at the same time to allow a level of plausible deniability. The physical infrastructure disruptions were claimed to be due to lack of passengers, repairs, and safety concerns rather than retribution. The cyberattacks were attributable to unknown patriotic hackers rather than a government or military group that could be held accountable. While in some cases it may be that governments and militaries truly were not involved, in the cases in which they were and attempt to deny their involvement, it is likely in many cases that this is due to fear of being cut off from global networks themselves. Ene Ergma, the speaker of the Estonian parliament at the time, claimed in an interview that "attacking us is one way of checking NATO's defenses. They could examine the alliance's readiness under the cover of the statue protest."[23] While Estonia did not invoke Article 5 of the NATO treaty, which outlines countries' responsibility of mutual defense, NATO responded by creating the NATO Cooperative Cyber Defence Centre of Excellence in Estonia's capital.[24] The creation of the Centre of Excellence served to reassert Estonia's position in a network of mutual defense, from which it was believed that Russia was attempting to sever Estonia. Thus this conflict can be read as a series of actions aimed at severing and reasserting Estonia's connection to global flows of information, capital, people, military assistance, and goods.

It is also clear from these attacks that we are witnessing a significant blurring of the distinction between civilian, military, and political spheres. Just over a year after the Estonian crisis, when Russia entered a kinetic war with Georgia over South Ossetia, a wave of cyberattacks against Georgian targets followed Russian physical attacks. Like the Estonian attacks, the degree of Russian involvement was largely indeterminable. These attacks followed a similar logic of attempting to disconnect Georgia from global networks and also to assert the legitimacy of the Russian cause, perhaps with the hope of winning the global media's blessing and thus support for maintaining global connections.[25] In both these conflicts, it is evident that cyberwar does not merely seize upon an increasingly connected world but rather intervenes directly in global space itself to attempt to define, create, and undermine spaces of connection and disconnection. The increasing military and state interest in cyberwar is, then, not simply a result of the rise of global networks but rather an active force that both promotes and attacks such connections. Although the attacks in Estonia and Georgia were in response to geopolitical (and networked) change, they sought actively to reshape a set of interconnected networks and spaces.

OPERATION ORCHARD AS MICROSCOPIC WAR

A few months after the attacks against Estonia, on September 6, 2007, Israeli fighter jets attacked a supposed nuclear installation in Syria. The jets entered Syrian air space, destroyed the site, and returned without being fired upon. Despite the two countries technically being at war since 1948, both downplayed the event, which is now known as Operation Orchard.[26] One of the most noteworthy elements of the attack was that a state-of-the-art radar system completely failed to detect the Israeli airplanes. Although it is unclear why the radar system failed, a number of commentators have suggested that the most likely cause was an advanced electronic attack on the system. Some sources even suggested it was possible that the computer chips that ran the radar system were fabricated with a "back door" so that they could be forced to malfunction.[27]

Even if this was not the case in the Israeli attack on Syria, chips being compromised during their production is becoming a growing military concern. The U.S. military has been working to create verified production facilities within the United States, but the growing number of commercial chips used in military equipment has complicated these efforts. There have been attempts to create systems to verify chips after production, but with current technology, it is nearly impossible to guard against a back door that is only triggered under specific conditions.[28]

There arises in cybersecurity a numbers game that generally favors attackers over defenders. For instance, microchips have become so complicated that a few transistors arranged in such a way that they can be activated for some malicious purpose are almost impossible to detect in chips now made of billions of transistors.[29] Furthermore, even if it were possible to check chips for insecurities, it would be possible to limit the number of compromised chips to a small number in a production run, requiring that nearly every chip be checked to guarantee security (and one would, of course, have to guarantee that the system that checked the chips had not been compromised itself).

Two important phenomena emerge from the insecurity of supply chains in a digital and globalized world. First, the space and time of war spread outside war itself in an even more insidious way than we saw previously. Cyberwar, especially as it includes physical points of intrusion into chips, requires, in a sense, that the war start before the war. The trap must be laid long before a conflict breaks out. The War then extends along the entire supply chain. Any place that weapons, infrastructure, or any systems containing chips are designed, assembled, and stored becomes a potential battle space in a future conflict. Though sabotage has always been a threat for warring parties, the globalization and commercialization of the computer chip market mean that a country may end up fighting the very country that designed and manufactured the majority of its computing power. Prior to the growth of computer-based weapons, it may have been possible to sell low-quality armaments or steel to a potential future enemy, but hiding such built-in failures was difficult. Now the situation is inverted, and the work required to find faults and back doors in chips is substantially greater than the work involved in creating and hiding them. It is, then, not only that a nation or group can be disconnected from global flows but also that these global flows can be turned against an adversary, quickly turning supply chains and capital flows into potential threats.

Second, new, more complicated gaps open between knowing and seeing. The military reliance on more and more complicated technology has, over the course of the past century or so, pushed military operations beyond the field of sight. With the introduction of computer chips, and especially chips that could be attacked or sabotaged, the battle space now includes the microscopic. Moreover, technologies like radar and other advanced warning systems now rely exclusively on these technologies, and thus attacks that are imperceptible and microscopic can disrupt one's ability to see on a macroscopic level. This is precisely what is believed to have happened in Syria. As Richard Clarke said of the attacks, "the view seen by the Syrians bore no relation to the reality that their eastern skies had become an Israeli Air Force bombing range. Syrian air defense missiles could not have been fired because there had been no targets in the system for them to seek out."[30] While war can now happen at every level from the microscopic to the global, defeat on one level easily spills over to all the others. Not only does war expand into cyberspace as a new domain of battle but other domains with their own geographies—including the macroscopic geographies of supply chains and the internal microscopic geographies of chips themselves—become realms of war and localized battle spaces.

War becomes rhizomatic and spreads out in all directions, including downward to the microscopic and imperceptible. Supply chains have always been important to war efforts, but what has changed is both the depth and breadth of global supply chains. Following World War II, the European Coal and Steel Community was created with the express purpose of tying French and German markets together to prevent another war, but this relied on the products of coal and steel being perceptible and war being a macroscopic phenomenon.[31] Now supply chains are intertwined on an imperceptible, molecular level, making their interdependency a potential source of instability rather than stability.

While nuclear weapons harness the microscopic power of atoms to create unprecedented levels of destruction, they are anathema to any type of precision, rendering them useless in any conflict short of all-out warfare. Cyberweapons act to counter this lack of precision. Instead of releasing the maximum power from atoms, bits are manipulated, corrupted, and destroyed with exacting precision. Not only are precise sites and types of machines selected for destruction but levels of destruction are dialed in to precisely determine the possible responses. This is not to say that these political calculations are always, or even often, done well or to the benefit of anyone. Nor is it to say that what is precisely chosen and destroyed will not create results that will spiral out of control. Still, interventions are weighed and aimed at specific nodal sites in global networks, moving these calculations away from geopolitics toward a nodal politics.[32] This networked political calculus does not replace the geographic but rather embeds geopolitics in what Virilio calls "metageophysics."[33] Ultimately, war in this new nodal space spreads out in every perceptible and imperceptible direction, intertwining with the civilian and the everyday. It follows the supply chains of advanced industrial nations all over the world, increasing the possibility that an imperceptible war could be fought unbeknownst to all observers. War then atomizes and moves along these multiple geographies, both spatial and aspatial, exploiting global flows and seeking infinitesimal advantages.

STUXNET AND THE STRATEGIC VALUE OF SLOWNESS

In June 2010, a virus was discovered that exploited a never before known vulnerability in the Windows operating system. The following month, news of the virus, dubbed Stuxnet, was picked up by a security blogger, who reported that it seemed to be targeting a Siemens device for automatic control of large industrial operations. While there were multiple variants discovered alongside substantial and often contradictory reporting, the virus is believed to have originated as early as 2007 and been aimed at Iran's uranium enrichment capabilities. The virus functioned by infecting Windows machines through flash drives. The virus then searched for a specific Siemens industrial controller. If the computer was not connected to such a controller, the virus did nothing aside from attempting to infect other computers. If the controller was detected, malicious code was installed onto the controller, which would eventually begin destroying the physical infrastructure of the plant, all while making it appear as though the system were operating normally.[34]

Researchers, analysts, and computer security firms are still attempting to assess the exact target or targets as well as the ultimate impact of the virus. Ralph Langner, one of the leading security experts studying Stuxnet, claims that, based on the Siemens controllers the virus was seeking, the sole target was an Iranian enrichment facility at Natanz. Although the exact extent of the damage has been hard to assess, it seems likely that roughly one thousand centrifuges (over 10 percent of the operational capacity at Natanz) were destroyed as a result of the virus altering the speeds of the centrifuges.[35]

A number of observers noted that the attack was most likely carried out by a state actor owing to the complexity of the virus. Some estimates suggest that it took multiple person-months or possibly even years to program a virus that complex.[36] Not only were advanced hacking skills required to break in to the Iranian networks but intimate knowledge of the Siemens control structure was necessary to cause anything more than mere annoyances. It was widely believed that the virus had to be of either U.S. or Israeli origin. In June 2012, the New York Times published a lengthy article claiming that the virus had been developed under George W. Bush's presidency as part of a program named "Olympic Games" and that Barack Obama decided to accelerate the program. According to the Times, the United States built a replica of Iran's enrichment facility, using P-1 centrifuges they acquired when Muammar Gaddafi dismantled the Libyan nuclear program in 2003, to test the virus.[37] It has also been disclosed by anonymous government sources in the United States that a similar attack was attempted against North Korea around the same time, but the virus was incapable of entering any North Korean facility, likely because of the extreme isolation of North Korean communication networks.[38]

The expense of deploying Stuxnet indicates the vast resources required to cause physical damage with a computer virus. There has been a growing concern, at least in the United States, of cyberterrorism and the opening of low-cost attack vectors to individuals or small groups around the world. For instance, Joseph Nye, former U.S. assistant secretary of defense and chairman of the U.S. National Intelligence Council, has claimed "that the diffusion of power away from governments is one of this century's great political shifts. . . . Dependence on complex cyber systems for support of military and economic activities creates new vulnerabilities in large states that can be exploited by non-state actors."[39] Given the cost and complexity of Stuxnet, these sentiments are, at least for now, overstated. At this point, Stuxnet is one of the only cyberattacks thus far to effectively cross the border into the physical world and cause substantial damage. A secret uranium enrichment facility is likely more difficult to attack than many other industrial systems, but the resources required to understand the physical structure in such a way to effectively compromise it and create enough damage before someone notices are not available to lone individuals or small groups. Furthermore, even though a computer virus can be programmed in relative secrecy, understanding a complicated industrial control system, let alone building a replica of an industrial facility, is difficult to achieve without the resources of a state or a well-financed and well-equipped group.

Stuxnet in many ways represents the state of the art of cyberwar and also suggests some of the key political–strategic considerations surrounding cyberwar. As an attack, the virus exists outside the bounds of traditionally understood war. Along these lines, David Gregory has argued that in addition to the United States entering a forever war, as evidenced by the War on Terror and the militarization of the United States–Mexico border, the United States is also engaged in an everywhere war.[40] He includes cyberwar and the ability of state-based hackers to reach across the globe instantaneously in his examples of this growing everywhere war. He suggests that new advances in cyberwar capabilities, such as the Stuxnet virus, allow cyberattacks to become precision weapons that can target specific countries or groups. We can extend Gregory's argument by adding that while cyberwar marks an everywhere war, it is not a placeless war. Gregory suggests that rather than "carpet bombing" cyberspace, the cyberweapons that are being designed and used are stealthy and precise weapons. They thus mark a specific synthesis between precision and global reach. This is not to suggest that these weapons, like other so-called precision weapons, are not capable of producing excessive damage to civilian lives and infrastructure purposefully or accidentally. Rather, they are purposefully targeted and, as such, rely on selecting specific places. Though the twenty-first-century army extends its capabilities over the globe, it selects and acts in specific places. These global war machines do not engage in a battle over the entire globe; rather, they select atomized battle spaces that exist potentially for only seconds at a time or, in other cases, sit dormant for years as a mere possibility that a conflict will erupt and a planned vulnerability will be exploited.

Thus cyberwar has an odd relationship with the space of war; it reconfigures the relationship between space and territory, but not by eviscerating it. Space and territory are given over to a networked reorganization that can be exploited for military, political, and economic ends.[41] Although war has always spilled outside its bounds, and states have never had a pure monopoly over war, the global War on Terror and the growing number of incursions in cyberspace mark a shift away from the battlefield to a global battle space. Moreover, the declaration of war seems to have been replaced by a series of global conflicts in which the state's (and especially the military's) monopoly over war has been broken up and redistributed to police forces, terrorists, paramilitaries, and private security firms to an unprecedented degree.

The technological limits on the space of the battlefield were of course destroyed long before Stuxnet by the invention of airplanes, battleships, and ballistic missiles, but wars were still fought within a territorial framework. The logic of territory as a place of war appears to be eroding. Traditional political alliances no longer constrain the space of war. The United States even supposedly hacked into then president of France Nicolas Sarkozy's office, including the computer of his chief of staff, shortly before the end of his presidency.[42] More important than military technology, perhaps what has changed and created this constant everywhere/forever war are the growing linkages across the globe. The rise of global capitalism has drastically increased the importance of disparate parts of the globe to each other. The interlinkages of supply chains, financial flows, information networks, climate, and labor flows create an increasing interdependency of the globalized world.

Insomuch as this global war machine selects certain atomized sites of intervention, the primacy of these sites seems to be not so much their geographic location as their location in a multiplicity of global networks. Global power projection, intervention, and exploitation are now organized around nodal sites. The United States's growing drone war in remote mountains and deserts is an attempt not to maintain control of territory but rather to disrupt what the program's architects see as critical nodes in a globalized network of terrorism.[43] Even before this, Virilio said of NATO bombings in Serbia that

> the logistics of perception on all fronts has won out over the logistics of weapons targeted along a particular front, or rather along that absence of front characterizing this absence of declared war. . . . By bombing the Serbian television building in Belgrade for the first time, NATO inaugurated a nodal war, which is merely the obverse of the total war of the mid-twentieth century.[44]

Virilio says little about what constitutes a nodal war, but the example of the NATO bombing of a television building suggests what he has in mind. The building functioned not as a geographic place, although it clearly exists in geographic space as well, but as a critical node in television and propaganda networks. It was selected for bombing precisely as a result of its existence in these networks. Its selection as a target along with its use for broadcasting in these multiple networks and spaces speak to its importance in network space. Thus what differentiates nodal war from traditional war is the shift toward focusing on these multiple and often nongeographic spaces. Cyberwar appears, then, as the epitome of what we could term nodal politics. Cyberwar attempts to completely short-circuit the need to engage with the enemy's territory and instead control, destroy, or corrupt certain critical nodes in the networked infrastructure of the enemy.

In this light, Stuxnet can be read as an attempt to engage specific nodes in the political, economic, and social network of Iran without intervening in Iran's territory. It exemplifies the manner in which cyberwar confounds the traditional space of war. Stuxnet did not completely overcome space, duration, or territory, as it was aimed exclusively at Iran. Still, the virus marked an attempt to apply military pressure to a precise node in a whole network of diplomatic, economic, and military relations. Geography still maintains a level of importance, but as one type of connection among many. A physical place like the Suez Canal may be politically important as a result of its geographic location, but what marks it as such is determined by being a critical link in a global shipping network. The type of network over which one attempts to assert power mediates geography's importance. For instance, maintaining control over intellectual property in a networked world becomes detached from geography and requires technological and networked solutions. Still, legal regimes surrounding copyright differ, and because these legal regimes are tied to territorial spaces, political and economic pressure comes to bear on nations as territorial entities even if their geographic proximity becomes less relevant.[45]

Moreover, while speed grants advantages to adversaries, Stuxnet suggests that speed alone may not always be all that matters. The virus was explicitly designed to move only through flash drives, and an infected machine was set only to infect three other machines. Stuxnet was purposefully slowed down so as not to attract too much attention. A virus that replicated at the speed of SQL Slammer would have been detected almost instantly. The slowness of Stuxnet not only decreased the likelihood of detection but also minimized its geographic spread. The vast majority of infected machines were in the Middle East, with 60 percent of infections within Iran.[46] There is still value in being able to stay in place, to move slowly and deliberately. One of the greatest difficulties of getting a virus into the uranium enrichment facility was that the networks that controlled the facility were air gapped, meaning they had no outside connections. While on average being well connected to networks may provide myriad benefits and facilitate nodal power projection, being disconnected from certain networks can also be an advantage. In confronting a disconnected target, the creators of Stuxnet were required to slow down their attack to match the slowness of their target. Rather than pure speed being advantageous, in a cyberwar, the ability to operate at multiple speeds and frequencies becomes critical. A successful attacker must be able to match the target's frequency, connection for connection and disconnection for disconnection, ultimately constructing a battle space that provides ideal speeds, connections, and disconnections. Deleuze and Guattari put it well when they discuss nomads, saying, "The nomad knows how to wait, he has infinite patience.

Immobility and speed, catatonia and rush."[47] It may be that those who move too fast or too slow tend to be disempowered, but this is always relative to an ideal speed for the parts of the networks one inhabits and in which one acts.

Sites of intervention then maintain their geographic nature, largely as a result of a variety of networked considerations, purposefully, as in the case of Stuxnet, or accidentally, as in the case of Moonlight Maze. Stuxnet demonstrates another level at which power becomes primarily nodal and networked rather than territorial and geographic. The international outcry surrounding Stuxnet was surprisingly muted, with even Iran downplaying the entire event. A number of legal scholars have suggested that, despite Stuxnet being an attack against a sovereign nation outside of a war, there may in fact be little illegal about the action. As one writer explained, the minimal amount of disruption Stuxnet caused meant that "it appears not to reach the threshold of illegality pursuant to public international law and thus to be a 'legal masterpiece.'"[48] Stuxnet is a precision weapon in that, not only was it able to disrupt specific types of equipment, but also it was precisely calibrated to fall under the international threshold for the use of force. It, in a sense, exploited a complicated network of international law and norms to maximize its effectiveness while minimizing the negative implications for the attacking nation.

Stuxnet and the decision to deploy the virus thus occupy sites across a spectrum of networks—geographic, imperceptible, perceptible, technological, and legal—and intervene within these networks at precise points. Military force is deployed at precisely chosen nodal sites and through equally precise connections in a wide array of networks that intertwine to control and exploit a variety of global and local flows. Thus geography does not simply disappear. Rather, it is overrun by a variety of additional networks that define, shift, and reshape the power of geography.

THE MULTIPLE NAMES OF COMMENT CREW

Starting around the same time as Moonlight Maze, in the late 1990s, there was a constant string of unattributed attacks against military and corporate networks both within the United States and globally, with the presumed aim of stealing military and commercial technology. Many of these attacks went unreported, as corporations were afraid of the negative publicity, but increasingly these attacks were investigated by both law enforcement and private security firms. One of the most interesting of these investigations by a private security firm, Mandiant, led to a report, published in February 2013, accusing the Chinese military of overseeing a series of attacks against U.S. companies. The firm traced more than 150 attacks since 2006, which they believed were carried out by the same group, often identified by the moniker Comment Crew. Mandiant traced the attacks to a neighborhood in Shanghai housing the headquarters of the Chinese army's Unit 61398. Mandiant, which also published an earlier report in 2010 where it stated that it was impossible to determine the extent of involvement by the Chinese government, ultimately concluded in the more recent report,

> Our analysis has led us to conclude that APT1 [Advanced Persistent Threat 1—the name Mandiant uses for the group they are attempting to identify] is likely government-sponsored and one of the most persistent of China's cyber threat actors. We believe that APT1 is able to wage such a long-running and extensive cyber espionage campaign in large part because it receives direct government support. In seeking to identify the organization behind this activity, our research found that People's Liberation Army (PLA's) Unit 61398 is similar to APT1 in its mission, capabilities, and resources. PLA Unit 61398 is also located in precisely the same area from which APT1 activity appears to originate.[49]

The report even claims to have identified some of the individuals working in Unit 61398 because they logged in to Facebook or Twitter from the same machines they were using for the attacks.

Thus a few traces (a shared server, a common technique, a reused exploit) are linked together and given a proper name—Moonlight Maze, Comment Crew/APT1/Unit 61398, Stuxnet, and so on—and a certain argument is put forth about someone's responsibility. The skill by which these traces are assembled into a proper name is always questionable. For instance, one security expert pointed out that the address Mandiant claimed belonged to Unit 61398 actually housed a preschool.[50] While it still seems likely that most of Mandiant's claims are accurate, even the specifics of how the threat is assembled provoke and call for different responses. The question of whether these actions are criminal or military does not have a correct answer; an interpretation must be created and convince a large number of diverse actors. It is in a sense a social process that mirrors the technical process of computer forensics. A semiotic threat network must be assembled from electronic traces to produce a threatening body, be it an individual, an organization, or a state. In a way, the work of attributing cyberattacks mirrors the work of the hacker; one organizes tiny mistakes and oversights into a coherent narrative, and the other organizes similar mistakes into an attack.

While there is a tendency in a variety of fields to associate networks with completely fluid, dynamic, and horizontal structures, it is more often the case that self-organized networks produce clusters and create structures that are flexible, but at the same time redundant and robust.[51] This can happen in all types of networks, be they technological, social, or biological. In many cases, the cost of making connections among nodes tends to favor structures with many local connections and few long-distance connections. Still, critical systems often collapse if there is only a single long-distance connection. Thus, although there tend to be few of these long-distance connections, there are often enough so that even were one or two to be cut, the network would still continue to function. In a sense, the creation of tight clusters out of long-distance networks is ultimately what hackers and forensic analysts achieve. They form out of so many disparate traces, mistakes, and perhaps even purposefully deceptive clues a theory or an attack vector that may fail or succeed, depending on the skill with which it was assembled, the current political climate (in the case of forensic analysis), and the acumen of the target's network administrators (in the case of hacking). Mandiant's analysis pulls together a variety of threads to make a relatively compelling argument that the Chinese military was involved in this series of attacks. The security expert who claimed the address referred to a preschool begins to loosen the cluster of arguments in support of Mandiant's hypothesis, but it seems unlikely at this point to be enough to completely nullify Mandiant's claims and destroy the cluster of traces it pulled together.

In a small article about a Tomás Saraceno installation, Bruno Latour suggests something similar:

This is not to say that spheres are made from different stuff, as if we must choose between habitation and connection, between local and global, or indeed between Sloterdijk and, let's say, actor-network theory. What Saraceno's work of art and engineering reveals is that multiplying the connections and assembling them closely enough will shift slowly from a network (which you can see through) to a sphere (difficult to see through). Beautifully simple and terribly efficient.... Instead of having to choose between networks and spheres, we can have our cake and eat it too. There is a principle of connection—a kind of movement overlooked by the concepts of networks and spheres alike—that is able to generate, in the hands of a clever artist, both networks and spheres; a certain topology of knots that may thread the two types of connectors in a seamless web.[52]

This metaphor of spheres born of intertwined networks is an apt description for what is at stake in a cyberwar. On both sides, adversaries attempt to weave together tightly clustered networks, be they sets of computer servers or arguments about history, and adversaries attempt to destroy or modify these spheres to their advantage. We can take Latour's argument one step further and posit that these tightly woven spheres then become the nodes at the next level of analysis. There exists a network of nations with their various relationships, but these nations are themselves networks of individuals, organizations, laws, goods, and so on. In the case of Unit 61398, Mandiant has woven a tightly coupled sphere out of so many traces, producing new units of analysis. Politicians, analysts, and strategists can act as though Unit 61398 is a thing in and of itself that needs no further proof of existence. In fact, Mandiant's analysis has put considerable pressure on U.S. politicians to respond to believed Chinese military incursions into U.S. networks.[53] Of course, there is always the risk that someone would be able to successfully dispute these claims and thus tear asunder the node Mandiant or another actor attempts to create. As Galloway and Thacker note, "any instance of naming always produces its shadowy double: nominalism, that is, the notion that universal descriptors do not adequately represent the referents they are supposed to name or demarcate."[54] Any node always bears within it the possibility that other, uncontrollable traces will destabilize it; that it will cease to hold together; and that its descriptor will fail to name it convincingly.

War and politics in this realm then begin not only to fix upon the most important nodes in various economic, legal, and military networks but also to reshape the connections and nodes of these networks to their advantage. War becomes the ability not only to occupy and control nodes or connect and disconnect parts of the network but to shape the space and networks that underlie the global battle space. Perhaps this is part of the reason that late-twentieth- and early-twenty-first-century war begins to fixate so heavily on the spectacle. It may be that, rather than war becoming a purely virtual phenomenon, war has instead taken the naming of reality itself as its object. If one can effectively intervene in the multiple networks that define the twenty-first-century globe, it may now be possible to win conflicts without even fighting them. Through these attempts to win by defining the battle, war has become actively engaged in the process of representing both the world and the ability to destroy it. In that sense, we must add a provision to Galloway's claim: "There is one game in town: a positivistic dominant of reductive, systemic efficiency and expediency. Offering a counter-aesthetic in the face of such systematicity is the first step toward building a poetics for it, a language of representability adequate to it."[55] These dominant forces are equally invested in destroying this game, in upsetting the positivist investments of their enemies. War machines, states, and corporations are already invested in representing the complex space of these networks and in destroying both networks and their representations. The cases of Comment Crew and Stuxnet demonstrate that there is not merely a reductive system of efficiency. Rather, the powers of war and conflict are invested in both speed and slowness; pure unnamed flow and the poetics of representation; construction and destruction. Thus any resistance to these forces of war and control, while it certainly must utilize these tactics, cannot rely solely on representation and slowness against the speed and complexity of war and domination.

INTERNATIONAL LAW AND TERRITORIALITY

The speed at which these spaces are created and reconfigured creates dynamic forces that threaten to destabilize the institutions that exist within these spaces. One need only look at the difficulty that governments face in legislating and regulating networks to see how destabilizing these spaces can be. The constant reconfiguration of the technological, topological, and conceptual nature of these spaces impedes their integration into legal frameworks. For instance, the attribution problem stems from the reach and speed with which individuals can connect and disconnect from the global Internet. This particular difficulty is often taken up in legal discussions surrounding cyberwar. Although the problem of attributing attacks affects the security of systems, it is more often a political and legal problem. If it is impossible to assign responsibility for an attack convincingly, political and military responses become difficult. A number of legal solutions to both the attribution problem and this more general destabilization of quickly shifting spaces have been proposed, but many quickly run into challenges.

One potential legal remedy to the uncontrollability of networks has been to make individual nations responsible for attacks originating in their territories.[56] This attempt to solve the attribution problem shifts the burden of responsibility to the countries from which attacks emanate, regardless of their political or military involvement in the attacks. Although a number of legal scholars, especially from the United States, have suggested this potential approach, their optimism is usually tempered by the admission that the vast majority of attacks traverse networks inside the United States owing to the density of well-networked (and often insecure) computers in that country.[57] It seems ultimately unlikely that the United States or many other countries would actually push such an agenda on an international level, because they would then be responsible for a vast number of attacks and compromised machines. Aside from the question of whether such a solution is politically viable or would actually serve to decrease the rate of attack, it is interesting in that it attempts to reassert the geographic territoriality and responsibility of nations over the network. Moreover, these attempts mark a willingness among these authors to give up identity in favor of a new territoriality. The proponents of this plan seem so frustrated by attacks that they are willing to forgo knowing the identity of attackers (whether they are military, paramilitary, rogue agents, etc.) by assigning responsibility to those with national political control over territory.

An American legal scholar and a computer scientist, Jeremy and Ariel Rabkin, have gone so far as to suggest that the United States reintroduce the practice of issuing "letters of marque" to counter cyberattacks. Letters of marque were a practice for dealing with pirates up until the middle of the nineteenth century. With a letter of marque, a privateer would be authorized by a government to attack and capture pirate vessels. Thus, while the government did not take responsibility for the reprisal, it would offer legal protection for privateering. The notion proposed by the Rabkins would have the U.S. government offer letters of marque to domestic hackers to attack particular hackers in other countries. They are clear about the claimed benefits of privateering, both historically and contemporarily: "In practice, letters of marque often were issued to those who had learned the craft of capturing prize at sea without any government authorization. Governments issuing authorization brought these raiders under more state control in return for offering them more state protection."[58] The extent to which some scholars of cyberwar are willing to go to reassert state and territorial control over its complicated existence in cyberspace is at times astounding. This is not to suggest that an unraveling of state control over cyberspace or territory is inevitable. The opposite may be true: that we are condemned to live in a bordered, nationalized, territorial world for centuries. What is surprising about the Rabkins' suggestion is the intensity of their response to the fear that an uncontrolled military force might grow outside of the state's control. Rather than rethinking the relationship between state, territory, and war, they seem to reach for any legal metaphor to recapture these events in the space of law and territory. They are keenly aware that one of the effects of letters of marque is to bring privateers under some state control. They are willing to return to privateering so as to guarantee that everything falls into the state/territorial system at least to the highest degree possible.

Both of these attempts appear to try to reinscribe cyberspace into the space of the nation: the first simply by using the physical location of servers to inscribe cyberspace in national law and the second by treating cyberspace as analogous to the high seas and legalizing privateering. In both cases, the authors see war located on the Internet as problematic for state control. This fear testifies to a loosening of the state's control over space, or at least the new spaces created through modern communication technologies.

This is not to say that such a process is historically unique but rather that cyberwar can be understood as part of a process of militarization creating smooth space, Deleuze and Guattari's term for an open space across which forces are able to move uninterrupted. They define this type of space against striated space, the space of law and the state, in which one is held in place and blocked from movement. Their concepts of smooth and striated space share much with Castell's distinction between spaces of flow and spaces of place. The distribution and configuration of these spaces are central to contemporary politics. As Deleuze and Guattari suggest, the state "does not just go from the smooth to the striated, it reconstitutes smooth space; it reimparts smooth in the wake of the striated. It is true that this new nomadism accompanies a worldwide war machine whose organization exceeds the State apparatuses and passes into energy, military-industrial, and multinational complexes."[59] This is not to suggest that these are necessarily spaces of liberation or freedom. Rather, these spaces can become the most terrifying sites of state violence. One could easily imagine that smooth spaces inhabited by pirates and privateers could be more violent than the interiors of state control. Thus we must draw a distinction between the spaces in which the state acts and spaces the state can control. These spaces that are opened for military intervention often turn into spaces in which the state acts but is ultimately unable to control and is thus forced to appropriate and integrate privateering, piracy, and other forces that exceed the state and potentially destabilize it.

The militarization of new spaces is not unequivocally on the side of expanded state control. Rather, it appears that the expansion and distortion of the space of war may ultimately undermine the state's relation to its territory, requiring the creation of novel legal regimes or the reintroduction of old institutions, such as privateering, to reappropriate these destabilizing spaces to state control. These spaces are not frictionless networks over which the state unceasingly expands its control. It is the complexity, multiplicity, and polyvocal nature of these spaces and those systems that inhabit them that continually challenge state attempts to fix, stabilize, and manage them.

CYBER-RANGES

In addition to legal attempts to police quickly shifting network spaces, lawmakers and military planners are inventing other strategic ways to operate within and control these spaces. While the military has begun to consider cyberspace a "domain" of warfare, similar to air, sea, land, and outer space, what precisely is meant by cyberspace being a domain is only now becoming clear.[60] It has become popular for the military, and even businesses, to have "live-fire" cyberexercises. These exercises are normally carried out on a cyber-range, where an underlying system (which is, under the rules of the game, off limits for hacking) simulates multiple computer systems. Typically a blue team is responsible for maintaining basic operations on the simulated computer systems (e.g., a Web server, e-mail, databases), whereas the red team attempts to hack into the systems or disable them.

In November 2012, the SANS Institute established, on behalf of the U.S. military, a cyber-range named CyberCity. The idea behind it was to move beyond the notion of just defending networks and offer training exercises where physically embedded networks control critical infrastructure, such as electric grids and transportation systems. As the director of the SANS Institute, Eric Bassel, said of the need for this training, "When you lose control of cyberspace, you lose control of the physical world."[61] To provide this training on a multifaceted network embedded in a city space, a scale model of this imagined city was created using a model train set connected to a server.

CyberCity is a novel example in that it marks one of the first attempts to simulate cyberwar in a network with a physical spatiality, but what is most notable about the creation of CyberCity was one of the example missions identified in interviews with its creators. The training mission involved a researcher, acting as a foreign special forces operative, attempting to access systems at the hospital to assassinate a patient by altering his medication schedule. To prevent this, trainees on the blue team were asked to gain control of the hospital networks in order to block these attacks.[62] Rather than the normal practice in these live-fire exercises, in which the blue team is tasked with defending a network, in this exercise, the blue team is required to defend a physical asset (a human) by attacking a network.

This marks a sea change in thinking about cyberwar. Instead of implicitly imagining networks within a territory as networks that should be defended (or ignored in favor of higher-value military networks), this opens up the possibility that a military or security agency would hack into a domestic network to further strengthen it. In much the same fashion that the notion of urban warfare has conceptually turned the city from a fort that must be defended to the space of battle itself, cyberspace has quickly been turned from a set of networked forts to be defended to a literal battle space. Networks and computer systems now become a potential (and quickly shifting) backdrop to a battle, where the military cares little about the functioning of these networks outside the scope of the battle. Furthermore, this logic marks a theoretical abandonment of the fantasy of total network security. Instead it appears as an admission of the unavoidable insecurity of even our most critical networks.

The difficulties in completely securing network space have encouraged this shift from seeing networks as assets to be defended to a neutral battle space where fortifications may be created and as quickly abandoned. This movement toward conceptualizing networks as a battle space marks a new development in the spatial relationship between networks and geography. Rather than creating national territories in cyberspace, the U.S. military, along with the SANS Institute, is pushing toward recognizing a second-order networked battle space, where the connections of this space are created and sabotaged for the purposes of winning global conflicts.

Rather than a series of networked forts with topological connections, the attack and defense of this space's topology itself becomes an object of war. To put it in Deleuzian terms, we are witnessing a smoothing of space. Places where entrance is denied or permitted are being replaced by a smooth network fabric where the military comes and goes as it pleases, unconcerned with whose network it has commandeered. This then marks a military commitment to smooth space, or existing in spaces of flow, to use Castell's term. The military fixes not on their territoriality but on the flows they process and their relation to global networks.

Eyal Weizman, in an article about the Israeli Defense Force's (IDF) conceptualization of military strategy in Deleuzian terms, depicts the way in which the IDF was able to operationalize Deleuze's concept of the smooth and striated to rearrange urban battle spaces. Recounting an incursion into Nablus in 2002, Weizman explains that the IDF conceptualized its strategy as "smoothing" the striated spaces of households and barricaded alleyways. At the same time, Palestine was striated from without by travel restrictions, sanctions, and so on. Ultimately, the IDF and the Israeli government had more resources available for creating smooth and striated spaces and the ability to flow through space overcoming what striations existed. A whole military strategy arises then out of smoothing and striating spaces. Though some spaces are smoother than others, some individuals and groups also are able to move or flow more easily through both smooth and striated spaces. Moreover, there are those who are able to flow through the preestablished networks of global capitalism, and there are those who are able to create new smooth spaces (such as the IDF in Weizman's article) and those who are able to create new striated spaces. In some cases, these may be the same individuals, and in other cases, individuals may be adept at only one or even none of these operations.

In this light, cyberwar functions in two distinct but interrelated modes. First, as was the case in Estonia, the aim of the cyberattacks was to striate the network space of Estonia and cut it off from global flows. On the other hand, attacks such as Moonlight Maze and those carried out by Unit 61398 were designed to smooth the space of certain networks to allow advantageous information to flow out of protected networks, making it accessible to the attackers. Furthermore, in the case of the Stuxnet attack, flows were slowed down in an attempt to striate the space of its spread, attempting to limit its effects to the territory of Iran. Cyberwar works through reconfiguring space, creating smoothness and striation, and blocking or freeing flows. Moreover, cyberwar attacks the security flaws enmeshed in both spaces of place and flow to rework them toward the attackers' aim.

We should note that with the realization that it is advantageous to smooth and striate spaces according to one's strategy, and with the increasing ease with which this can be done, there may be a general smoothing of global space. In this regard, Deleuze and Guattari say, "The world became a smooth space again (sea, air, atmosphere), over which reigned a single war machine, even when it opposed its own parts. Wars had become a part of peace. More than that, the States no longer appropriated the war machine: they reconstituted a war machine of which they themselves were only the parts."[63] This decidedly does not mean that either smooth or striated space is always strategic or desirable. The strategic value of each depends on its location and time in the network.

VULNERABLE SPACES AND TEXTS

The smooth and striated spaces that are at stake in cyberwar are not only geopolitical but exist within the systems that are attacked as well. The flows of data within programs, databases, and servers are subjected to striations that are meant to keep the program secure, and at the same time, smooth spaces are opened up to allow the flow of data and commands. Attacking these systems often involves smoothing the space of the program to allow unintended flows of data and code. For instance, on September 19, 2007, a group of anti-U.S. hackers based in Turkey, known as m0sted, were able to break into servers belonging to the U.S. Army Corps of Engineers. Although it does not appear that they were able to access sensitive data, they redirected Web traffic to their own website. Investigators believe that the hackers likely were able to gain control of the system through a Structured Query Language (SQL) injection attack.[64] The attack itself seems to have done little serious damage, but the likely means of entry are indicative of the ways in which vulnerabilities can be exploited to reshape the space of networks and programs.

SQL injection vulnerabilities are a major threat to interactive websites, as they can allow an attacker remote access to the databases that control the website. They are part of a larger class of vulnerabilities, known as injection attacks, that work by inserting code into the computer where the program expects data. Younan reports that in the twenty-five years between 1988 and 2012, injection attacks were the fourth most common type of vulnerability, and if one looks only at vulnerabilities that pose high severity threats, they were the second most common.[65] It is worthwhile to spend a little time exploring the precise mechanism by which such an attack occurs, both because of the frequency of these types of vulnerabilities and because these attacks can concisely demonstrate how a vulnerability exploits the textual nature of a program.

An injection attack leverages the ambiguity between data and command within code at the location where two different programming languages communicate with each other.[66] Often this involves a database language, such as SQL, that receives commands from a different language. Imagine a database that consists of usernames and passwords. A simple SQL command to look up the password of a user "ada" might look something like this:

```
SELECT 'password' FROM 'users' WHERE 'user' = 'ada';
```

This bit of code will return the password from the table "users" that corresponds with the user named "ada" so that a program could check

if the user inputted the correct password.[67] Aside from how the passwords are stored, this code has no remarkable security vulnerabilities,
but often it is another programming language that creates these queries. For example, PHP, a relatively common programming language
for interactive websites, might be used to get a username from a Web
form and query the database. The code could look something like this
(note that this structure of creating queries has largely been deprecated
as newer versions of libraries have been created to mitigate the risk of
injection attacks, but the older insecure form demonstrates most clearly
how these vulnerabilities work):

```
$user = $_GET['username'];
$query = "SELECT 'password' FROM 'users' WHERE 'user' =
'" . $user . ';"
$result = sql_query($query);
```

In PHP, the $ is used to specify a variable; so the first line takes data from
a user-submitted variable ("get" is a way for passing data to a website)
and stores the data in the variable "user." The second line then takes this
value and uses it to construct a query string. The periods concatenate
multiple strings together; literal strings are enclosed in double quotes,
and variables, such as $user, are left on their own. The third line then
sends this query to the database. So, if we pass the username "ada," the
second line effectively becomes

```
$query = "SELECT 'password' FROM 'users' WHERE 'user' =
'"."ada"."';"
```

which is the same as

```
$query = "SELECT 'password' FROM 'users' WHERE 'user' =
'ada';"
```

Once this is executed, it works in the same way as our initial SQL query,
but with the added benefit that the same code can handle any username.
This all works fine, until someone inputs a username like

```
'; UPDATE 'users' SET 'password'='newpassword
```

Once this string is concatenated into the query, it ends up like this:

```
$query = "SELECT 'password' FROM 'user' WHERE 'user' =
'" . "'; UPDATE 'users' SET 'password'='newpassword" .
';"
```

If we concatenate the string, we get

```
$query = "SELECT 'password' FROM 'users' WHERE 'user' =
''; UPDATE 'users' SET 'password'='newpassword';"
```

So, instead of the single select command, the database is now given two commands (the semicolon indicates the end of a command) to execute. The first attempts to select a blank user, and then regardless of the outcome, the second, injected command now sets everyone's password to "newpassword." Injection attacks can be prevented by properly sanitizing the data that are passed to the database, making sure the data contain no characters that would allow the input to be executed as commands. Sometimes this takes the form of escaping special characters, such as quotes (putting a slash or other character in front of it so that the database knows it is just character data rather than a command). Although these and other defenses can be effective, they only work if they are applied rigorously every place data can enter the system and if they are designed with full knowledge of exactly how the database language will interpret every command and character that is passed to it.

These types of attacks can take many forms and produce different outcomes from revealing the secret data in databases to giving an attacker complete control over a system. Regardless of the ultimate goal, these attacks succeed by sending commands (e.g., change all passwords) where the programmer expected only data (e.g., a username or a block of text) and exploiting the different interpretations of text between two languages (such as a single quote in our example). Injection vulnerabilities exist in neither one language nor the other but rather in the border between the two. The space between the two languages is assumed striated, such that aside from the predetermined query, only data and not commands should pass between them. Between these two languages, in translation, in the unstable space between data and command, the quotation mark is fundamentally polyvocal. Its meanings multiply, and the programmer can never fully control the input. It floats between the two languages, a surplus of inscription that opens a lacuna in the program, neither data nor command. The mark precludes the closure of the program, guaranteeing its textual ambiguity. This singular mark smooths the space, opening the border between the two, giving the attacker unfettered access to all sorts of digital spaces inside the machine and potentially even the physical space of its environment.

The stray quote mark rearranges the space and regulation of the system, but it does so with the insertion of text. We will turn to the textual aspects of cyberwar shortly, but for the time being, it is important to note the entanglement here between text and space: the spacing of text, as Derrida would say, but also the textuality of space. Especially with digital networks, it is often text, password, command, and data that control access to digital and physical space. Computation exists within a spatialized textuality and a textualized spatiality that is put into play by a rogue inscription.

THE HIGH-DIMENSIONAL BATTLE SPACE

Cyberwar advances with the accelerating breakdown of the traditional space and time of warfare. This is not to suggest that cyberwar as a military strategy is solely responsible for this breakdown; rather, cyberwar appears to be one of the more symptomatic elements of this larger shift. A whole host of growing interconnections, from communication networks to globalized trade, is creating new vulnerabilities, interdependencies, and opportunities. It is precisely this late-capitalist, post–Cold War geopolitical situation that is forcing practitioners of war to reconceptualize the means and even the ends of war. Still, cyberwar is at the leading edge of exploring and exploiting this breakdown of warfare. As a strategy, it quickly moves warfare beyond the space of the battlefield, allowing it to seep into economic, political, and diplomatic networks. Furthermore, if cyberwar is taken in its broadest sense to mean a mode of war that fixes on systems and their functioning, then cyberwar can be understood as precisely that type of war that fights in an ever-expanding realm of multiple spaces and ways of being in space.

Of course, the practitioners of warfare have always been concerned with the economic and political, but, since the early 1990s, an explosion of military discourse has concerned intervention in traditionally nonmilitary affairs. Following what was seen as a stunning victory of technological domination in the Gulf War, military strategists in the United States began to consider how future conflicts would unfold in light of such technological asymmetries. Picking up on Sun-Tzu's famous dictum "to subdue the enemy without fighting is the acme of skill," one of the conclusions a number of strategists began to reach was that warfare would focus less on fighting and more on other forms of coercion. For example, in 1994, a U.S. Air Force colonel, Richard Szafranski, wrote an article about what he termed "neocortical warfare," invoking Sun-Tzu's theory of war and arguing that we should view "war not as the application of physical force, but as the quest for metaphysical control."[68] His article goes on to explain that the purpose of war is to subdue the enemy's will and that achieving this goal only through "destroying the enemy's brain" is rather shortsighted. He suggests learning as much about the enemy as possible so that the opposing force can be subverted before a conflict even begins. This is precisely the military logic we have been tracing. War as metaphysical control, with the aim to win before even beginning, moves war completely outside of itself. As this logic pushes war beyond and outside itself into a multiplicity of networks, war atomizes and moves into all aspects of global space and time.

Two colonels in the Chinese PLA, Qiao and Wang, have developed similar theories in a text that was translated into English as *Unrestricted Warfare.* Their theory of warfare, they say, is based on the American strategies on display during the Gulf War, but they believe the Americans did not take the logic far enough. Suggesting a theory similar to the notion of metaphysical control, they argue that military strategists must expand the domain of war, considering all domains as potential spaces of military innervation. They argue that war takes place in these multiple dimensions and that the enemy can be defeated in any of them. Ultimately, Qiao and Wang aptly describe this proliferation of spaces of conflict and their increasing interconnection, stating,

> Technology is doing its utmost to extend the contemporary battlefield to a degree that is virtually infinite: there are satellites in space, there are submarines under the water, there are ballistic missiles that can reach any place on the globe, and electronic

countermeasures are even now being carried out in the invisible electromagnetic spectrum space. Even the last refuge of the human race—the inner world of the heart—cannot avoid the attacks of psychological warfare. There are nets above and snares below, so that a person has no place to flee. All of the prevailing concepts about the breadth, depth and height of the operational space already appear to be old-fashioned and obsolete. In the wake of the expansion of mankind's imaginative powers and his ability to master technology, the battlespace is being stretched to its limits.[69]

The battle space is thus transformed into a high-dimensional space that complicates the primacy of geography and supplements it with an ever-increasing set of spaces that intersect and interact with previous networks.

In one sense, this military investment in "metaphysical control" and new battle spaces is a continuation of ancient strategies of deception, sabotage, and manipulation, but still this contemporary explication seems to mark a qualitatively new level of abstraction and expansiveness. As DiNardo and Hughes, two military historians and theorists, have warned, this focus on a metaphysical battle space marks a military–strategic investment in the complete inversion of the Clausewitzean formula in which politics is war by other means.[70] In a 1995 article in *Airpower Journal,* they worry that the military focus on information warfare and subduing the enemy outside of traditional fighting lends itself to a complete military intervention into politics and civilian life. Chun's insight that software functions as ideology is thus important in another regard: both software and ideology, along with law and economics, become sites of intervention that risk their symbolic functioning being turned against them.[71]

Although war spills over into all aspects of everyday life, it is decidedly not total war. It is almost the opposite: a war so constrained and reserved that it nearly goes unnoticed. As is argued in *Unrestricted Warfare,* growing global interlinkages, including international law, the shared biosphere, a highly connected global economy, and the threat of global thermonuclear war, serve to constrain many global actors. This is not to suggest that these constraints are always or even often effective or that they are positive forces, but they add additional costs that complicate political and military calculuses. All of these serve to put political limits on military options. Instead of vertical escalations of conflict to ever more violence, we are witnessing a horizontal escalation to ever more varied modes of conflict. As war spreads, it escalates horizontally and strategists attempt to open new domains. Thus "fighting" begins to look little like previous conflicts. For instance, the existence of both domestic and international law opens the possibility that one force would be able to limit another force's strategic options by litigation (a strategy occasionally referred to as lawfare).[72] These global interconnections have raised the cost of military escalation, often forcing states to fight within specified rules and domains for fear of upsetting the global order and unleashing potentially more destructive forces or disconnections from global spaces of flow.

Rather than a completely accessible global battle space where war would rage unhindered, we are witnessing the growth of a metaconflict where strategists, legal experts, and public relations experts are constantly attempting to define and constrain war for each side's strategic advantage. The concept of war has now become part of war itself. As Qiao and Wang argue, the means to contemporary victory in war involve combining limited ends with unlimited means. They are careful to say that this is not total war. Rather, it is a war that weighs means and is not afraid to use any of them, but always to achieve limited rather than total ends. This must be at least part of what Virilio calls "pure war," or elsewhere the "race to the absolute essence of war"[73] as military goals become increasingly limited while strategy expands infinitely, culminating in "the war with zero deaths for the military, but also zero victories in political terms."[74] Rather than an all-out war, we are witnessing with the rise of cyberwar a war that spills outside the bounds of traditional warfare while remaining vertically constrained. This is not to say that these conflicts cannot become horribly violent; for the further afield these interventions stray, the more they may be likely to spiral out of control.

CONCLUSION: ACTING IN THE SPACE AND TIME OF NETWORKS

Cyberwar, when defined broadly to mean war that fixes on systems and networks, does not simply function in a nongeographical space of networks. Rather, it succeeds as a strategy because of its ability to identify, exploit, create, and destroy a multitude of spaces. Practitioners of cyberwar attempt to connect and disconnect themselves and their adversaries from global networks while reshaping these networks and the traces that flow through them to achieve their desired ends. While it may appear that it is the ease of covering up networked attacks that allows states to execute attacks outside of the space and time of declared war, the situation is much more complicated. Cyberwar functions within *new* spaces and *new* times, not just outside of specific spaces and times. Its theorists and backers seek out new "attack vectors" in the highly networked space of global capitalism. They seek new spaces to attack and reconfigure, be they geographic, technological, imperceptible, economic, or even conceptual and philosophical. In doing so, they open up spaces of metaconflict that allow wars to be fought and won on multiple levels. Although there may be an increasing number of connections and interlinkages between and within these spaces, cyberwar does not always fight on the side of connection or disconnection, speed or slowness. Successful strategies seek out specific sites of intervention, creating connections and disconnections alike. Like Deleuzian nomads, they vary their speed: the slowness of geography and earth here and the speed of light there.

Ultimately, these adventures in high-dimensional warfare and the reconfiguration of both macro and micro metageophysics are inevitably destabilizing. While we are not in the least witnessing an end to geography or territory, the speed with which cyberwar moves into and out of geographic spaces confounds state-based attempts to understand and conceptualize it. While thinkers of state policy are quickly dreaming up new and old methods for constraining and appropriating these new strategies, which are undermining older ties between law, state, and territory (while attempting to maintain the possibility for states' utilization of them for their own ends), it is unclear to what degree they will succeed and what if any legal regime will capture these forces.

It is often suggested that the rise of network technologies is rapidly decreasing geographic distance, increasing global connections, and ultimately speeding up our shared existence. Among the more nuanced readings of this situation, it is argued that this phenomenon is not evenly distributed and that some individuals have access to these growing networks while others are excluded. Virilio says there are "classes of speed like classes of wealth."[75] Castells develops his theory that some individuals have access to spaces of flow, while others are relegated to, or choose, spaces of place where one has far fewer opportunities. Likewise, Boltanski and Chiapello argue that the new mode of global capitalism rewards those who are flexible and mobile, while exploiting those who either refuse or are not able to flow through these global networks.[76] The rise of cyberwar suggests that the situation is even more complicated. Those who are able to take advantage of these new global spaces and connections are not only the well connected; rather, three distinct operations become central. First, the ability to reshape connections and disconnections in conceptual, economic, legal, geographic, and technological networks becomes critical. Second, identifying both the most important networks and the most central nodes as sites of intervention allows actors to control the space of conflict. Moreover, the ability to select nodes and assemble varied network connections and traces into nodes or spheres that are able to resist dissolving is essential. Finally, as was seen especially in the case of Stuxnet, one must not always bet on speed or slowness but choose the most advantageous speed for the site and means of intervention. Although on average, flexibility, flow, and speed may benefit global capitalism and the atomization of military force into these networks, it does not follow that speed and flow are the only strategies. Nor does it follow that slowness or disconnection could serve on its own as an efficacious strategy of resistance to this logic of militarization and global capital. Cyberwar exploits and proliferates a vast heterogeneity of multiple times and spaces that destabilize these networks. Though militaries, states, corporations, and other groups rush in to stabilize and destabilize these spaces, in the face of these modulations of space and time, it increasingly appears as though it is networked mediatic systems themselves that engage in these conflicts and invariably fall to pieces.

2

Injection Attack:
Writing and the Information Catastrophe

The systems that are attacked through cyberwar are dual entities: on one hand, they are defined by a series of connections, and on the other hand, they are defined by the text of programs and messages that are sent through the network. The networked structure of the global Internet allows malicious programs to quickly propagate, but it is the insecurity of individual systems and the computer programs they run that are exploited to attack these networks. Without the insecurity of these programs and messages, cyberwar would never be a strategic possibility.

While computer programs are often considered to be overly deterministic and simply a series of rules for a machine to follow, the very existence of cyberwar suggests that programs are not so straightforward. Programming is a textual and linguistic practice that is always carried out in languages and at levels of complexity that preclude complete mastery over what is written. Cyberwar infiltrates and subverts these programs, turning the text and logic of the program against itself. To fully grasp what is at stake in cyberwar, it is then critical to understand the logic of writing, especially the logic of writing at its most vulnerable. In this light, cyberwar is ultimately a process of deconstructing programs and undermining them from within their own logical and linguistic systems. As such, it is a form of writing itself, a writing that is aimed at both shoring up and deconstructing other texts.

To understand cyberwar in this way, then, also requires a reconceptualization of deconstruction and its functioning. Admitting the textual nature of code and the machinic force of deconstruction overwhelms any attempt to maintain that deconstruction has ever been an exclusively theoretical matter or could ever be secured against its possible usage by the state and military. Cyberwar, in harnessing and exploiting the vulnerable and machinic nature of writing, is thus both a form of deconstruction and a deconstructive threat to deconstruction itself. Still, this threat to deconstruction and the logic of writing does not spell the end of deconstruction but rather guarantees its continued importance to the history of both writing and metaphysics.

GLIMPSES OF THE FUTURE CATASTROPHE

One of the earliest glimpses of the possible impact of an all-out cyberwar occurred in June 1997. A small team of hackers using publicly available tools and programs was supposedly able to gain access to the power grid in nine U.S. cities, those cities' emergency response systems, and a number of critical Pentagon networks, including those that managed military supply chains and the command-and-control structure. According to James Adams, who has written at length about these attacks,

> the hackers also managed to infect the human command-and-control system with a paralyzing level of mistrust. Orders that appeared to come from a commanding general were fake, as were bogus news reports on the crisis and instructions from the civilian command authorities. As a result, nobody in the chain of command, from the president on down, could believe anything. This group of hackers using publicly available resources was able to prevent the United States from waging war effectively.[1]

Luckily, the series of attacks, which have been code-named Eligible Receiver, were carried out by the National Security Agency as an unannounced test of military and civilian digital infrastructure. The attackers, who were working as part of a No-Notice Interoperability Exercise Program, were asked only to prove what was possible and not actually to destroy anything.

Though the military provided no substantial evidence about Eligible Receiver, aside from interviews with the media and vague congressional testimony, for a while, Eligible Receiver was repeatedly referenced as a brief glimpse of future war and the dark nature of our digital technologies.[2] Of course, there were those who were sure it was merely the media-security complex displaying its newest boogeyman. In a hacking publication titled *The Crypt Newsletter,* whose provenance and history seem to have gone the way of dial-up modems but which still lingers in search-engine-indexed text files in various parts of the Internet, Joseph K refers to Eligible Receiver as "a Pentagon ghost story repeated *ad nauseum* to journalists and the easily frightened in which ludicrous or totally unsubstantiated claims about menaces from cyberspace are passed off as astonishing deeds of techno-legerdemain performed by cybersoldiers working within a highly classified wargame."

Although Joseph K meant to dismiss Eligible Receiver, the discourse surrounding it still tells an interesting ghost story, especially if it is treated as such and read not as baseless but as a myth that functions even without proof. John Arquilla summed up the state of the public relation to the event aptly when, in an interview with PBS, he said, "Eligible Receiver is a classified event about which I can't speak. What I can say is that when people say there is no existence proof of the seriousness of the cyber threat, to my mind, Eligible Receiver provides a convincing existence proof of the nature of the threat that we face."[3] This Kafkaesque claim is telling: he cannot tell us what transpired, but its existence, despite being under classified erasure, proves his point. This event appears in this light not then as an attack against military information systems but instead as an attack against our belief in the digital systems that increasingly provide the fabric of our everyday lives. Perhaps in Adams's claims that no one could believe anything from the president on down, we should read a warning that we, too, outside the wargame, can no longer believe anything—that, ultimately, the collapse of the entire system may already be upon us. It takes little extra imagination to suggest that the implied result is some catastrophic social collapse, which may already be under way. It is not merely our military communication technologies that are at stake in Eligible Receiver but the entirety of society.

Computer systems, especially when seen as data storage devices, function to guarantee that past inscriptions persist into the future. Computer security is often discussed as being founded on the "CIA triad," standing for confidentiality, integrity, and access. Confidentially requires that only authorized users have access to information. Integrity is the need that the information that is put into a system is the same information that is retrieved, and access suggests that if authorized users cannot retrieve information, no matter how secure that information is, the system is useless.[4] All of these function not just in the present but as guarantees of past and future. For a system to be secure under these conditions, the system must assure that the data entered in the past extend into the future and avoid unauthorized compromise. Cyberattacks instantly call all three of these into question in the past, present, and future. The futurity of a "real" attack like Eligible Receiver infects our belief in these systems in the present.

Garrett Schubert, of EMC's Critical Incident Response Center, tasked with protecting EMC's data centers from cyberattacks, describes his work directly in relation to a change in temporality: "When I started in my career, the idea was, we wanted to stop a bad thing from happening. Now, we assume that the bad thing has already happened. Every single day, we walk in and we assume there is an active attack going on."[5] The future catastrophe has become a part of the daily operations of our technologies. As Parikka claims, the inscription of information in media is the invention of the accident of information erasure.[6] The database always contains within it the immanent possibility that the data are, or may be, corrupted. As much as this unannounced test exercise may have been a test of military security, it is also a test of our belief in the future of our digital world.

Joseph K's mocking dismissal then appears, like a pithy sermon by an unknown sage of our digital belief, to reassure us that these events are merely phantasms thought up to terrify the gullible and will never come to pass. At the same time, the complete dismissal of this ghost story bifurcates the future: on one hand, the possibility of utter collapse, and on the other, complete faith and resilience. Likewise, it doubles the structure of belief and skepticism. Are the believers those who put faith in our technological world or those who blindly take the military's word that the catastrophe is around any corner? If we cannot believe "anyone from the president on down," how can we believe those who call that belief into question?

THE INFORMATIONAL UNCANNY

We arrive at an impasse that mirrors the Cold War nuclear catastrophe, not in terms of the destruction of life but in terms of the destruction of meaning. Though the relationship between the digital and the symbolic is complex, if the material support of meaning—be it magnetic bits, flashes of light in a fiber optic cable, or paper writing—is destroyed, then so too is the possibility of meaning. If the bits that store our digital writing are effaced, so too is any message they may carry. A nuclear catastrophe destroys meaning by destroying potential readers and the material of writing, whereas a digital catastrophe destroys meaning and inscription by destroying the microscopic material support. As these digital communications are entrusted more and more, what is at stake is the whole system of believing in the integrity of one's information, and with it the integrity of all systems. We arrive, then, at a similar situation to what Paul Saint-Amour refers to as the nuclear uncanny: "Because it offers the possibility of a future without symptoms, without a symbolic order—in other words, no future at all—the nuclear condition can, in a sense, only cause anticipatory symptoms."[7]

Likewise, the militarized digital catastrophe shapes the present by its future possibility. Saint-Amour's argument is helpful in that it places the futurity of such events clearly in the present. He suggests that such a catastrophe, especially because it destroys the symbolic, must produce its effects in the present. If this future catastrophe undermines the symbolic in the present, we begin to enter a space of what we could call militarized deconstruction. The ability for any program, database, or text to control its meaning and intent is instantly destabilized. As Parikka argues, "apocalypses reveal new temporalities, new layers for a media archaeology of the present."[8] The possibility of a catastrophe places the full meaning of programs and networks always in the future but their symptomatic expression in the present. Their complete meaning can only be understood after their looming breakdown. In short, despite the linear and programmatic nature of a program's execution, the deferral of meaning and the non-self-sameness opened by its potential insecurity guarantee that the relation between the text of the program and its action in the world is governed by play, *différance*, and the impending possibility of its deconstruction.

This catastrophic threat to the future of databases suggests that they are ultimately shaped by the structure of what Derrida calls arche-writing (the originary structure of non-self-presence and externalization that shapes all existence—the violence of our being in the world). When Hägglund explains arche-writing, we could easily imagine that he is speaking about a computer rather than a human subject:

Such exterior support risks erasure in its very becoming and makes the subject essentially liable to betray itself as well as any other: to exclude, overlook, and forget. To think arche-writing is thus to think how death, discrimination, and obliteration are at work from the beginning and do not overtake an already constituted subject.[9]

Computers and digital networks, like all writing, rely on exterior support that is always under the threat of both erasure and betrayal. On its most basic level, computation partakes of the structure of arche-writing. It does not constitute a totality that risks corruption; rather, computation and the human subjects who engage it are born of finitude and exposed to obliteration. It should be added that while the future catastrophe is immanent to these technologies, its effect is not because of any inevitability but precisely because of its undecidability and unknowability.

Derrida, in a short article about the nuclear condition, which Saint-Amour cites in his article on the nuclear uncanny, suggests something similar:

Here we are dealing hypothetically with a total and remainderless destruction of the archive. This destruction would take place for the first time and it would lack any common proportion with, for example, the burning of a library, even that of Alexandria, which occasioned so many written accounts and nourished so many literatures. The hypothesis of this total destruction watches over deconstruction, it guides its footsteps.[10]

While Derrida claims that deconstruction and this catastrophe belong to the nuclear era, it belongs just as much to the information age, as the increasing digitization of information increasingly exposes the archive to a systemwide catastrophe and destabilization from within. Especially if we take cyberwar to mean war against systems, we arrive, then, at a situation that is not limited to the digital but infects all systems with a potential militarized catastrophe. In short, nuclear war appears as a specific example of a larger structure of catastrophe that threatens to destroy the symbolic. There exists, then, an accidental or military catastrophe for every system in which our lives are embedded: ecological collapse, speculative bubbles, new drug-resistant diseases, market crashes, global warming, and so on.[11] All of these systems, be they networked technology, banking, or law, function like computer systems, not exclusively in the present but as a result of their guarantee across time. We arrive not at the Cold War possibility of a nuclear mutually assured destruction but rather at the immanence of an information war–induced state of mutually assured deconstruction.

MILITARY DECONSTRUCTION

Cyberwar in its catastrophic futurity opens up a space that constantly threatens symbolic systems with deconstruction. While Derridean deconstruction aims at *the* metaphysics of presence, binary structures, and the desire for pure origins, cyberwar utilizes a similar set of operations aimed against any strategically important system. Moreover, cyberwar—especially if taken to include Szfranski's claim that war must aim not only for physical but also for metaphysical control—inaugurates a militarization of metaphysics itself. Cyberwar, in attacking systems and metaphysical structures, doubles the logic of deconstruction as a military strategy, turning it against computer programs and network infrastructures as a means of war. Thus, what is at stake in cyberwar is the future of deconstruction and metaphysics itself.

The attacks of cyberwar push systems beyond their creators' and authors' intentions. Both the adventurous programmer and the malicious military hacker attempt to read and write digital systems against themselves. It is as Derrida says of deconstruction: "The movements of deconstruction do not destroy structures from the outside. They are not possible and effective, nor can they take accurate aim, except by inhabiting those structures."[12] The attacks against digital systems carried out in cyberwar trace the most minute logic and text of the systems and programs they attempt to subvert. They intimately inhabit these systems, subjecting their code to a sort of close reading that intimately traces their spatial, temporal, and textual logics.[13]

These attacks, despite coming from the outside in a sense, inhabit systems and structures, turning their intended aim against itself. For instance, in the case of Stuxnet, one version of the virus recorded the data stream of a PLC when it was functioning correctly so that it could play back realistic data while destroying the centrifuges. Cyberwar functions not simply by destroying but instead by inhabiting, learning, and modifying the forces inherent in digital systems. Programs of any complexity inevitably slip out of the programmer's control, and even those that run perfectly interact with other programs and other systems that compromise any perfect security. This is precisely what Derrida says of language: "The writer writes in a language and in a logic whose proper system, laws, and life his discourse by definition cannot dominate absolutely."[14] The programmer never writes in a language or computer logic that she can dominate absolutely. There are always gaps and breaks that can be exploited and turned against the system or program.

Under the threat of this insecurity, we are faced with the realization that the data and code with which we interact may have been written by someone else, from some other place and time. Cyberwar functions, then, in this mode to explicate the necessary insecurity of writing. Computer programming, like all writing, exteriorizes texts, exposing them to nonpresences and insecurity. In their insecurity, our digital systems come to express a type of *différance,* the combination of deferral and difference that is so central to deconstruction. The possibility that the execution of a program could produce an unexpected result, either accidentally or as the result of malicious code, injects into computation the possibility that it differs from itself. The exact same code run at a different time or in a different place bears the possibility of different results. This potential difference simultaneously indicates a necessary deferral: we can never know what a program does or means until it is executed. Every use of the program risks the full meaning of the program.[15] Thus cyberwar attests to a *différance* that inhabits even our most programmatic and machinic writing. It is the insecurity that is inherent in a given system, the traces that always point to absences, that undermines these digital systems from within. While, of course, it requires an army or an individual hacker to exploit a security vulnerability, it is increasingly becoming the rule that exploits will be discovered and utilized. What initially appears as an intentional intrusion by a state or individual into a digital system that merely executes a program, now under threat from a future event whose arrival is always uncertain, appears as an autodeconstruction immanent to the logic of the program. The system fractures of its own accord.

READING/WRITING METAPHYSICAL WAR

Cyberwar, and with it militarized deconstruction, operates in a multiplicity of metaphysical, communicational, social, and physical systems. To operate across systems requires the work of translation or projection, mapping high-dimensional spaces to different spatialities. Each system creates its own internal space of communication, language, and movement that is never completely under the control of the system itself and is even further absent and obfuscated from an outside observer. For example, the code for Windows XP consists of 45 million lines of code, an entirely incomprehensible amount of code for any programmer to grasp in its entirety.[16] One who approaches this system from the outside, with only the finished program and without the underlying source code, is even further from being able to understand and map the system space of the program.

Maturana and Varela, two biologists and cyberneticians, offer a notion of autopoietic systems that is clarifying in this regard. The two developed the theory to describe the difference between living systems and nonliving systems. At its most basic, their notion is that a living (autopoietic) system works to maintain its own organization, whereas a nonliving (allopoietic) system produces and organizes something other than itself. While this distinction is likely problematic (it is unclear if a chicken reproduces its own organization or if it is a factory for eggs; conversely, does an automotive factory produce cars or primarily reproduce its own socioeconomic relations and make cars as waste?), their discussion of the space and dimensionality of systems is elucidating.[17]

They describe the space of autopoietic systems (for these purposes, we should consider all systems of at least moderate complexity) as only definable from within the dimensionality of that space:

> An autopoietic organization acquires topological unity by its embodiment in a concrete autopoietic system which retains its identity as long as it remains autopoietic. Furthermore, the space defined by an autopoietic system is self-contained and cannot be described by using dimensions that define another space. . . . We interact with the components of the autopoietic system through the properties

of their constituting elements that do not lie in the autopoietic space, and thus, we modify the structure of the autopoietic system by modifying its components.[18]

The space of a system for Maturana and Varela is self-contained. As such, we never interact with the system in and of itself, but we have access to the components that constitute the relations of the system. As a result, it becomes impossible to completely secure a system because we never have complete access to its functioning. Instead, we always interact with these systems in translation, across the gap of its autopoietic enclosure.

This process of operating across and within systems becomes one of the most significant challenges for militarized deconstruction. We are always stuck within and between systems, never fully able to grasp their logic and functioning. What arrives, then, under the names metaphysical control, militarized deconstruction, and cyberwarfare is akin to Derridean deconstruction but does not aim at a specific metaphysics or logos; rather, it operates under a similar program, but aimed at diverse sites of intervention. Cyberwar appears as a process of fortifying, weaving, and destabilizing spheres born of loosely coupled networks. Along these lines, Derrida, invoking the etymological relationship between text and textile, explicitly places deconstruction and writing in relationship to both organisms and weaving in "Plato's Pharmacy":

> The dissimulation of the woven texture can in any case take centuries to undo its web: a web that envelops a web, undoing the web for centuries; reconstituting it too as an organism, indefinitely regenerating its own tissue behind the cutting trace, the decision of each reading. There is always a surprise in store for the anatomy or physiology of any criticism that might think it had mastered the game, surveyed all the threads at once, deluding itself, too, in wanting to look at the text without touching it, without laying a hand on the "object," without risking—which is the only chance of entering into the game, by getting a few fingers caught—the addition of some new thread.[19]

We could almost imagine Derrida writing these words about cyberwar. One is always acting within the global network of communication, capital, information, and so on, and any who believe they have mastered the game or grasped it from the outside are already lost. Cyberwar takes place across an interconnected and woven battle space made of both tightly and loosely connected nodes, and any interaction with this network, like Derrida's woven texts, can never step outside the game. Both deconstruction and cyberwar act within this global network that is constituted across time and space only by following, weaving, unweaving, and getting caught.

This web as it is unwoven is simultaneously rewoven and regenerated as tissue. The web of the text and the program is given over to a complexity that forecloses the possibility of it being mastered or understood in a singular and objective spatiality. The system autopoieticly closes upon its own local spatiality. Derrida explicitly denies the possibility of a pregiven geometric objectivity, stating that it "is an object or an ideal signified produced at a moment of writing. Before it, there is no homogenous space."[20] Any objective geometry is always the result of projection and translation, which are subjected to the same vulnerabilities as texts. Every program and system risks itself in this complex multiplicity of spaces.

In its linkage of weaving and writing, "Plato's Pharmacy" begins to elucidate what is at stake in the connection between deconstruction and cyberwar. Cyberwar reinforces certain readings and texts (and programs), all while it attempts to disentangle and destroy others. We should remember here the training mission offered in CyberCity, where the goal is to break into a hospital network to defend a patient from another hacker who is attempting to alter the medication schedule to kill the patient. It is the untranslatability between the systems, the organisms and the webs, the unique dimensionality of each, that can never be crossed or secured completely and can only be accessed through the constituent parts that make such a conflict conceivable. Were it possible to create a secure network of programs and machines, or a text that an author completely controlled, such opportunities for these interventions would rarely, if ever, arise.

PROGRAMMING WRITING

Despite the impossibility of controlling computer code, Derrida opposes over and over again deconstruction to the program and machine. In an attempt to aid the translation of the term deconstruction into Japanese, he states, "Deconstruction is not a method and cannot be transformed into one. Especially if the technical and procedural significations of the word are stressed. It is true that in certain circles (university or cultural, especially in the United States) the technical and methodological 'metaphor' that seems necessarily attached to the very word deconstruction has been able to seduce or lead astray."[21] Many have followed Derrida in this insistence that deconstruction is not a method or an operation that can be carried out and that one risks being led astray from the insights of deconstruction by the seduction of a program.[22] Moreover, from the first reference to deconstruction in the grammatology, it is opposed to a machine:

> Within the closure, by an oblique and always perilous movement, constantly risking falling back within what is being deconstructed, it is necessary to surround the critical concepts with a careful and thorough discourse—to mark the conditions, the medium, and the limits of their effectiveness and to designate rigorously their intimate relationship to the machine whose deconstruction they permit; and, in the same process, designate the crevice through which the yet unnameable glimmer beyond the closure can be glimpsed.[23]

Deconstruction is thus from the start aimed at a machine that it is intimately related to but must always be protected from the seduction of becoming a machine itself. A careful and thorough discourse is required to prevent deconstruction from becoming machinic, technical, or methodological. Derrida even argues here that one must carefully mark the media through which deconstruction can operate. In these attempts to demarcate deconstruction and avoid this seduction, we can glimpse another deconstruction that always haunts it.[24] Here one must rigorously designate to avoid the rigor of the machine. But, if programming produces numerous unmasterable languages, as the existence of cyberwar attests, it becomes difficult to exclude a deconstruction that would work on and through these digital and programmatic forms of writing, simultaneously risking the exposure of deconstruction to its own programmatic other.

Of course, Derrida is aware of this machinic force that haunts both writing and deconstruction and at times writes directly of it, offering it a proper name, but a proper name that has already been named as the opposing force of a radical other who would preclude the programmatic.[25] In relation to Joyce's *Ulysses,* referring to two Elijahs that inhabit the work, he states,

> No longer Elijah the grand operator of the central, Elijah the head of the megaprogramotelephonic network, but the other Elijah, Elijah the other. But this is a homonym, Elijah can always be either one at the same time, one cannot call on one without risking getting the other.[26]

In this sense, Derridean deconstruction both requires this machinic other and surrounds itself with a protective discourse that aims to resist the seduction of the programotelephonic Elijah that would make of deconstruction a machine that repeats the machine of metaphysics. One always risks the mutual contamination of these two Elijahs, and in response deconstruction attempts to refuse the machinic Elijah. While Elijah the grand operator is never able to exclude or refuse Elijah the other, any who would ally himself with the other must carefully avoid this force of alterity itself being haunted by a megaprogramotelephonic network. Derrida says, "I hear this vibration as the very music of Ulysses. The computer today cannot enumerate these interlacings, despite all the many ways it is already able to help us. Only a computer which has not yet been invented could answer that music in Ulysses."[27] For Derrida, no extant programming language or computer could ever integrate the beautiful ambiguity and musical vibrations of historical writing—only a computer to come.

Still, in Derrida's work, ground is constantly given to the machinic other of deconstruction. Deconstruction for a moment becomes a machine bound by rules when Derrida describes deconstruction to be "a sort of strategic device, opening onto its own abyss, an unclosed, unenclosable, not wholly formalizable ensemble of rules for reading, interpretation and writing."[28] Likewise, especially in his essay on Freud and the mystic writing pad, writing itself is conceived of as a machine, and the trace is described as "a two-handed machine, a multiplicity of agencies or origins."[29] This two-handed machine of writing, spacing, deferral, and erasure sounds surprisingly similar to the read/write head on a modern hard drive.[30] In the text on *Ulysses,* the novel itself is seen as a "hypermnesic machine capable of storing in a giant epic work, with the memory of the West and virtually all the languages of the world, the very traces of the future," and we are reminded that "hypermnesic interiorization can never close itself on itself."[31] Near the end of this text, Derrida imagines a computer that would count and categorize all of the words in *Ulysses,* and all the words in all of Joyce's texts. But, even without this imagined computer, he declares, "I could keep you for hours describing what I have myself computed with a pencil."[32] This computer and its program are thus already at work in the computing of the text by pencil and its spoken instantiation. Thus the point is not to reproach Derrida for the exclusion of this programmatic other that haunts deconstruction and writing-in-general but rather to listen to it explicitly both within Derrida's work and in the threats that are today written by cyberwar.

Retaining the distinction between writing and code and, with it, a distinction between calculation and the incalculable has allowed a certain reading of deconstruction to conserve a relationship with authorial intent; as long as the program is neither deconstructable nor a force of deconstruction, one can maintain, even if in covert fashion, that deconstruction must proceed exclusively as an authored theoretical activity. Minimizing the nonhuman agency of code produces a corollary effect, reifying the sanctity of the subject who writes in human languages. This distinction is thus central to a deconstruction that would attempt to secure an authorial importance while disavowing the danger of its military and political usage. To fully deconstruct this binary both threatens deconstruction and guarantees deconstruction's continued importance to the future.

Stiegler explicitly notes this relationship between calculation and the incalculable in the history and openness of writing: "Historiality, the horizon of every truth, also proceeds originally from this repetition that governs both the possibility of an access (to the already-there as already-there) and a concealing that is this very disclosure: the *grammē* is simultaneously calculation, determination and letter, indeterminacy."[33] Stiegler here, like Derrida, can be read as either naming two different but homonymous Elijahs or, alternatively, naming a history of deconstruction and writing that refuses to separate the programmatic from the indeterminate. Cyberwar, and the militarized corruption of computers, injects a deferral and difference directly into this division, making the calculable as indeterminate and unpredictable as any letter or writing. To recuperate programming to writing is not to somehow save it or defend it but rather to trace its deconstruction and at the same time expose deconstruction to this programmatic other.

THE GEOSPATIALITY OF DECONSTRUCTION

As cyberwar repeats Derridean deconstruction and appropriates its function, it does so as a critique of any deconstruction that would attempt to maintain this distinction between program and text. By structuring war along these lines, cyberwar reimagines deconstruction and inhabits the interior of deconstruction. It recodes deconstruction in a manner similar to a computer virus. To trace what is at stake in such a maneuver, it is fruitful to find a potential location in Derridean deconstruction that may have allowed for such an inversion, a place that structures and allows the distinction between program and text.

One possible candidate for the attack vector, to put it in terms of computer security, is a slippage Derrida makes in *Of Grammatology* when discussing the spacing of language. He says at one point, referring to Rousseau, "One will not be able to distinguish the question of the morphological classification of languages, which takes into account the effects of need on the form of a language, from the question of the place of origin of the language, *typology from topology.*"[34] In talking about the development of language in Rousseau's work and geographic spacing, Derrida uses the term *topology*. It is notable because geographic space is rarely what is meant by topology. Topology is the mathematics of space under continuous deformations. It focuses on spaces as connected, bordering, or disconnected but explicitly excludes distance as a necessary term.[35] It is a science of regions that border or do not border but have no distance between them.

Later Derrida says something similar but uses the term *topography*: "One cannot therefore describe the structure or the general essence of the language without taking topography into account."[36] His description of Rousseau's argument is nearly exactly the same, but here topography, the study of geographic features often including the elevation of landmasses, replaces topology. In one instance, Rousseau is read as distributing language and its formation in topological space, a space without distance, and then again, Derrida suggests that Rousseau distributes language throughout topographical space. This slippage between topology and topography immediately suggests one of the central concerns of cyberwar: the movement between connected and disconnected spaces, spaces for which distance matters and spaces of nearly instantaneous movement, or to put it in Castell's terms, spaces of place and spaces of flow.

Within Derrida's text, it is unclear what the relationship between the two is and how deconstruction operates within and between the opposition. It should be noted that both topography and topology offer an objective space open to mathematical calculation; it's just that one incorporates distance and the other does not require distance. The replacement of topology with topography suggests a move from *topos*, meaning "place," as *logos* to *topos* as writing and grapheme. But what is at stake between topology and topography cannot simply be the difference between *logos* and writing. Both open the space of deconstruction, but if language requires localization and spacing, it is because spatiality, or spacing, as Derrida says, is a critical component of deconstruction. Thus the shift between topology and topography can never be secondary to the movement of deconstruction. Derrida says,

> The neume, the spell of self-presence, inarticulate experience of time, tantamount to saying: *utopia*. Such a language—since a language must be involved—does not, properly speaking, take place. It does not know articulation, which cannot take place without spacing and without organization of spaces.[37]

This slippage cannot simply be discovered or put into motion by deconstruction; rather, it defines a difference within deconstruction itself. The question arises, then: how do language and deconstruction function in topological space, and how do they function in topographic space? More broadly, if language is spaced, deconstruction must be as well. This is not to suggest that the difference between topography and topology is rigid or originary but rather that different spatialities must constitute a difference within deconstruction.

As Hägglund suggests, deconstruction, trace, and any number of Derrida's other concepts are first and foremost concerned with spacing, or the becoming-space of time and the becoming-time of space.[38] The point is not that Derrida fails to account for space but that a multiplicity of spatialities and temporalities threatens to make deconstruction even more destabilizing. The proliferation of spaces threatens to break careful discourses, which would maintain deconstruction apart from machines and programs. Within the space of topography, of duration, spacing acts as a delay and a deferral; the greater the spacing, the longer one must travel and wait. Conversely, in topological space, spacing, the production of a gap, is a radical cut with no duration. Two computers sitting directly next to each other in geographic space, but with no connection between them, might as well be thousands of miles apart. The central question of spacing in deconstruction is immediately a question of which spaces. Likewise, cyberwar is a question of the spacing of networks and the programs that run on them. The multiple spaces and spacings of writing, inscription, and computation constantly threaten both computer networks and any theory of either computation or writing. The mutability of space is simultaneously the mutability of deconstruction itself.

Erasing the difference between multiple spatialities ultimately provides the ground for readings of deconstruction that would insist on a single space of literature and text that could exclude the program. A deconstruction that insists upon a single spatiality, or a simple equivalency between multiple spatialities, easily becomes a deconstruction that resists the mutability of deconstruction and its historical openness to new technologies of writing. Malabou suggests the importance of this mutability with what she calls "plastic reading":

> Structural plastic analysis thus calls deconstruction to recognize its *metamorphic debt*. It is in this sense that it continues deconstruction, paradoxically by leading it to the most originary. The structure or form of a thought—the alterity of philosophy to both its tradition and its own destruction—is both *the specter of its history* and the outline of something within it that is *not yet born*.[39]

Deconstruction is always metamorphic. It varies over time, and we must add that its metamorphic debt is spatial as well as temporal. The form of deconstruction is not fixed. It metamorphizes over both space and time as well as over different spatialities and temporalities. Malabou comments, in discussing Derrida's essay "Différance," that "Derrida does not recognize an essential, even if banal, meaning of the word 'difference,' namely 'change,' 'variation,' or 'variant.'"[40] It should be noted that this metamorphic possibility means that a historical act of writing, deconstruction, or cyberwar can attack and disfigure metaphysics in the fullest possible sense. The advent of a new type of writing can reconfigure both deconstruction and the metaphysical structures it confronts.

It is here, then, in this space between topography and topology, that cyberwar opens a possible vector into Derridean deconstruction. If deconstruction must be localized rather than a global phenomenon that "never takes place," it is by necessity subject to appropriation, misappropriation, reconfiguration, and infection. Derrida says the same of writing: "This absolute contingency [writing] determined the interior of an essential history and affected the interior unity of a life, *literally infected* it."[41] This infection of these multiple spatialities threatens deconstruction with the machinic force of the program that constantly haunts it. The proliferation of a multiplicity of spaces and times of deconstruction pushes deconstruction beyond its relation to Western metaphysics and opens the text of the program to both its own deconstruction and the possibility of other deconstructions.

The entire notion of a single closed metaphysical system is called into question by this slippage of spatiality and the requirements for locality. Derrida says,

> I think that *all concepts hitherto proposed in order to think the articulation of a discourse and of an historical totality are caught within the metaphysical closure that I question here,* as we do not know of any other concepts and cannot produce any others, and indeed shall not produce so long as this closure limits our discourse.[42]

Even to think a closure requires a single measurable spatiality. The metaphysical closure, which Derrida claims recourse to here, mirrors a belief in absolute security.[43] Despite this, it is, as Derrida argues elsewhere, always already infected.[44] The notion of closure is a global phenomenon that is destabilized by the localization in different non–directly translatable systems and localities. Deconstruction can never protect itself from a military appropriation or exclude the program from its texts because it differs over time and space. In sliding so easily between topology and topography, we risk ignoring the spatial specificity of deconstruction and the other deconstructions that lie within these multiple spatialities, temporalities, and modes of writing. Cyberwar slides into this place between global deconstruction, invents a local and machinic deconstruction, and attacks not "metaphysics" but the specific metaphysics or program of a chosen system.

THE WAR MACHINE MODEL

To better grasp what is at stake in military deconstruction and cyberwar, it is fruitful to explore a slight variation on the standard model of deconstruction. Deleuze and Guattari's notion of the war machine may begin to suggest what is at stake in these military forms of deconstruction. Deleuze and Guattari argue in *A Thousand Plateaus*,

> They are the principal elements of a State apparatus that proceeds by a One-Two, distributes binary distinctions, and forms a milieu of interiority. It is a double articulation that makes the State apparatus into a *stratum*. It will be noted that war is not contained within this apparatus. . . . As for the war machine in itself, it seems to be irreducible to the State apparatus, to be outside its sovereignty and prior to its law: it comes from elsewhere. *Indra, the warrior god, is in opposition to Varuna no less than to Mitra.* He can no more be reduced to one or the other than he can constitute a third of their kind. Rather, he is like a pure and immeasurable multiplicity, the pack, an irruption of the ephemeral and the power of metamorphosis. *He unties the bond as he betrays the pact.* He brings a *furor* to bear against sovereignty, a celerity against gravity, secrecy against the public, a power against sovereignty, a machine against the apparatus.[45]

Rather than disrupting binary systems from within, the war machine arrives from outside of the binarized interior of the state. The war machine adds a third term to deconstruction. This "war machine model" of deconstruction disrupts not from the inherent imbalance or relationship between the One-Two but rather by a force that comes from the outside and exploits the varied relationship between inside and outside. It should be noted that we are likely not so far from Derrida's model, but the war machine moves the emphasis between the binary relation to its outside.[46] It is possible to read the war machine into Derrida's description of deconstruction, but for the moment, to develop a theory of militarized deconstruction, it will be fruitful to read Deleuze against Derrida's claim that deconstruction always operates by inhabiting the inside of binary systems.[47] Moreover, the terminology of the war machine expressly suggests the possibility of a deconstruction that would function directly through machines and programs rather than exclusively by way of a textuality opposed to the program. Derridean deconstruction, at least in the sense given to it by a certain reading, operates within binary structures, for instance, speech–writing, and opposes them first by inverting the hierarchical relationship between the terms and then by placing the binary under erasure.[48] This reading must be complicated, but let us first broach it from the outside by way of Deleuze and the machinations of twenty-first-century military strategists.

For Deleuze and Guattari, the war machine is always outside of the state apparatus, which is both binary itself and produces binaries. It is possible for the state to appropriate a war machine and turn it into a military apparatus, but even so, the state always runs the risk that it will "reimpart a war machine that takes charge of the aim, appropriates the States, and assumes increasingly wider political functions."[49] Even when the third term is captured and appropriated inside the binary structure of the state, it always threatens the state and binary structures. Thus the war machine model puts forth the possibility that the force that destabilizes a binary does not necessarily arise from within. Rather, it names a force of deconstruction that, while carefully attuned to the texts it interacts with, militarizes them and unleashes an outside and machinic force of deconstruction.

This difficulty with the war machine is not merely theoretical but expresses itself repeatedly in cyberwar. The politics and science surrounding cryptography, a field that is not far from Derrida's concerns with writing and speech, may suggest some of what is at stake in the relationship between the state and the war machine. While for centuries cryptography (the science of making secret messages unreadable) was a specialized technique often used to obfuscate messages during times of war, it now plays a critical role in securely using digital networks. But often the security concerns of the state and of the war machine diverge. One of the most blatant examples is a system known as Tor (originally called The Onion Routing Network). Tor is often a source of frustration for law enforcement, as it allows criminals and others anonymity. The opportunities and difficulties presented by Tor directly suggest the contentious and destabilizing nature of these technologies even in the space between the state and an appropriated war machine.

Tor functions by routing traffic through multiple servers and encrypting the data in layers (hence the onion), so that each server only knows the previous server and which server is next in the communication chain. Thus the server that handles the initial request only knows the source of the initial request and the next server in the chain. Likewise, the final server only knows the preceding one and the final destination of the data. Thus the multiple layers of encryption prevent any server or anyone listening to the communication between servers from knowing both the source and the destination of communication or from knowing the content at all. Tor thus prevents both the content of messages and the metadata about messages from being known.[50] Metadata is the information about a message aside from its content, for example, its source, time, size, and frequency. Increasingly, this information about with whom individuals are talking, what websites they are reading, and other aspects surrounding the nature of their communication, without considering the content, is being used to pick out suspicious individuals and create assumptions about their social connections.[51] Tor serves to prevent the ability for security agencies to gather this information, and thus it is used by various groups who hope to avoid having their activities being detected.

One of the most interesting aspects of Tor is that most of the initial funding for the project was provided by the Office of Naval Research and the Defense Advanced Research Projects Agency.[52] The project additionally received funding from the Broadcasting Board of Governors, the U.S. government agency that runs Voice of America and Radio Free Europe, and the State Department.[53] The U.S. military intentionally developed it as a public tool, mainly because anonymization techniques are significantly more effective the more people use them. If only the military were using Tor, it would be easy for those watching to tell where U.S. military personnel were operating from. Thus the military not only developed this relatively easy-to-use software to prevent other governmental agencies from tracking individuals on the Internet but also made sure it was accessible to anyone who would like to use it. Even a highly appropriated war machine, such as the U.S. military, works at odds with the aims of the state and actively seeks to undermine their attempts at surveillance. While the state may construct binary oppositions between privacy–surveillance, licit–illicit messages, legitimate–illegitimate cryptography, and so on, the war machine intervenes from the outside with the invention and distribution of a technology to disrupt the balance and set it again in motion.

The early work of Norbert Weiner, a pioneer in the field of cybernetics, provides another example of this relationship. One of Weiner's earliest projects was an attempt during World War II to use computational methods to improve the targeting of antiaircraft guns. Though no immediate practical applications came out of this work, one of the major theoretical shifts that Weiner brought was to think of planes and pilots as a joint system. He says of this work, "The pilot does *not* have a completely free chance to maneuver at his will. For one thing, he is in a plane going at an exceedingly high speed, and any too sudden deviation from his course will produce an acceleration that will render him unconscious and may disintegrate the plane."[54] This early cybernetic project, aimed at thinking through the feedback and communication within a plane–human machine and influenced by the exigencies of the war effort, like much of the early work in computation and cybernetics, suggests the method by which war machines can act as outside agents of deconstruction. Weiner, faced with the philosophical distinction between human and machine, approaches this binary distribution not from within the system but from the possibility of their future destruction. The human–machine binary is thus destroyed twice: once through its philosophical deconstruction and again through its physical destruction.[55] The binary is overcome through directly technical means, demonstrating that no single component controls the overall system.

The human–machine binary is not deconstructed to some philosophical end; the goal is their physical destruction, but they are intimately linked. The successful physical destruction of the plane–human is the proof of its technical deconstruction. One sees in the plane falling out of the sky the verification of their impossible separation. This deconstruction moves from the radical outside attacking the internal dynamics of the system as it destroys the external manifestation of the system. As war machines move into the space of cyberwar and deconstruction, new modes of confronting, destabilizing, and even destroying oppositions open and are exploited by the military, the state, the market, and also those opposed to these systems. Ultimately, to come to terms with the future opened through cyberwar and our explosion of communication technologies requires recognizing the multiple movements of individuals, armies, and states, along with the material, textual, programmatic, metaphysical, and real aspects of these nested systems.

DE(CON)STRUCTION

It may seem, especially in the light of Weiner's attempts to destroy airplanes, that calling these military interventions deconstruction risks stretching the boundaries of deconstruction beyond a meaningful limit. To include cyberwar and cybernetic antiaircraft guns seems at first to conflate deconstruction with simple destruction. But the successful culmination of Weiner's project would not only result in the destruction of a given aircraft but ultimately forces a reconsideration of the autonomy of the pilot apropos the machine. While destruction may serve as the sign that verifies a given deconstruction, the implications of this work travel through various networks and texts, affirming that neither pilot nor machine is in control of the other. Likewise, with cyberwar, as we have seen, all attacks must become visible. Even in the case of attacks such as Stuxnet and Operation Orchard, it is ultimately the creation of visible and mediatized effects that constitutes cyberwar and represents the deconstructive, hidden, and nonpresent aspects of these military actions.

More important, these actions do not presuppose a subject that chooses or autonomously sets them in motion. In what Galloway and Thacker refer to as the dissolution of enmity into the swarm of networks, it becomes increasingly difficult to attribute attacks or even to maintain the concept of an attacker.[56] It increasingly appears as though technologies are falling apart from their own internal contradictions and insecurities. While nations or individuals may organize attacks, cyberwar in its relationship to deconstruction calls into question the coherence of a subject who would carry out an attack. As Wark suggests, "every hacker is at one and the same time producer and product of the hack, and emerges as a singularity that is the memory of the hack as process."[57] The subject who carries out an attack is as much a product of the deconstruction as the ensuing destruction.[58] Derrida states in his later work that "a subject can never decide anything: a subject is even that to *which* a decision cannot come or happen otherwise than as a marginal accident that does not affect the essential identity and the substantial presence-to-self that make a subject what it is."[59] A decision always decenters the subject by sending it racing through a series of unpredictable accidents from which it can never return the same. In attempting to disrupt the enemy's ability to compute, one must engage in computation and hence risk the same displacements and subversions. To grasp what is at stake in cyberwar and deconstruction requires beginning not from the subject that writes or codes but from topography, topology, and their inherent insecurity, the inherent deconstructability that constitutes the subject and the system.

Derrida puts this clearly in a slightly different light when he states, "Deconstruction takes place, it is an event that does not await the deliberation, consciousness, or organization of a subject, or even of modernity. It deconstructs itself. It can be deconstructed."[60] The deconstruction wrought by cyberwar is not a result of a subject who attacks a system; it is the autodeconstruction of a system. The deconstruction is not the attack but rather the fissures and gaps in the systems that are activated through an attack. What is at issue in this militarized deconstruction is, then, not the conflation of deconstruction and destruction but rather deconstruction giving rise to a destructive force and destruction marking the efficacy and danger of deconstruction. In *Of Grammatology*, "empirical violence, war in the colloquial sense," always points back to the arche-violence of writing that produces the loss of the full speech of law that has never taken place and the later violence of law that attempts to respond to arche-violence with violence.[61] In the same way, the destruction of cyberwar points toward the arche-violence of writing—the violence of our very existence outside ourselves inscribed in insecure systems. The destruction of cyberwar operates as a form of the violence of law that attempts to recuperate an origin safe from the insecurity and violence of writing itself. Instead, it only succeeds in instituting a new violence. While deconstruction should never be confused with destruction, deconstruction is always at stake in violence and "war in the colloquial sense."

Furthermore, in Derrida's claim that "it can be deconstructed," we can read the risk that deconstruction itself is exposed to deconstructive threats. The vulnerability of code touches directly on the arche-structure of writing itself. To include code and its exploitations within the structure of arche-writing threatens the last remains of a privileged relationship between writing and a "subject." When code partakes of the originary absence of writing, it refigures that absence and the metaphysical structure of writing-in-general. Inscription takes on a nonhuman agency that unleashes a deconstruction that threatens to outpace any theoretically delimited and authored deconstruction. In short, deconstruction becomes an autodeconstruction to which systems subject themselves. The self-deconstruction of the human–machine division produces both Weiner and the proposed machine. In sum, what constitutes the relationship between deconstruction and cyberwar is not that a subject either writes deconstruction or carries out an attack, although both of these events clearly happen; rather, it is the existence of the fissures, nonpresences, and insecurities in the systems they attack that defines the relationship between a given system and its deconstruction.

This is precisely why the heterogeneity of the temporality and spatiality of deconstruction are such important features. The possible future subversion of a given system places the system under the threat of its own vulnerability. The event of a system's deconstruction is the continued possibility of an unknown event to come, an event that arrives from another place and time. It is a deconstruction that is fully a movement of the system itself. The *différance* inherent to writing names the gap between writing and the real, which exposes all writing—and with it all programs—to their future deconstruction. The full meaning and essence of a system exists only in its always deferred deconstruction and as a result of its self-difference. An insecure system, which has possibly been compromised, always risks running contrary to its intended purpose. Thus, while cyberwar militarizes and utilizes exterior forces, operationalizing a war machine, the deconstruction of which it takes hold is always immanent to the system itself.

THE GEOSPATIALITY OF THE WAR MACHINE MODEL OF DECONSTRUCTION

Without invoking a necessarily sovereign subject, the war machine model of deconstruction begins to suggest a difference between deconstruction in topological and topographic space, since the "outsides" of these spaces differ. We should note that Derrida destabilizes the distinction between the inside and the outside. He suggests, "It is precisely these concepts that permitted the exclusion of writing: image or representation, sensible and intelligible, nature and culture, nature and technics, etc. They are solidary with all metaphysical conceptuality and particularly with a naturalist, objectivist, and derivative determination of the difference between outside and inside."[62] Arche-violence and the metaphysical response to this violence divide the world into inside and outside. While problematizing objective distinctions between the outside and the inside is absolutely critical, and a strategic necessity for cyberwar, Deleuze attacks the issue from another angle. He says, "We must distinguish between exteriority and the outside."[63] Even here, instead of destabilizing the relationship between inside and outside from within the binary relationship, Deleuze invents a war machine, the outside that is more than exterior, to upset the binary between the inside and the exterior.

The notion of an exterior space is an especially topographical concept. A space that is further away requires a space of measurement and of distance. In such a space, it makes sense that there should be no outside. The topography of the text always leads to other contours and other texts. Alternatively, when space becomes topological, it must admit a radical outside. It is an outside that is totally disconnected, that cannot be accounted for in the space or connections of the network but always threatens to intervene. A network defines a series of objects and relations that constitute so many nodes and edges, but any network always exists in a nonspace that can never enter into its topology. A communications network that connects terminals with cables always exists in real geographic space, where a cable could be severed. The nonspace of the network always threatens the message's arrival or the possibility that the message may be intercepted. All writing, and programming by extension, functions in a multitude of topological systems, from networks of publishing to citations to hyperlinks, where the outside can always intervene to disrupt the functioning of the system.

It is this possibility of the intervention of the outside that sets the system into motion. Deleuze says, "Every inside-space is topologically in contact with the outside-space, independent of distance and on the limits of a 'living'; and this carnal or vital topology, far from showing up in space, frees a sense of time that fits the past into the inside, brings about the future in the outside, and brings the two into confrontation at the limit of the living present."[64] Thus topological space presents what Deleuze calls a fold. That which is the farthest away is always at the same time what is most close: "The most distant point becomes interior, by being converted into the nearest: *life within the folds*."[65] Cyberwar inhabits this fold. It turns the fold against itself. It arrives always from the outside, but to inhabit the innermost caverns of systems and their functioning. Cyberwar subverts systems by turning the system's logic against itself. The war machine folded inside the state apparatus becomes a cutting edge of deconstruction that is turned both against enemies and at times against the state itself. Thus these structures are always susceptible to destabilization, to a deconstruction of their internal metaphysical structure born of their non-self-sameness and inherent insecurity.

It is then the movement between topographical and topological space that opens the space of the outside and causes it to become an issue for deconstruction. The possibility of this outside denies the specificity of deconstruction and allows it to be taken up against any "metaphysical" system. The claim is not that the "war machine model" of deconstruction should replace Derridean deconstruction. On the contrary, we must localize deconstruction and elucidate its multiple modes of operation. The coexistence and constant movement between topological and topographical space allow a multiplicity of deconstructions that operate across and through these system spaces, always requiring translation and foreclosing the possibility of a speaker, writer, or programmer ever mastering the language she uses. Moreover, this heterogeneity of spatialities upsets the stability of the boundary between language and nonlanguage; the technologies of writing and reconfiguring space constantly fold and undercut this boundary, precluding metaphysically distinguishing writing from the program.

It should be noted in this regard that the purpose of confronting deconstruction with the war machine is not to attempt to synthesize Deleuze and Derrida. On the contrary, to trace cyberwar and militarized deconstruction is to accept the impossibility of an overarching system or a metaphysical closure. It is precisely the incompatibilities between Derrida and Deleuze that make tracing these various strategies fruitful. The aim is instead to find similarities and incompatibilities between strategic operations, to outline techniques that move between systems. Instead of confronting "metaphysics," we must outline a series of strategies that may prove useful either in understanding the maneuvers of military and state institutions or in the practice of reading, writing, and criticism as they move across metaphysical spaces.

THE DERRIDEAN WAR MACHINE

While the war machine model seems at first opposed to Derridean deconstruction, in many ways deconstruction already accounts for a third term that comes from the outside. The clearest example of this logic is the binary relation between writing and speech. Derrida, in *Of Grammatology*, names supplementarity as the logic by which binary systems are distributed and hierarchized. He states, "The logic of supplementarity, which would have it that the outside be inside, that the other and the lack come to add themselves as a plus that replaces a minus, that what adds itself to something takes the place of a default in the thing, that the default, as the outside of the inside, should be already within the inside, etc."[66] The supplement, while in binary relation to the primary term, has a relationship similar to that of the fold. The supplement, which in *Of Grammatology* is exemplified by writing as supplement to speech, is always an outside that deconstruction demonstrates to be folded into the inside. Writing is believed to be exterior, secondary, supplemental, but deconstruction traces the relationship elucidating the folded nature of the supplement to show that the outside is always already inside. In doing so, deconstruction demonstrates that this distinction responds to an arche-writing, in which all existence is founded on a primary exteriorization; there is no original presence or security, only a necessary insecurity.

The fold between speech and writing initially appears as a binary structure. The supplementary outside is shown to be folded into the absent-center of the primary term. Derrida says this of writing repeat-edly in *Of Grammatology*: "Now we must think that writing is at the same time more exterior to speech, not being its 'image' or its 'symbol,' and more interior to speech which is already in itself a writing."[67] In the definition that Derrida provides in *Positions,* deconstruction fixes upon metaphysical and hierarchal binaries and proceeds by first inverting the hierarchy and then marking the interval between the opposed terms such that the minor term is demonstrated to be critical for the major term.[68] Thus, metaphysics always presents thought in terms of binary structures, but the process of deconstruction that is brought to bear works simultaneously within this binary structure and by marking a ternary structure that adds to the binary the spacing between them.[69]

While, in a sense, *Of Grammatology* deals with the binary of read-ing and writing, this is done by the introduction of a third term; what is called "writing" is differentiated from "writing-in-general," which Derrida equates with arche-writing.[70] Derrida says, "If 'writing' signi-fies inscription and especially the durable institution of a sign (and that is the only irreducible kernel of the concept of writing), writing in general covers the entire field of linguistic signs."[71] Writing itself becomes bifurcated into the writing that is separated from speech and as the separation itself. The name "writing" signifies a certain institu-tion of the sign, whereas writing-in-general describes both writing and the general logic of the speech-writing system. Thus deconstruction is directly concerned with the third, writing-in-general, as that which structures, through its absence and erasure, the relationship between the One-Two (speech–"writing"). Thus "the law of the addition of the origin to its representation, of the thing to its image, is that one plus one makes at least three."[72]

In one sense, writing-in-general names the logic of the relation-ship between speech and writing, and alternatively, it appears as a third term that disrupts the relationship between speech and writing.[73] Thus writing-in-general is for Derrida an "arche-violence, loss of the proper, of absolute proximity, of self-presence, in truth the loss of what has never taken place, of a self-presence which has never been."[74] It is an origin that can never provide a full presence or a stable essence; it is a fall that only afterward produces a before, a loss of what has never been.[75] Thus writing-in-general produces speech with a nonpres-ence in its core that is both exposed and treated by colloquial writing.

Derrida says, "It is that very thing which cannot let itself be reduced to the form of a *presence*."[76] While arche-writing structures writing and its vulnerability, its nonpresence simultaneously allows new historical forms of writing, such as the program, to reconfigure the form of this metaphysical structure. Thus writing-in-general functions as a third term in the relation of speech to writing both temporally as a before and spatially by way of a gap between speech and writing, but in both cases always as an opening to what would arrive and reconfigure its structure.

This dual function of writing-in-general thus replicates the relation between topography and topology. Writing-in-general both folds the topological relationship between the two terms and spaces them, instantiating a duration, a distance, a topographical difference. Within the space of topology, the miniscule distance of spacing appears as an unbridgeable cut, a disconnection between speech and writing that appears infinite. At the same time, in topographic space, writing-in-general serves as a fold that, like a Möbius strip or Klein bottle, frustrates meaningful distinctions between interior and exterior space. In this sense, there do not exist pure spaces and times of topography and pure spaces and times of topology. Rather, space is always in the process of becoming topological or topographic. The insecurity of writing-in-general, of all programs and all networks, places the relation between program and network, topology and topography, into an unstable state of play. Each collapses in upon the other as the insecurity of both is operationalized. The space of the outside is always shifting and always opening anew.

This logic of the supplement touches directly on the production and distribution of space.[77] If the "outside" is the space of the supplement, it then has a nothingness that is analogous to that of the supplement, of which Derrida says, "The supplement *is* not, is not a being *(on)*. It is nevertheless not a simple nonbeing *(mēon)*, either. Its slidings slip it out of the simple alternative presence/absence. *That* is the danger."[78] The same should be said of the outside: though the outside is not a transcendent elsewhere, it is at the same time not a simple nonbeing. Just like the supplement, what is named as the outside is a space that slips out of the alternative between presence and absence. Moreover, in "Plato's Pharmacy," he suggests, "We do not believe that there exists, in all rigor, a Platonic text, closed upon itself, complete with its inside and its outside."[79] The inside and the outside of the text are not closed; they fold into each other as the text is inscribed between topological and topographic spaces. But still nonpresent outsides always threaten even the most oppressive closure, including the supposedly fixed text of the program.

The space between topology and topography, or more accurately, the constant slippage between topology and topography, never allows deconstruction to rest and forecloses the possibility of a metaphysical distinction between program and language. The constant shifting of spatializations refuses the possibility of a metaphysical closure that would be both the impossibility of deconstruction and the guarantee of a safe deconstruction beyond military and state appropriation. Deconstruction and metaphysics are both opened and localized, never captured by a language anyone is in control of and thus subject to attack and counterattack.

Derrida states much of this explicitly in the preface to *Dissemination*. He outlines the importance of the three, not as the holy trinity of the Hegelian dialectic, but as a strategic partition and mark that cuts across the field of binary oppositions:

> The "three" will no longer give us the ideality of the speculative solution but rather the effect of a strategic re-mark, a mark which by phase and by simulacrum, refers the name of one of the two terms to the absolute outside of the opposition, that absolute otherness which was marked—once again—in the exposé of *différance*. Two/four, and the "closure of metaphysics" can no longer take, can indeed never have taken, the form of a circular line enclosing a field, a finite culture of binary oppositions, but takes on the figure of a totally different partition. Dissemination *displaces* the three of ontotheology along the angle of a certain refolding [*re-ploiement*].[80]

For Derrida, binary relationships are destabilized not exclusively from within but rather from the strategic refolding or repartitioning of space that introduces a third. He proceeds here by way of a war machine that arrives from the absolute outside. This third appears at once as the spacing between the two terms and as an outside force that militarizes and explodes the internal interval. Derridean deconstruction, even if it has at times downplayed its machinic and military potential, has always produced war machines that disrupt systems both from outside and from the very distinction that creates the outside.

Ultimately, deconstruction names and exploits a certain slippage between heterogeneous spaces. It is precisely the movement between topographical and topological space and the instability of any space that is always in the process of folding the outside inside. As a result, deconstruction can never exteriorize the program from text. This distinction, through the violence of cyberwar, is continually deconstructed from within both deconstruction and the war machines that exploit its insecurity. This is what makes deconstruction dangerous: it opens a multiplicity of spaces, temporalities, metaphysics, and systems to a play that can at once unhinge hierarchies and set free meaning, but also destroy systems, infect them, corrupt them, turn them against those who created them, and perhaps most devastatingly, turn them against those whose continued existence depends on them. This is the danger of both deconstruction and these new modalities of war.

THE PLASTICITY OF CYBERWAR

Cyberwar and deconstruction thus name a certain morphology of space, a strategic or accidental reconceptualization of the structure of local spaces, a plasticity, to invoke Malabou's term. Malabou defines plasticity as designating three related aspects: "On the one hand, it designates the capacity of certain materials, such as clay or plaster, to receive form. On the other hand, it designates the power to give form—the power of a sculptor or a plastic surgeon. But, finally, it also refers to the possibility of the deflagration or explosion of every form."[81] In many ways, plasticity describes the global networks over which cyberwar is waged. Although these networks are often thought of as completely reconfigurable and formless, they require massive physical, economic, and informational infrastructures that both give and receive form. Digital and other networks function not as completely malleable material but rather as plastic material that both receives and gives form to the networks that they create. Through the construction of these networks, the accidents that can befall them, and the possibility of military intervention, they both allow for transformations and resist other transformations. Finally, they are always susceptible to the destruction of their form.

While in many ways Malabou's focus in invoking plasticity is to contemplate change and transformation over time, it should be stressed that this notion of plasticity also describes the changes both over space and of space itself that cyberwar invokes. A spatial plasticity thus describes the local nature of systems and the constantly shifting spatialities of our networked world. It is the form of the spaces and the connections within and across them that define the networked geopolitical landscape. Malabou suggests that plasticity requires us to think form: "It is not form that is the problem; it's the fact that form can be thought separately from the nature of the being that transforms itself.... The critique of metaphysics does not want to recognize that in fact, despite what it claims loud and clear, metaphysics constantly instigates the dissociation of essence and form."[82] Networks, topological connections, and the reconfiguration of space all require the thinking of form as essence. The connections themselves create the nature of networks. And it is also this form of plastic connection that is vulnerable to accident or purposeful attack. Cyberwar's strategies are built on the spatiotemporal plasticity of networks. Cyberwar attempts to rework the various physical, informational, and epistemological networks within which we exist.

This raises a question that we briefly broached through the work of Maturana and Varela regarding autopoeisis, namely, what constitutes organization? The inability to translate directly between systems and their spaces also raises a question as to what constitutes a system. It must be concluded that there is, properly speaking, no such thing as "a system" or "organization" in the cybernetic sense. It is always a product of writing, reading, and assembling topologies and topographies. To speak of a system is to create one, to define, but always in translation, a space and a time. It is, as Malabou says, creating form from traces, as she "affirms the *mutual convertibility of trace and form*."[83] It requires constructing a network out of traces and giving it a proper name, as in the case of Comment Crew in the preceding chapter. To speak of the organization of a system is to name that system and translate it, but never from a space completely external to the system. Systems are defined by "*the spontaneous organization of fragments*," and if we include the explosive possibility of negative plasticity, we must also include the spontaneous disorganization of fragments. One must infiltrate a system to know it and name it. To do so requires weaving oneself into the system, to bisect its space and become part of it, but always as the creation of a new system, through new connections and new topologies. Thus the structure, the topology, always comes after and never forms the system a priori—"this means that structure is not a starting point but an outcome."[84]

Thus this morphological potential describes both the structure of metaphysics itself and its mutability. Especially insomuch as arche-writing is simultaneously a structure and the nonpresent outside of structure itself, what is essential to deconstruction is the lack of a fixed structure. Derrida states,

> Difference by itself would be more "originary," but one would no longer be able to call it "origin" or "ground," those notions belong essentially to the history of onto-theology, to the system function-ing as the effacing of difference. It can, however, be thought of in the closet proximity to itself only on one condition: that one begins by determining it as the ontico-ontological difference before erasing that determination. The necessity of passing through that erased determination, the necessity of that *trick of writing* is irreducible.[85]

The structure of arche-writing as originary difference precludes the possibility of a fixed determination of the boundary between the onti-cal and the ontological. It is, then, through this trick of writing, that an ontical act of historical writing touches directly on the ontological structure of arche-writing. Cyberwar therefore amounts to a histori-cal development, a new trick or technology of writing, that plastically reconfigures the ontological structure of writing. The discovery of code as a form of writing and the later historical discovery of its vulnerability and nonpresence in the advent of cyberwar do not merely reenact a fixed ontology of writing. Rather, these discoveries reconfigure metaphysics and deconstruction themselves, pushing writing and its autodeconstruc-tion even further from the primacy of human agency.

THE PLACE OF PLASTICITY

This naming and structuring of topologies, networks, and structures do not ultimately touch on a global metaphysical structure. There are merely local interiorities and exteriorities that exist only from the standpoint of a created system. Despite this lack of a transcendental outside, it in no way engenders some global closure, as Malabou insists that there exists "a point of sheer randomness [that] dwells within essential being, within 'original substance.'"[86] There exists in the heart of all systems a random center, the nonpresence of arche-writing; hence essence becomes accidental and the accident becomes essential. Deleuze suggests something similar in describing the nature of the fold, which contains "an outside that is farther away than any external world, and hence closer than any internal world. Must this outside be called Chance?"[87] Though Deleuze insists on referring to this randomness as an outside, it in no way represents a transcendental outside; rather, it names this "point of sheer randomness" that upsets all fixity and writes contingency into the center of all systems.

Malabou puts this directly in relation to deconstruction, stating, "The deconstruction of presence does not arise from the presence *of an outside,* an event or an accident that belatedly affects it; rather, the aforementioned fissures are originally within it. Hence, the dislocating force of deconstruction is always localized within the architecture it deconstructs."[88] In this light, it becomes evident how the ambiguity between accident and attack makes theorizing cyberwar so difficult. The militarization of the microscopic fractures within systems and the lack of mastery over the language in which individuals program ultimately confuse the distinction between the accident and the attack. It is always possible that what appears as an accident could be a carefully hidden attack or that what was claimed as an attack is merely an accident, such as in the case of the Soviet pipeline explosion. The essences of systems are defined by being always open to their possible future destruction. Thus, although there is no global transcendental outside, each system is susceptible to a deconstruction that moves along the fold of its interiority.

It is precisely the space of the exterior and the heterogeneity in relation to other systems that prevent any system from becoming completely secure or in control of its language. Exteriors can always be woven into systems. Larger systems can incorporate smaller ones. Transistors and their exteriors are organized into computers, computers into local networks, local networks into global ones, and so on. Thus it becomes completely indeterminate whether these systems are destroyed from within or without, and deconstruction names both the internal destabilization of a system and the possibility of a force from elsewhere effectuating the already existing fractures.

One can move into exteriors, into other systems and other spaces, but the radical fold of the contingent inside–outside can never be recuperated and mastered. The outside does not provide a place of escape, only the impossibility of flight: "Metamorphosis by destruction is not the same as flight; it is rather the form of the impossibility of fleeing. The impossibility of flight where flight presents the only possible solution."[89] It is these situations of metamorphic destruction that cause systems to move toward an in-existent outside, toward an outside that is never present but still announces itself as the impossibility of closure and as the possibility of transformation through accident and contingency. It is precisely this inability to flee, the need for transformation of systems that cannot escape, that allows them to be destroyed in place, but always under the guidance of a contingency that can never be reached nor made present.

Cyberwar and the creation of global networks thus take place in the plastic space between topography and topology, in relation to a nonexistent outside that is always folded inside and provides the possibility of destroying, transforming, reading, writing, and translating systems between spatialities and temporalities. It was suggested earlier that such a process is a writing and reading of the system by weaving, but for Malabou, we have passed beyond writing into plasticity. Malabou states, "Today we must acknowledge that the linguistic-graphic scheme is diminishing and that it has entered a twilight for some time already. It now seems that plasticity is slowly but surely establishing itself as the paradigmatic figure of organization in general."[90] Although this seems unequivocally to be the case, and we can note it in the movement from spaces of place to spaces of flow and the valuation of the latter in global capitalist economies, it is important to note that the one does not replace the other. Ultimately, they vary over time and space. Topology does not simply replace the topographic; spaces and times are constructed and assembled as both. This deformation exposes texts and systems to a deconstruction that pushes beyond any meaningful distinction between text and program, between topology and topography. Cyberwar, while affirming the convertibility between trace and form, announces, outside the space of carefully authored theoretical treatises, the global strategic investment in that convertibility and the local possibility of destruction and deconstruction of both network and text.

AUTHENTICATION AND THE FUTURE OF IDENTITY

Cryptography again offers a fruitful example of the relationship between the war machine and deconstruction. One of the powerful uses of cryptography is the ability to determine the identity of an interlocutor over a network. The way in which this is achieved and the problems that arise demonstrate what is at stake in our digital writing and the deconstruction of the spaces traced by cryptographic authentication. A common technique for verifying the identity of someone sending information over the Internet, for instance, a banking website, is to use a technique known as public-key encryption. Public-key encryption works through the use of an asymmetric encryption algorithm, which creates key pairs. One of the keys is "public" and the other "private." Using the public key to encrypt a message produces a message that can only be decrypted with the private key, so even someone else who knows the public key cannot decrypt the message. This allows someone to openly publish her public key and receive an encrypted message without the need to set up a key for each person with whom she communicates. Another benefit of public-key encryption is that the system works in the opposite direction. A message can be encrypted with the private key and then only decrypted with the public key. While at first this may seem unimportant, because anyone could then decrypt the message, this ability plays a critical role in network security. Because only the holder of the private key can encrypt a message with her private key, anyone with the public key can then verify both the sender of the message and that the message has not been modified. As long as one is confident that the sender is the only person who knows the private key, the cryptographic schema is secure, and one has the correct public key, it is impossible for anyone else to have sent the message.[91] It is of course possible that an adversary could break the cryptographic system, but at least for the time being, it is believed that currently used public-key cryptographic systems are strong enough to require sufficiently large amounts of computation time to make breaking the encryption unlikely in most day-to-day applications.[92]

Thus, in addition to allowing interlocutors to communicate secret messages, public-key cryptography also provides a strategy for verifying the identity of individuals, websites, systems, and so on, on the public

Internet. As more and more tasks are moved to the global Internet, being able to establish the identity of another computer becomes critical for security. If an adversary were able to convince a user that she were a bank, an automated software update service, an e-mail provider, and so on, it would be a trivial task to destroy or subvert nearly any networked system. One could steal a target's banking information, force her computer to automatically install malicious software, intercept and forge e-mails, and so on. Though a multitude of attack vectors open up potential network insecurities, it is not an overstatement to say that without the ability to verify the identity of machines over the Internet, computer security on open networks would be an impossibility. The successful functioning of these encryption algorithms is thus critical to the secure and continued operation of the modern Internet.

Despite the general efficacy of encryption for establishing identity, a critical difficulty arises. To trust the computer with which one believes he is communicating, it is necessary to already have the public key of the signer. It cannot arrive with the message; otherwise, anyone could send a public key that would match his private key. One of the most common exploits of this problem is referred to as a man-in-the-middle attack. By being present between two communicating parties at the beginning of the encrypted or signed conversation, it is possible to appear to both parties as the other party. If Alice is attempting to send a message to Bob, Eve can send public keys to both parties so she appears as Alice to Bob and as Bob to Alice. In doing so, it is possible both to eavesdrop on encrypted communication and to pretend to be another party.[93] It is thus necessary to provide public keys through other verified channels. For many Web applications, this is achieved by a trusted certificate authority that, through using its own digital signature, verifies the digital signatures of other known parties, who currently pay to register their signatures with the certificate authority. This, of course, requires that one believe one has the appropriate public key for the certificate authority. For the most part, certificate authorities' public keys are provided with Web browsers that come with computers. Thus one makes at the beginning a leap of faith into a system of trust and authentication. If the system was corrupted from the beginning, it is possible that all is already lost. Moreover, it is always possible that somewhere along these chains of public keys, a mistake was made.[94]

In the systemization of determining and authenticating identity over the open Internet, a whole new identity politics plays out. It is not an identity politics of groups but rather the identity of absolutely unique identities (in terms of being computationally distinguishable) assured under the sign of an empty secret. The secret string of numbers that makes up the private key signifies nothing and only functions so much as it is kept secret. Likewise, the identity it confirms signifies nothing other than the possession of the secret. Over the network, all one really knows about an authenticated interlocutor is that she knows the secret she claims to know. The two slide into each other: the secret says nothing other than that one is the one who knows the secret. Likewise, identity says no more than that one possesses the secret that verifies one's identity. As the secret and identity become synonymous in the space of the network, the play between the two is at the same time disrupted from the outside, called into question by the topological networks that attempt to stabilize the secrets and verify the authenticity of the secret itself. The text of the secret requires the support of a network of supplementary secrets. The textual practice of the identity-secret is embedded in the network space of exchange and flow. Neither is primary; rather, the two support each other. The textual secret creates authenticated exchanges over the network, and the network distributes and verifies the secrets themselves.

Kittler states, "The interception of correspondence is as old as correspondence itself."[95] Contemporaneous with the origin of writing lies the attack on writing; interception and subversion mark the originary difference endemic to writing. The program, like all writing, does not occur immediately in a single space; it is stretched over time and space. The whole system thus functions in the interplay between space and text. It cannot be reduced to one or the other. To reduce it to either is to ignore the fundamental insecurity of the system, the possibility of its internal or external deconstruction. The system always slips into its exteriors. The fantasy of complete security is analogous to the fantasy of an independent text or the sovereign individual unaffected by the surrounding world. To believe that a system can be isolated and reduced to the topographic or the topological constitutes a dual movement that both erases the necessary translation between system spaces and, in doing so, constructs the imagined possibility of the total security and sovereignty of the system.

CONCLUSION: WRITING IN THE SHADOW OF THE CATASTROPHE

This militarized, machinic, and programmatic deconstruction is likely not far from Derrida's description of deconstruction. Still, if this militarized deconstruction pushes beyond Derrida's intent, it is important to note that he would never have been able to control what deconstruction was to become. Derrida in many ways opposed the attention and attempts at interpreting deconstruction that followed his use of the term. Gasché says of deconstruction that "it is a word, he has said elsewhere, that he has never liked, and whose fortune has disagreeably surprised him. Only after others valorized the word in the context of structuralism—which, Derrida claims, did not primarily determine his usage of the word—did Derrida try to define deconstruction in his own manner."[96] In a certain sense, Derrida's attempts to delimit deconstruction and insist against its programmatic possibilities appear as an attempt to recuperate the term after it had already begun, like a rogue computer virus, to spiral out of control.

Thus it is possible to detect in Derrida's claims about the space of metaphysical closure a securitization of metaphysics. Derrida's generalization of a metaphysics of presence and insistence on its pervasive nature lead him to conclude that we are trapped in a global space of metaphysical closure. While such claims of closure were problematized by Derrida, their existence at points—like attempts to shield deconstruction from its machinic possibilities—suggests a hope for a safe form of deconstruction. The concept of this metaphysical closure risks, like those who may believe in the absolute security of the identity-secret over the network, ignoring how any system is localized and embedded in both topographic and topological space and the impossibility of fixing the nature of writing, excluding the program from its purview. This belief in the closure of the system sanitizes deconstruction. Deconstruction, if it can be enclosed within a single space and with a circumscribed notion of text, both supports the belief that one can never escape metaphysics and also guarantees that it will provoke no interest from war machines and states. The closure of metaphysics is only possible if one ignores the multiple spatialities, temporalities, and textualities of deconstruction and its movement between them. Once this can no longer be ignored, and the advent of cyberwar declares the political–historical recognition of this fact, deconstruction can no longer be limited to the inside of closed systems or a single machine of metaphysics but rather opens to attacks against systems from all angles, all forms of inscription, all insides and all outsides.

Cyberwar thus arrives from any possible space and any possible future to disrupt the functioning of every system we may name. Despite the immanent possibility of these disruptions and deconstructions, programmers, writers, and armies invested in metaphysical conflict continue to produce and defend networks and systems. They continue despite the future deconstruction that potentially awaits them. Derrida explains in his text on nuclear war that although the catastrophe (or, as he calls it, "the apocalypse without revelation") may destroy the archive, it becomes at the same time the final referent of all writing:

> The only referent that is absolutely real is thus of the scope or dimension of an absolute nuclear catastrophe that would irreversibly destroy the entire archive and all symbolic capacity. . . . This is the only absolute trace—effaceable, ineffaceable. The only "subject" of all possible literature, of all possible criticism, its only ultimate and a-symbolic referent, unsymbolizable, even unsignifiable.[97]

The future cybercatastrophe produces the same structure. All writing—and by writing we must include programming, databases, and so on—is written against and toward the ineffaceable trace of the destruction of the trace. We write, code, create data, and so on, against and in light of the catastrophe. Out of the future digital effacement of writing grows the possibility of writing. It is not only writing that arises from this future. It is the creative possibility of both writing and plasticity, of text and network. The catastrophe that conditions this movement provides both the guarantee of the impossibility of the closure of any global metaphysics (although each system is a local closure defining its own space) and the possibility of military and state intervention into every system we may interact with or depend upon.

We arrive, then, at a global situation confronted with a horrifying mutually assured deconstruction. Cyberwarfare, as a generalized military logic of destroying systems by turning them against themselves, infecting them, changing their context, attacking from the inside and without, operates as a deconstruction that infects all systems. The program, code, and all digital technologies and systems in general, then, take on a dual structure, a doubled possibility: on one hand, an intensification of the militarization of information technology, and on the other hand, a writing, a creativity that writes both against and in reference to a possible cybernetic effacement. If this latter is to remain a possibility, it cannot be through the erasure of the *différance* that inhabits even the most programmatic writing but rather through the theorization of this deconstruction that lies there in wait. This dual possibility is both a threat to the future of deconstruction as it undermines any theoretical fixity, safety, or alliance with a particular political aim and at the same time a guarantee of the continued relevance of deconstruction.

Ultimately, any analysis of the digital must at least come to terms with its own effacement. The situation is not dissimilar to Derrida's description of cybernetics in *Of Grammatology*, where he states, "If the theory of cybernetics is by itself to oust all metaphysical concepts—including the concepts of soul, of life, of value, of choice, of memory—which until recently served to separate the machine from man, it must conserve the notion of writing, trace gramme, or grapheme, until its own historico-metaphysical character is also exposed."[98] While Derrida is critical of cybernetics and its logic, it seems to offer a similar dual possibility: supposedly being a science of control, but also being a science that, in attempting to theorize control, effaces itself, deconstructs itself, leaving only writing and trace. In this vein, Derrida argues, "the entire field of the cybernetic *program* would be the field of writing."[99] The program, even in its most cybernetic understanding, can never be held back and meaningfully separated from writing. Perhaps with the advent of cyberwar, we are seeing the final stage of this logic of cybernetics: a movement of atomized military investment into the everyday, and especially into the systems and technologies of the everyday under the logic of writing. It seems at least possible that against this militarization of writing and deconstruction, but always arising from the same place, a different and creative digital writing may take hold precisely where these systems of militarism efface themselves in their blind rush toward a mutual and antagonistic deconstruction.

3

Distributed Denial of Service: Cybernetic Sovereignty

While much of the discourse surrounding cyberwar focuses on conflicts between states, to fully explore what is at stake, it is important to consider the impact that systems of security and insecurity have on individuals and the experience of the everyday. Especially as war slips outside the time and space of declared war and intervenes into the microscopic spaces of our technical systems, it touches upon our daily lives directly. The media, technology, and texts that are at stake in cyberwar are ultimately the same systems that serve as the substrate for our contemporary society and the technologies that control populations today. This confluence means that cyberwar is simultaneously a means of fighting between states and a means of fighting between states and their populations.

Siegfried Zielinski suggests that today the media function as a site of control and domination:

> Now that it is possible to create a state with media, they are no longer any good for a revolution. The media are an indispensable component of functioning social hierarchies, both from the top down and the bottom up, of power and countervailing power. They have taken on systemic character.... Many universities have established courses in media design, media studies, and media management. Something that operates as a complex, dynamic, and edgy complex between the discourses, that is, something which can only operate interdiscursively, has acquired a firm and fixed place in the academic landscape. This is reassuring and creates

professorial chairs, upon which a once anarchic element can be sat out and developed into knowledge for domination and control.[1]

Increasingly, the media, when they work properly and when they are attacked, appear only to serve the forces of domination and control.[2] Still, Zielinski notes that there are peripheries from which it is possible to undermine and criticize these uses of media. In this sense, cyberwar appears as a logic of control and domination, but one that achieves its ends by exploiting and releasing these peripheral forces that threaten to destabilize this static and controlling mediatic system. The military engagement with these media inevitably finds a complex set of networks and texts that always slip outside any attempt at fixing them and simultaneously threaten to release systemwide catastrophe. Recently it was discovered that Russian state-backed hackers attacked the servers of the Democratic National Convention in the United States and released private information in order to destabilize the 2016 elections.[3] Such attacks demonstrate the potential for cyberwar to intervene directly in the relations between states and their own populations.

It is here, as cyberwar explicates a logic of power and control over the everyday, that it becomes possible to see both the complex interactions between space, time, writing, and the machinic nature of these systems and also the fundamental risk that any sovereign entity takes as it attempts to act within this space. The deconstructability of these systems simultaneously creates the conditions of cyberwar and problematizes any simple logic of control. As we shall see, cryptography again proves a fruitful example of the immense difficulty that these networks, systems, and modes of digital writing create for any force that may attempt to control them. Ultimately, while increasing state intervention into the microscopic digital networks of the everyday threaten to subject us all to complete control, the war machines that are simultaneously engaging in these spaces, and the spaces' complexity, testify to the impossibility of these systems and networks ever being completely closed or under any sovereign control.

CRYPTOWARS

As computation increasingly becomes a globally networked phenomenon, the ability to establish secure and trusted lines of communication has become vital for the continued functioning of governments, society, and everyday life. The means of this security, cryptography, was briefly discussed earlier, but to explore the relationship between security, cyberwar, and the everyday, we must further explicate the relationship between networked systems and cryptography. As cryptography, and its subversion, underlie many attempts at networked security and attack, exploring its inner workings is critical to understanding the implications of cyberwar and digital writing. If network traffic can be observed unencrypted, it can then be faked, allowing unfettered access to any system that accepts commands or data from elsewhere. In the case of Stuxnet, viruses were able to get into the microcontrollers because they required no cryptographic signature to update the software.

While extensive histories are available, it is elucidating to recount a few key points from the history of public access to cryptography in the United States. For millennia, encoding schemes for military and government secrets have mainly been kept secret themselves, as it is easier and more effective to keep messages secret if adversaries do not understand the system by which messages are encoded. In the United States following World War II, the National Security Agency (NSA), which grew out of wartime cryptography efforts, became the central agency in maintaining the government's and military's ability to send secret messages and decrypt adversaries' secret communications. Until the early 1970s, the NSA was able to maintain a near-monopoly on knowledge about advanced ciphers, but concurrent with the growth of public and university access to computers, public interest in cryptography arose.[4]

The NSA responded initially by attempting to stifle this conversation through efforts to establish systems of review for academic work on cryptography, occasionally claiming cryptographic patents as government secrets and banning their dissemination, along with enforcing a law classifying cryptographic methods and implementations as munitions that were illegal to export. While a growing group of academics and hobbyists built a public knowledge base around advanced cryptography, the computer industry began to realize the importance of secure networked communications and data storage. By the mid-1980s, various companies, such as IBM and Lotus, began integrating cryptography into their software and hardware.[5] Struggles ensued between industry, the government, and hobbyist cryptoactivists. As part of these disputes, the government relied heavily on the Arms Export Control Act to attempt to slow the dissemination of cryptographic knowledge. Companies that included cryptography in software and hardware were allowed to export some cryptographic systems, but with intentionally short keys, weakening the cryptography. They were thus forced either to provide weak cryptography to all clients or to produce separate domestic and export versions of software.[6]

Under pressure from both industry and activists, by the late 1990s, this system of control began to break down along a number of fronts. In 1996, a graduate student asked U.S. courts to rule that the source code for cryptographic systems could be published on free speech grounds, despite export controls. The courts ruled in favor of the graduate student, but the decision was withdrawn and the case rendered moot as the government moved to make new regulations liberalizing the export and publication of cryptographic algorithms.[7] Around the same time, a government attempt to create a national hardware-based key escrow system known as the Clipper Chip completely failed. The plan, pushed by the Clinton administration, called for the creation of a system of hardware-based cryptography and the storage of secret keys for each chip in escrow, such that law enforcement could recover the keys with a warrant and descramble any communications that had been encrypted with the chip. The plan ran into a host of problems, including technical errors, concerns about the security of the escrow facility, and privacy complaints. One overarching issue continues to frustrate all of these plans for putting back doors into cryptographic systems: any attempt to require the ability to decrypt a secret message by a third party is akin to legally mandating insecurity. As Whitfield and Landau put it, attempts to circumvent cryptographic security systems on the Internet "present a clear risk of introducing vulnerabilities into Internet communications. After all, wiretapping is a legally authorized security breach, and introducing a security breach into a communications network always entails serious risks."[8]

Thus it appeared in the late 1990s that strong, publicly available cryptography was inevitable. It was not merely access to cryptography that changed in this period but also the way in which cryptography was described and understood. In the mid-1970s, the U.S. government decided that it required a standardized system for cryptographic communications. The system, which was developed and published as a national standard, was known as the Data Encryption Standard (DES). While the algorithm was made publicly available, the design considerations that went into it were kept secret, and many believed the NSA had tampered with the design to make it weaker. It was later revealed that the NSA was aware the original design was susceptible to differential cryptanalysis—a technique that was not known to the public at the time—and so the NSA changed the design to make it stronger, without releasing any information about differential cryptanalysis.

At the end of 2001, DES was replaced by a new standard, the Advanced Encryption Standard (AES). The process of developing this replacement began in the late 1990s and spoke to just how different the public understanding of cryptography had become. While DES was developed almost completely in secret and aimed to provide just enough strength for nonclassified materials, AES was developed through a completely public process and designed to be as strong as possible. Of all the teams that submitted proposals for AES, only one team consisted of all U.S. citizens. The submission that was finally accepted was put forth by a team from Belgium. Moreover, where DES was described in a series of engineering specifications laying out the required operations to encrypt information with a number of the components' purposes left unexplained, AES was described in primarily mathematical terms. Where AES included descriptions of how to implement the algorithm, these elements were all justified by the mathematics.[9]

Over the course of about thirty years, cryptography moved from a set of secret national systems that were believed to be hard to crack to publicly available and openly discussed, mathematically provable formulas. Contrary to centuries of belief about the nature of keeping secrets, it appears now that the strongest systems for keeping secrets are in fact publicly advertised and reviewed systems rather than those that are themselves shrouded in secrecy. This was not the only cryptographic orthodoxy that collapsed. The invention of public-key cryptography, discussed earlier, overturned the widely held dogma that any public disclosure of part of an encryption key would clearly expose whatever secret one was trying to keep. During this period, cryptography quickly became a "public science" in more ways than one, all while shifting from a series of engineering designs to abstract mathematical systems that defined what was possible. The growing use of the Internet, especially with corporate interest in systems for secure online shopping and other monetary transactions; the ability to remotely access and manage computer systems; and even the post–Cold War need for common military systems to support ad hoc alliances all created a demand for strong public cryptography. Thus it appeared as though cryptography was a technology that, despite the NSA's desire, could not be uninvented.[10]

These conflicts over cryptography point toward the irreducible complexity of working in and through these networked digital spaces. The textual practices, sovereign powers, networked topologies, technical systems, mathematics, and texts that define the possibilities of these systems all mutually implicate each other and define the enfolded space of these systems. To attempt to reduce what is at stake in cyberwar exclusively to texts, networks, states, or machines would inevitably mean simplifying these systems and losing the thread of their importance to our current time. Thus, in proceeding, we must hold open all of these questions and delay deciding on the nature or essence of these systems, as that is always produced only after the fact.

THE ABSTRACT MACHINE OF CRYPTOGRAPHY

Though cryptography is clearly a technical–mathematical problem, it exists immanently, but in a complex manner, within networks of machines and politics. WikiLeaks founder Julian Assange has stated that "the universe believes in encryption. It is easier to encrypt information than it is to decrypt it."[11] Ultimately, this is because of the existence of a number of one-way functions. One-way functions are easy to compute in one direction, but given an output of the function, it is extremely difficult (meaning, in computational terms, time consuming) to reconstitute the input. For instance, multiplying two large prime numbers is an easy operation, but taking the output of such an operation and trying to factor it to determine the original prime numbers requires essentially trying a large number of primes until one has found the right pair. The existence of this class of functions means that it is possible to easily convert a message into its encrypted version and decrypt it with the secret key, but trying to reverse the process without knowing the key is incredibly time consuming. For a number of currently used encryption algorithms, it would take modern supercomputers longer than the current age of the universe to crack one encryption key.[12]

Assange's claim raises a number of important philosophical questions about the nature of technology, writing, and encryption. To believe that the universe believes in encryption is to state that there are certain physical tendencies, to use Leroi-Gourhan's term, that shape our technical world. In short, it is to believe that there exists what Stiegler calls a technological *maieutic*:

> There is here an actual techno-logical *maieutic*. Certainly, what is invented, exhumed, brought to light, brought into the world by the object exists in the laws of physics. But in physics they exist only as possibilities. When they are freed, they are no longer possibilities but realities, irreversibly.[13]

With cryptography, we see a certain set of possibilities that, once discovered, cannot be overturned.[14] Cryptography represents a possibility in physics, or in the laws of the universe as Assange puts it, that creates both a technological inevitability and a set of political realities that no sovereignty can undo. It is in Stiegler's terms a maieutic, a truth that exists and can be uncovered through questioning our physical reality. Cryptography operates, then, not as an accidental arrangement but as a fundamental truth of the universe that is discovered and operated upon. Deleuze suggests something similar using the term *abstract machine*:

> [The] abstract machine is the map of relations between forces, a map of destiny, or intensity, which proceeds by primary non-localizable relations and at every moment passes through every point, "or rather in every relation from one point to another." Of course, this has nothing to do either with a transcendent idea or with an ideological superstructure, or even with an economic infrastructure, which is already qualified by its substance and defined by its form and use. None the less, the diagram acts as a non-unifying immanent cause that is coextensive with the whole social field. . . . It is a cause which is realized, integrated and distinguished in its effect.[15]

An abstract machine functions as a destiny that appears as a cause only after the effects are discovered. The abstract machine is not a transcendent concept but rather a tendency that is realized and revealed in every point of the social field.[16] The abstract machine as a possibility in the laws of physics cuts across the social–political field and predetermines a set of possible arrangements. The development of such an abstract machine can be seen clearly in the movement from DES, which was designed in secret and distributed as a series of engineering specifications, to AES, which was designed publicly and distributed as a series of mathematical formulas. We move slowly through a maieutic process of questioning and revealing toward an abstract machine that defines an entire class of relations and concrete machines. Cryptography as abstract machine sets up a certain set of possible arrangements that are then translated into a whole series of concrete machines. Deleuze refers to the diagram, another name he uses for the abstract machine, as "a machine that is almost blind and mute, even though it makes others see and speak."[17] The universal possibility of cryptography is nearly mute, but it can be made to irreversibly reveal its secrets. So we move from a chance engineering specification to an abstract set of mathematical laws to actual software that is capable of encrypting data and an assemblage of social relations that allows individuals to use this software and technology.

While it appears that the universe may "believe in encryption," Assange goes further. He claims that this universal movement toward encryption constitutes "our one hope against total domination. A hope that with courage, insight and solidarity we could use to resist."[18] His wager, then, amounts to believing cryptography as abstract machine is a truth too powerful for tyranny. Cryptography as abstract machine is thus for him the only machine that might resist domination. As Assange says, "no amount of coercive force can solve a math problem."[19] But immediately, this assertion seems overly hopeful. Although, of course, no sovereign can will away the laws of gravity (or of computation), historically, political power has functioned despite its inability to control gravity. Moreover, as the Cold War space race suggests, political power functions quite well as it struggles against gravity and other physical laws.

ABSTRACT MACHINES AND POLITICAL *TECHNĒ*

Though Assange is undoubtedly right that violence or coercive force cannot solve a math problem, it seems questionable that math would necessarily favor liberty and freedom. Assange's assertion linking cryptography with political liberation rests on two questionable assumptions often overlooked by advocates of cryptography as a political good. First, even if the math favors secrecy, there is no guarantee that the state or various war machines will not figure out other ways to extract secrets or undermine the implementation of mathematically sound cryptography. Second, even if everyone is able to communicate with associates in complete secrecy, there is no reason to assume that secret discourse alone will necessarily alter the current economic–political organization.

For a number of years, the first concern was only speculative, and there were those in the cryptography community who believed that the NSA had secretly conspired to undermine public access to cryptography. While it is clear that the NSA played a role in cryptography and was invested in being able to read at least some communications, those who really believed the NSA was controlling everything and undermining the strength of commercial cryptography were often seen as conspiracy theorists not to be listened to.[20] It has recently become clear that those critics were not so far off. Even those who worked in cryptography and believed that the math could be implemented in such a way to offer complete secrecy have been surprised by how effectively their efforts could be circumvented.

In summer 2013, Edward Snowden, an NSA contractor working for a private company, Booz Allen, traveled to Hong Kong to provide a small group of reporters with documents detailing NSA and other security agencies' programs to collect and monitor Internet traffic. One of the major revelations of the Snowden documents was that the NSA was spending more than $800 million annually to guarantee its ability to read encrypted messages. This has primarily been achieved through collaboration with technology companies to ensure that communications presented to consumers as secure are actually decryptable.[21] In addition, the NSA worked to ensure that at least one encryption standard adopted by the U.S. National Institute of Standards and Technology (NIST) had built-in insecurities. This standard applies not to encryption itself but rather to an algorithm known as dual elliptic curve deterministic random bit generator (or Dual_EC_DRBG), which is used to generate the random information upon which various encryption schemes are based.[22] One of the difficulties of encrypting information is that the encryption key must be selected at random (otherwise, an adversary would have an advantage in guessing the key), but generating truly random numbers is difficult for computers designed to follow deterministic rules. Computers generally use complicated algorithms and lookup tables to generate pseudo-random numbers, but these are often not random enough to be cryptographically secure. Thus a number of systems for generating cryptographically secure pseudo-random numbers have been invented. By encouraging NIST to recommend an insecure pseudo-random number generation algorithm, it became significantly easier to decrypt information using encryption schemes based upon that algorithm.

Both actions have significantly undermined the security of Internet traffic as well as global trust in the standards used for encryption. Most security experts believe that the math behind cryptography is still generally secure, but the implementation of these mathematical formulas is now suspect. As Bruce Schneier, a leading computer security expert, stated, "the math is good, but math has no agency. Code has agency, and the code has been subverted."[23] The ability of the NSA to so thoroughly undermine the efficacy of cryptography without defeating its underlying mathematics—but by breaking it at the level of code—means that even if there exists some technological tendency or an abstract machine of cryptography, its inscription into concrete machines is both a political act and a site of potential military intervention. While the universe may "believe" in cryptography, it seems, at least given our current geopolitical arrangement, that this belief cannot suffice for an efficacious politics on its own. Even if the laws of the universe contain the possibility for strong cryptography, the translation of this possibility into real systems is always vulnerable to political and military intervention.

The possibility of subverting cryptography suggests the complicated relationship between abstract machines and the political interventions in their modes of "being made to speak." While the diagrammatic nature of an abstract machine may delimit a certain set of possible sociotechnical arrangements, the implementation of these nearly mute universal tendencies is ripe with locations for potential subversions and interventions. The history and complications of cryptography suggest the unstoppable unfolding of abstract tendencies but also the impossibility of relying exclusively on any given tendency. Even in its most abstract mathematical expression, cryptography is still a writing that is never fully closed. It is, like all writing, always given over to being turned against itself and deconstructed. While it appears chilling that the state or military can devise ways to decipher our most closely guarded secrets, these developments also suggest an important truth about the most technical and deterministic mathematics or programs. Even an abstract machine founded on the mathematical laws of the universe is subject to movements of deconstruction that destabilize the fixity of these algorithmic texts and the spaces through which they circulate.

THE CRYPTOSTATE

As the state summons a counterwriting against the tendencies of the universe, it increasingly risks itself in the process. As we saw in the example of Tor, it is often the war machine that takes advantage of this counterwriting against, or at least outside, the state. Both the state and the war machine have an uncertain relationship to cryptography and the ability of citizenry to write in secret. The state appears at once to promote and develop cryptography, especially as a support for modern networked-based capitalism, and at the same time it moves to undermine and defeat cryptography. Moreover, since the invention of public-key cryptography, when we speak of the desire for and promotion of cryptography, we must remember that we are referring to the ability not only to send secret messages but also to authenticate and prove one's identity. Thus both states and war machines arrive at the public realization of the universe's tendency toward strong cryptography in a difficult situation. If, as Foucault suggests in his lecture series *Security, Population, Territory,* the function of the modern state is to secure the population, the state both requires cryptography to secure digital spaces and the digital population but must then defeat cryptography to secure its physical population. The ability to guarantee secrets becomes critical for maintaining long-distance communication networks but at the same time threatens to empower secret conspiracies that would turn against the state.

To better understand what is at stake in the state's relation to cryptography in particular, and more generally in relation to cyberwar and the militarization of networks, it is helpful to trace these developments through Foucault's work on the state vis-à-vis its population.[24] Foucault outlines three historical modes of operation of the state: sovereignty, societies of discipline, and finally, societies of security. He cautions, "There is not a series of successive elements, the appearance of the new causing the earlier ones to disappear . . . what above all changes is the dominant characteristic."[25] Still, the most contemporary in this list, security societies, has as its most notable element the creation of a population that must be secured as a whole. Foucault says of security,

> Security will try to plan a milieu in terms of events or series of events or possible elements, of series that will have to be regulated within a multivalent and transformable framework. The specific space of security refers then to a series of possible events; it refers to the temporal and the uncertain, which have to be inserted within a given space. The space in which a series of uncertain elements unfold is, I think, roughly what one can call the milieu.[26]

To control this milieu, the state intervenes in a population that is treated as a biological entity. Norms and limits are discovered against which to measure the population. In contrast to previous forms of the state,

> the milieu appears as a field of intervention in which, instead of affecting individuals as a set of legal subjects capable of voluntary actions—which would be the case with sovereignty—and instead of affecting them as a multiplicity of organisms, of bodies capable of performances, and of required performances—as in discipline— one tries to affect, precisely, a population. I mean a multiplicity of individuals who . . . essentially only exist biologically bound to the materiality within which they live.[27]

Security thus takes a space and a biological population that exists within that space and attempts to maintain control over the uncertain events of the milieu and the embedded population. The population, as biological entity, is measured against a norm and securitized to maintain the desired norm. This relation, between the state and a population that must be accounted for as a whole, radically changes in our contemporary era, especially under the threat of cyberwar.

The advent of cyberwar, especially with its cryptographic concerns, adds to the complexity of the state's desire for security. As more and more of our daily activities occur online and more infrastructure is supported and made vulnerable by its connection to the global Internet, the state becomes responsible for a digital milieu and a digital population as much as it is responsible for a biological population. The state's quest for security becomes bifurcated between a topographic and topological space, a biological population and a digital population. Cryptography bifurcates along similar lines and now fills a dual function. On one hand, cryptography has become the linchpin to security online. Without the ability to both send secure messages and identify individuals, there would exist no way to use the Internet for any but the most trivial functions. Cryptography thus becomes a requirement for security online and for the physical infrastructure connected to these digital networks. On the other hand, cryptography allows the exchange of messages across the globe beyond the watchful eyes of security agencies and militaries. Cryptography, in a sense, cuts between the war machine and the state, becoming a necessity and a threat to both.

The problem posed by cryptography is not an entirely new problem for the state. While, on one hand, it is a problem of spatiality, between topographic space and topological space and between a digital population and a biological population, it is also a problem of the relationship between the mass and the individual. Cryptography is critical for the security of the mass of online functions, for the global totality of the Internet, but an individual's use of cryptography can easily threaten the digital or physical whole. Cryptography thus repeats a central problem Foucault outlines in relation to the rise of security and the art of government, or governmentality, as he refers to it. Foucault traces the roots of the modern security state to the Christian pastorate, which he claims to be

> paradoxically distributive since, of course, the necessity of saving the whole entails, if necessary, accepting the sacrifice of a sheep that could compromise the whole. . . On the other hand, and this is the paradox, the salvation of a single sheep calls for as much care from the pastor as does the whole flock; there is no sheep for which he must not suspend all his other responsibilities and occupations, abandon the flock, and try to bring it back.[28]

Both the mass and the individual must be saved, and each at the expense of the other. For Foucault, the pastoral problematic does not stumble upon an already constituted individual who is opposed to the mass it constitutes; rather, the pastorate "is a form of individualization that will not be acquired through the relationship to a recognized truth, [but] will be acquired instead through the production of an internal, secret, and hidden truth."[29] The Christian pastorate constructs both an individual and mass that come to be diametrically opposed and require salvation both through and against the other.

Foucault goes on to say that as this system of pastoral power is adopted by the state, its logic disregards the problem of the mass and the individual.[30] Thus, for Foucault, the state as an institution of governmentality does away with the problem of the mass and the individual. It decides clearly on the side of the mass at the expense of the individual. But he also notes that as the state becomes a more liberal institution and its aims become "a matter of insuring that the state only intervenes to regulate, or rather to allow the well-being, the interest of each to adjust itself in such a way that it can actually serve all,"[31] the issue of this relation between mass and individual is maintained as an aporetic concern of the state. We see it arise precisely in the relation between the state, cryptography, and its defenses against cyberwar. The whole requires cryptography to function in a digital world, but the individual's access to cryptography threatens the whole. At the same time, the individual, as potential threat to the mass, must somehow be barred from full access to digital security. The paradox the Christian pastorate stumbles upon returns as a key aspect of the apparatus of security. Moreover, even if the state were to find an optimal balance between the two, the war machine's attempts to both secure its own systems and disrupt the security of enemy systems further destabilize any technopolitical balances.

The state as an institution of security arrives at precisely the issue that Maturana and Varela have outlined in relation to systems. The whole of both the state and the population upon which the state operates functions as an autopoietic system whose spatiality cannot be accessed directly. The whole cannot be the object of intervention. The state, to enforce or realize some biological (or digital) norm for the population, can never intervene in the population as such; rather, its interventions are always on the level of the constituent parts. Indeed, Foucault says something along these lines in his lecture series *Society Must Be Defended,* arguing that the state's investment in the population as a biological reality created a normalizing society:

> The normalizing society is a society in which the norm of discipline and the norm of regulation intersect along an orthogonal articulation. To say that power took possession of life in the nineteenth

century... thanks to the play of technologies of discipline on the one hand and technologies of regulation on the other, succeeded in covering the whole surface that lies between the organic and the biological, between body and population.[32]

Here the move toward something other than discipline does not do away with discipline, the technology of individual bodies, but rather utilizes it "by sort of infiltrating it, embedding itself in existing disciplinary techniques."[33] Thus security, especially as power over the human as a biological species, or biopower, does not do away with the paradox of the mass and the individual. Rather, two mechanisms are invented, perhaps asynchronously and for different original purposes, and ultimately end up addressing along a diagonal that cuts between the two the need for the apparatus of security to address the problem of both the mass and the individual.

Thus the relationship between the mass and the individual still exists as a major problem for the state. Security and biopower may shift the focus from the individual to the mass of individuals, but to intervene and affect the mass, it must continue to work upon individual bodies and technologies. Deleuze says of the end of traditional disciplinary institutions, such as the military, hospital, school, and so on, that "everyone knows these institutions are finished whatever the length of their expiration periods."[34] Despite this—and this suggests the accuracy of Foucault's observation that security has infiltrated disciplinary institutions—we are currently witnessing a proliferation of prisons and incarceration in the United States. Apparatuses of security have not overcome the paradoxical relationship between the individual and the flock.

This paradox is clear in the struggles over cryptography. Even as states set up apparatuses of security to control populations, they end up in our digital age confronting a complicated relationship not only between the individual and the population but also between different digital and biological populations. Despite whatever interventions the state or military may invest in, the spatial aporias of systems, from writing to populations, continue to assert their irreducible and inherent complexity.

SOCIETIES OF CONTROL AFTER SECURITY

A little over a decade after Foucault's lecture series *Security, Territory, Population,* Deleuze, in a short text titled "Postscript on the Societies of Control," suggested, while citing Foucault's work, something similar to the notion of security:

> Controls are a modulation, like a self-deforming cast that will continuously change from one moment to the other, or like a sieve whose mesh will transmute from point to point. This is obvious in the matter of salaries: the factory was a body that contained its internal forces at a level of equilibrium, the highest possible in terms of production, the lowest possible in terms of wages . . . but the corporation works more deeply to impose a modulation of each salary, in states of perpetual metastability that operate through challenges, contests, and highly comic group sessions.[35]

Deleuze argues that societies of control have come to replace the disciplinary societies that much of Foucault's work outlined. Control precipitates as disciplinary–security societies enter into crisis or fall out of fashion. As Deleuze suggests by invoking Foucault's extensive writing on these issues, disciplinary societies are organized around spaces of enclosure, where one moves from the school to the factory to the prison. It is a whole series of topographic spaces that are minimally yet definitively topologically connected. The school is a topographic space, a space of place, where one has a defined topological progression to the factory. Against this, control is organized around "a variable geometry," whereby, instead of always starting over in a new topographical enclosure, one is never finished with anything. Everything is modulated and made to flow, but also to stop, depending on the specifics of the situation. Deleuze, in developing this notion of control, links this new type of power explicitly to computation and communication technologies. These attempts by the state to control the population through digital technologies act as a cyberwar turned internally against the population. Thus, it is here, in the theory of control, that cyberwar entwines itself with the individualized forces that confront us through modern technologies.

The notion of control mirrors Foucault's conception of security and likewise develops upon the remains of discipline. Just like security, control modulates and rearranges to control the norm, the population, and the mass. It is curious that Deleuze does not mention Foucault's use of the term *security* in relation to discipline. Deleuze even remarks on Foucault's tracing the problem of the mass and the individual to the pastorate, which Foucault develops in the series of lectures on security.[36] It seems unlikely that Deleuze was unaware that Foucault had coined the term *security* for the type of society that had succeeded discipline. Thus, to understand Deleuze's theoretical development of the notion of control, it is critical to comprehend how it differs from security.

Control outlines a different pattern that must either replace the end point of sovereignty–discipline–security or add a fourth term that succeeds even security. Deleuze suggests that the major difference between discipline and control is the relationship between the individual and the mass:

> The disciplines never saw any incompatibility between these two [individual and mass], and because at the same time power individualizes and masses together, that is, constitutes those over whom it exercises power into a body and molds the individuality of each member of that body. (Foucault saw the origin of this double charge in the pastoral power of the priest—the flock and each of its animals—but civil power moves in turn and by other means to make itself lay "priest.") In the societies of control, on the other hand, what is important is no longer either a signature or a number, but a code: the code is a password, while on the other hand the disciplinary societies are regulated by watchwords (as much from the point of view of integration as from that of resistance). The numerical language of control is made of codes that mark access to information, or reject it. We no longer find ourselves dealing with the mass/individual pair. Individuals have become "dividuals," and masses, samples, data, markets, or "banks."[37]

For Deleuze, discipline does away with the mass–individual problem, or at the very least supplants it. In a certain sense, Deleuze's reading suggests something more closely aligned with the claims Foucault makes in *Society Must Be Defended* prior to his discussion of security. What

Foucault there calls biopower is a later historical development but still at least partially part of disciplinary societies. Foucault's earlier conception of discipline began to include an understanding of the mass. Regardless of how closely this aligns with Foucault, at least for Deleuze, discipline is a double articulation. On one hand, it intervenes on the level of the individual body, and on the other hand, on the side of the population. The signature is here critical, as it marks both the individual and her location in the mass; it translates between the two systems and marks one as a site of intervention for both disciplinary and biopolitical intervention. Thus, in this telling, security or biopower does not overturn the society of discipline but completes the system by supplementing it with a means to address the mass as well as the individual.

Despite the relevance of biopower, and especially statistical coding and management to control, Galloway claims that Foucault's theories are unable to explain our current situation. He states, "It is not simply Foucault's histories, but Foucault himself that is left behind by the societies of control. Foucault is the rhetorical stand-in for the modern disciplinary societies, while Deleuze claims to speak about the future."[38] For him, Foucault's concept of biopower is relevant for understanding control but, at the same time, is inadequate because it does not account for the complex forms of modulation to which the "dividual" is subjected, the forms of organization and modulation that far outpace biopower's focus on biological life.[39] Though it may not entirely be the case that Foucault is to be completely left behind, the important point is that Deleuze's insight adds something, even to Foucault's concepts of security and biopower, by stressing the production of new subjectivities. To account for the shift to societies of control thus requires accounting for the production of these new subjectivities and the contradictions that these subjectivities produce in the relationship between mass and individual. Especially given Foucault's extensive writings on biopower and statistical modes of managing populations, the break between discipline–security and control must be located in the shift in the subject that they engender and the problematic management of its relation to its mass rather than simply claiming the ascendency of modulation. If Foucault's concept of security appears to leverage similar technologies and methodologies as Deleuze's control, the essential difference is to be found in the shift from the disciplinary relation of mass and individual to a new relationship and the aporias that arise from this relation. In this light, cyberwar represents a crisis of the mass–individual and a symptom of the production of a new pair.

CRYPTOGRAPHY AND CONTROL

Cryptography illustrates the crisis disciplinary–security societies encounter as they confront the ubiquity of computation and communication technologies. Cryptography, which situates one within the mass, has a second function: it is the same technology that can be used to hide within the mass and to mask the proliferation of threats to that mass. Advanced cryptography does not destroy disciplinary and security societies; it is perhaps already too late for that. Cryptography, its secret writing, should be read instead as a requiem for disciplinary societies.

As we have seen, Deleuze claims that control functions both to reconstitute the relationship of the mass and the individual and also to constitute a new "dividual." There is, then, a break, or at the very least an inflection, in the long history of individualization that Foucault traces back to the pastoral subject and through to the subject of discipline–security. It is replaced here by the "dividual," which is overseen and marked by the code or password. The code controls access to information and to space. The code regulates the movement through topological space; it relegates some to flow and others to place. The modulation of the code directly ties the individual to a movement within and through topographic and topological space.

Deleuze claims societies of control do away with the signature. Recent events suggest, contrary to this, that it invents a new signature that is the inverse and complement of the code. The most telling example of the new importance of the signature is the United States's now infamous use of "signature strikes," in which drones launch missiles at individuals whose actions and behavior bear the "signature" of a terrorist (which can include the mere association of young men in somewhat secluded spaces).[40] The individual, about whom nothing is known, is killed for his "signature."[41] The individual who emits the signature is comprehended as a system that unintentionally emits information, analogous to the way a server might unintentionally publish information about its security configuration. Galloway suggests that one of the key results of the shift to societies of control is the move from "a condition in which singular machines produce proliferations of images, into a condition in which multitudes of machines produce singular images."[42] In the case of the individual, myriad data gathered by systems that span the entire surface of the globe assemble a corpus of data into a singular image. The individual is made into a signature that determines her fate without the individual's knowledge or active participation. The signature both marks individual bits of data for assembly and reductively attests to the meaning of the totality.

This new signature appears everywhere and acts like a fingerprint consisting of a person's habitual actions. The individual reveals his signature patterns of shopping, communicating, sleeping, and moving. These very marks become exactly who one is. Control functions through the utilization of the code, which the individual knows and keeps secret but can use at a moment's notice while utilizing a new type of signature that the individual emits and by which he can be identified, completely unknowingly. Ultimately, these codes and signatures serve to ease the ability of states and corporations to intervene in these systems in an increasingly insidious and fine-tuned manner. We can see in the rise of these techniques of capitalism, control, and military action the logic of cyberwar. These mechanisms of control attempt to intervene in the milieu of the everyday to subvert systems, inject malicious code, and interfere with systems and texts beginning with their innermost operations.

Deleuze hints at the contours of the subject of control but gives only the briefest of sketches. He first suggests that this subject is defined by access to information and places and, second, that this new subject is correlated with a new mass that is defined by samples, data, and markets. Deleuze uses the example of individual salaries set by performance rather than collectively negotiated as indicative of control. The subject is divided and specified by its relation to the mass, but it is not a one-way relationship. The subject is defined by a series of feedback loops; the group is constituted by individual subjects, and the individual subjects are divided out of the sample. In short, the subject of control is an ecological subject. It is a subject of a milieu even more fully than the subject of discipline–security. No longer is the individual, as a biological entity, embedded in a milieu, but the individual is constituted by its milieu.[43] Whereas the individual of discipline and security is measured against a population norm, the individual of control is measured against a local norm that is completely dependent on the milieu. The subject, under control, is thus comprehended as a topological system that can be affected and modulated in the same way that a technical system can be attacked.

Bateson explains the stakes well:

> The materialistic philosophy which sees "man" as pitted against his environment is rapidly breaking down as technological man becomes more and more able to oppose the largest systems. Every battle that he wins brings a threat of disaster. The unit of survival— either in ethics or in evolution—is not the organism or the species but the largest system or "power" within which the creature lives. If the creature destroys its environment, it destroys itself.[44]

The individual is no longer in the environment but is that environment. As Bateson argues here, every expansion of technological power, rather than increasing human control over the world, on the contrary explicates human dependency on the world. The ecological subject—or we could also say the cybernetic subject—is embedded in a milieu that it cannot be separated from. Just as Wiener's antiaircraft system deconstructed the boundary between man and machine, humanity's attempt to oppose the largest systems ends up deconstructing the boundary between the human and its milieu. The signature and the code thus articulate the relationship of the individual to its ecology. The code grants access and movement through the topographic and the topological spaces that constitute the milieu, and the signature is the sign of one's unique relationship to this milieu. The signature/code and the individual/mass thus intimately constitute and modify each other. The individual is controlled by a code and identified by a signature that is created out of a set of habitual relations to a milieu and mass; likewise, the milieu and the mass are modified and defined by the individuals who exist within and through it. Control thus constitutes a cybernetic subject, who can be attacked as part of this atomized warfare.

It is perhaps a mere historical accident, but worth noting: in October 1977, the Institute of Electrical and Electronics Engineers (IEEE) was planning an international symposium on information theory and intended to include presentations on encryption. A few months prior, the staff director of the organization's publication board, E. K. Gannett, received a letter warning that sending information abroad about cryptography would be a violation of export laws and subject to possible criminal prosecution. The conference proceeded, but individual presenters were warned about their potential liability. Several weeks after the letter arrived, it was discovered that the individual who wrote the letter to IEEE, Joseph A. Meyer, worked for the NSA. He and the NSA both have asserted that he wrote the letter as a private citizen and was not asked to send it. Meyer had previously written an article for an IEEE publication titled "Crime Deterrent Transponder System." The article outlined a system whereby radio transponders would be attached to paroled repeat offenders, allowing their constant monitoring and identification. Meyer believed this would create "an electronic surveillance and command-control system to make crime pointless."[45] Meyer was thus deeply involved in this shift toward societies of control. He took part both in these early attempts to control cryptography and also in efforts to turn the prison inside out. His utopian vision was of a topological prison, where individuals could be controlled and identified in their milieu rather than in the enclosure of the prison. It is telling that his fantasy of this society without crime was also a society with limited access to cryptography. In a sense, his hope was for complete control over both the cybernetic subject and her ecological milieu, of the mass and the individual.

This shift to an ecological and cybernetic subject does not undo the problem of the relation of the mass to the individual (pace both Deleuze and Foucault); instead, it radically changes its terms. No societies ever completely overcome the pastoral aporia of the relation of the mass to the individual. Rather, each constructs a system to deal with and relate different masses and individuals to each other. Technology, especially thought as abstract machine and including diverse technologies from the prison to cryptography, mediates and undermines these relations that define both the mass and the individual. Within a society of control, the individual and mass both become a set of feedback loops and embedded systems that continually interact and move between different spatialities and temporalities. The art of government becomes an almost incoherent attempt to put both individuals and populations in flow and in stasis, depending on the moment's objectives. Both the state and the war machine attempt to control a constantly fluctuating population and its individual components. To achieve this aim, it is thus no longer the individual nor the population that becomes the favored site of intervention. Instead, the networked connections and the coded writing that controls these flows become the loci of control. It becomes evident in the case of cryptography that these connections are not a simple or straightforward matter. Rather, a whole physical, social, technical infrastructure and an abstract machine or a mathematical teleology premise these connections, and all become part of the global battle space. In essence, the NSA, an organization that perhaps amounts to a war machine appropriated by the state, has attempted to allow cryptography to be just strong enough to allow the smooth functioning of the digital mass in its cybernetic milieu but weak enough not to disrupt the control of the individual. This careful balance, if it has ever been able to hold, is contested in every direction.

TRANSPARENCY AS ANTIGOVERNMENTALITY

The effacement of political and social possibilities in this shift toward societies of control appears as an unstoppable force. Both the smoothness of topological space and the "cyberneticization" of the subject suggest a historical effacement of the future and an ever more insidious closure. Hardt claims, "The passage from disciplinary society to the society of control is characterized first of all by the collapse of the walls that defined the institutions. There is progressively less distinction, in other words, between inside and outside. This is really part of a general change in the way that power marks space in the passage from modernity to postmodernity."[46] To return briefly to the spatial concerns from earlier, we must take issue with this perception of the total effacement of any differentiation of space. The belief in this effacement is the same fantasy that led Bill Gates to believe we were moving toward a "frictionless" form of capitalism, which is in reality only a redistribution of friction away from those who have access to spaces of flow toward those stuck in spaces of place.[47] Still the construction of this fantasy, the belief that the walls between inside and outside are collapsing, suggests the contours of the society of control. The society of control may break down the barriers between subject and environment, but at the same time, it creates new mobile barriers and blockages. Yet still, we are told everywhere the world is becoming faster and smoother and that all distinctions between spaces are breaking down. Thus we are doubly enclosed. First is in the fantasy of a smooth and frictionless world. The appearance of a completely open globe is simultaneously the image of a world-sized closure; there can be no escape from this pure openness. Second, and against this myth, blockages and barriers are erected everywhere, closing us into the microscopic spaces of control.

This closure is not only spatial but arises temporally as well in the face of threats of systemic catastrophe. The future has become infected with the possible collapse of any and all systems. Cyberwar threatens to destroy all of our systems, and so we are faced with an unknown and grim future. It is a future that is not merely unknown but contains both the possible catastrophe and the nonevent of the digital everyday. As such, the future appears closed. It is either a future of the total collapse of systems or the nonevent of the continuation of neoliberal capitalism. In the face of this future catastrophe, the only other possibility is survival, or at the very least the delay of the catastrophe. It becomes impossible to think a future that is not merely one more day of the present. The future becomes just an extended present and hence the continuation our current global arrangement. Thus, even in negating the catastrophe, the only option with which we are left is the logic of its mere avoidance. The only future that matters now is the future that is already here: the future of constant capitalist innovation that we are always already late for. Any other future is already lost.

These spatial and temporal closures within which we find ourselves enmeshed directly influence both political and counterpolitical discourses. It can be seen clearly in the shift of resistance from disciplinary–security societies to societies of control. Foucault, in his discussions of security and governmentality, suggests that the aim of governmentality is to modify the conduct of individuals. Against various modes of governmentality, he outlines a number of examples of what he terms *counterconducts*. In many ways, the counterconducts that he outlines (for instance, he sees certain modes of Gnosticism as counterconducts against pastoral power) attempt not to undermine governmentality but to create a space that is outside of the prescribed conduct. For Foucault, it is clear that even those counterconducts that attempt to undermine power do so by creating an alternative space for a different conduct. In light of the supposed effacement of the outside and the potential information catastrophe wrought by the threat of cyberwar, many resistances to the art of government offer not a counter-control but rather the breakdown of control itself. Resistance ceases to imagine another mode of conduct and instead sees itself as merely the disruption of current modes of conduct.

Nowhere is this clearer than in Julian Assange's writings on the relationship between states and secrecy. Assange has worked to allow citizen access to leaked government information. Since the mid-2000s, his organization, WikiLeaks, has provided access to a substantial corpus of government secrets. Assange's aim in providing access to these secret government documents is not exclusively greater transparency. Rather, Assange sees (and supports) these leaks as part of a broader attempt to destabilize world governments. In a short set of collected essays, Assange argues that unjust authoritarian governments act as conspiracies, trying to hide their true actions to avoid engendering resistance.[48]

While one could argue against this claim, especially considering the ways in which authoritarian regimes attempt to create public support for their actions, the most relevant part of Assange's claims is the conclusions he draws. He suggests that governmental conspiracies, as networks of conspirators, are essentially computational machines that compute the next action with the goal of maintaining the conspiracy. He then outlines a number of methods for decreasing a conspiracy's "conspiratorial power," most notably arguing that leaks force secretive organizations to limit internal communications and decrease their ability to understand the world. He suggests,

> The more secretive or unjust an organization is, the more leaks induce fear and paranoia in its leadership and planning coterie. This must result in minimization of efficient internal communications mechanisms (an increase in cognitive "secrecy tax") and consequent system-wide cognitive decline resulting in decreased ability to hold onto power as the environment demands adaption.[49]

Ultimately, he believes that this cognitive decline will cause an authoritarian regime to collapse like "a beast with arteries and veins whose blood may be thickened and slowed until it falls, stupefied; unable to sufficiently comprehend and control the forces in its environment."[50] In a sense, he argues for the exploitation of what Derrida refers to as the autoimmunity of systems, turning systems against themselves. While his application of network theory to authoritarian governments and the impact of leaks is novel and potentially useful, a practical problem with this thought becomes apparent. Some of the most ruthless and oppressive aspects of authoritarian regimes have arisen from those moments of cognitive failure. One would almost prefer an authoritarian regime that knew exactly what it was doing to a blind, confused, nuclear-armed state thrashing around our shared biosphere.

De Landa makes precisely this point; in a particularly relevant passage, he all but preemptively answers Assange's claims, fifteen years before Assange's writing:

> Armies have tried to reduce their uncertainty by centralizing information processing at the top, but the net effect is to increase the overall uncertainty about a situation. . . . A dysfunctional war machine is inherently self-destructive. We can afford an efficient army, but we cannot afford a suicidal one: in the nuclear age their suicide is ours as well.[51]

Assange's belief in the power of leak-induced "cognitive decline" appears not, then, as a counterconduct but rather as an antigovernmentality, or what Galloway and Thacker call a "counterprotocol practice."[52] Its aim is not to create another mode of action or a different subject but rather directly to disrupt the ability of the state to act as an agent of governance. This desire, especially without the construction of another conduct, appears, then, as symptomatic of the belief in a lack of any possible future. Assange's thought speaks to a certain claustrophobia. In the face of a global enclosure, there is, then, no longer any possibility aside from this attempt to destroy the entire system from the inside, even if it means the possible destruction of everything. No counterconduct can ever take hold if there is no other space, only a self-destructive antigovernmentality. These are precisely the stakes of the creation of a society of control that effaces any distinction between the inside and the outside and creates a pure topological space of completely frictionless exchange.[53]

The myth of complete connection and a frictionless world attempt to erase the possibility of any other space ever providing grounds for an alternative future. Hardt claims, "In this sense, the clearly defined crisis of modernity gives way to an omni-crisis in the imperial framework. In this smooth space of empire, there is no place of power—it is both everywhere and nowhere. The empire is an [*sic*] *u-topos,* or rather a non-place."[54] It is this belief in a pure nonspace of what he calls empire that power can be seen as coextensive with the entire topological field of existence that calls for Assange's politics of self-destruction. We arrive by way of Assange's resistance at the same point outlined in the preceding chapter, under the auspices of the military's Eligible Receiver program, practicing the collapse of digital networks. Eligible Receiver, like Assange's fear of an omnipotent control, functions to completely negate all other spaces and all other futures. The future is radically called into question and presented as a space of pure closure and destruction. Massumi puts this closure well when he describes the effect of the Bush doctrine and preemption on global politics: "The only certainty is that you have to act now to do everything possible to preempt the potential. In the vocabulary of Bush's Secretary of Defense, Donald Rumsfeld, the only thing certain is that you have to 'go kinetic,' even though you don't really know and can't know and know you don't know."[55] Any politics becomes either a dedication, not to the possibility of the future, but merely to the survival of the present or, alternatively, the destruction of the entire system. As long as power is believed to operate in a field either free of *topos* or rushing ever more rapidly toward a space of pure speed, flow, and connection (essentially a *u-topos* as pure movement effaces any place), there can be no future. The only possible resistance to the government of ecological subjects is the destruction of the entire system. Against such a closure, it is imperative to theorize both the heterogeneity of space and the contingent trace that exists in even the most programmatic writing.

IMPOSSIBLE CLOSURE

This closure of the future is on one hand spatial and on the other textual. Its supposed functioning relies on the transparency of space and time, on our ability to grasp them as homogenous, and at the same time on a deterministic program that would do exactly what its authors intend. Malabou puts this condition precisely, saying,

> We live out a teleology which is shattered because already accomplished. Such a future is both beautiful and terrible. Beautiful

because everything can still happen. Terrible, because everything has already happened. The situation creates the contradictory couple of *saturation* and *vacancy*. Saturation to the extent that the future can, in our time, no longer represent the promise of far-off worlds to conquer. . . . Paradoxically, this saturation of theoretical and natural space is felt as a vacuum. The major problem of our time is in fact the arrival of *free time*. Technological simplification, the shortening of distances—all heralded by Hegel with his notion of simplification—bring about a state where we must acknowledge there is nothing more to do. . . . But this promise is also a promise of novelty, a promise that there are forms of life which must be invented. If saturation follows from a closure of the horizon, vacancy, for its part opens perspectives. . . . Thus the possibility of a closed system to welcome new phenomena, all the while transforming itself, is what appears as plasticity.[56]

The feeling of spatial closure appears as saturation; there is nowhere left to go, because we feel we can go anywhere instantaneously, while the threat of temporal closure makes itself felt as the vacancy of a "there is nothing left to do."

Despite these appearances, it is in the midst of the saturation of the everyday by war, control, and the vacancy of boredom that entropic possibilities lie. At the heart of this vacant saturation, a point of sheer randomness, to use Malabou's description, is written as the most intimate rule of the system. Even Claude Shannon, the founder of information theory and an intellectual deeply embedded in the cybernetic project, found entropy at the heart of the most closed communication systems.[57] The vulnerability of the texts and the shifting spatialities through which communication and computation networks run write entropy, accidents, and militarized intervention into their very functioning. This is not to say that some, if not most, of these possibilities may be as or more horrific than the current global system. Still, this contingency holds open the space of possibility in the face of a catastrophic global cyberwar, oppressive systems of control, and the possibility of metaphysical closure.

Both the fantasy and fear of this closure are founded on the supposed ability of sovereign force to simultaneously survey the fixed space of its milieu and accurately compute the current and future states of this complex system. Against this certainty, cyberwar and the advancement of computation directly challenge this relation between calculation and perfect knowledge. The automatism of the program can no longer be a guarantee of perfect knowledge. While, for Derrida, calculation means that the outcome is predetermined, we can no longer be sure. Any automatism becomes—under the threat of intervention from some outside force—open, vulnerable, and unpredictable. While more often than not a computer will provide the same answer for a repeated calculation, the possibility that a machine has been subverted means that one always risks a different outcome. We saw this with Operation Orchard, in which Israel attacked a supposed Syrian nuclear facility and the Syrian radar system failed to detect Israeli jets crossing into Syrian air space. Despite whatever automatic decision the radar system and its program were supposed to initiate, an unauthorized bit of code likely subverted the entire system, destroying the applicability of a rule in the depths of its programmatic knowledge.

The calculable can only guarantee an outcome if the entire system is perfectly secure. The origin of the system, in the metaphysical sense and in terms of its location of manufacture and all of the software running on it, must be known and secured. Moreover, the system must be perfectly protected from all outside forces. Unless one were to able to guarantee such security, which is only possible in the nonplace of an impossible utopia of infinite security—a place precisely where nothing could happen—all calculation risks becoming unpredictable and unknowable. Thus, against Derrida's insistence that calculation is opposed to the incalculable, in the light of cyberwar, we must insist the exact opposite: calculation inevitably gives rise to the incalculable.

Furthermore, we have seen in the case of undecidable problems and also encryption that calculation itself can in mathematical and programmatic terms produce the incalculable. Encryption functions can be used to transform data to such a degree that all of the computing power in the world would take longer than the age of the universe to decrypt.[58] In a literal way, this ability to perform such computations provides a concrete demonstration of the ability to create out of the calculable something, which, through its shear entropy—in the sense of both the chaotic nonpresent outside and Shannon entropy, which measures the randomness of an encrypted message—is no longer, at least for those who do not know the secret key, calculable. Everywhere today, calculation resists being calculable; calculation itself harbors in its depths a non-self-sameness—the possibility that repeated calculations will not yield the same results—as it winds its way through space and time. The networked vulnerabilities that come from elsewhere and the time of computation that quickly scales beyond the age of the universe produce through calculation the very possibility of the incalculable.

INCALCULABLE CALCULATIONS

Despite these challenges to computation, many responses to this closure insist on the computability of computation—in essence the incorruptible power of abstract machines—and thus the necessity of some other metaphysical force that would resist computation. Derrida attempts to separate out the possibility of an unconditional decision from the power of sovereign force, ultimately to avoid the possibility of the decision collapsing into the program:

> Can we not and *must* we not distinguish, even when this appears impossible, between, on the one hand, the compulsion or auto-positioning of sovereignty (which is nothing less than *ipseity* itself, of the selfsame of the oneself, an *ipseity* that includes within itself, as the etymology would also confirm, the androcentric positioning of power in the master or head of the household, the sovereign mastery of the lord or seigneur, of the father or husband, the power of the *same*, of *ipse* as the selfsame self) and, on the other hand, this postulation of unconditionality, which can be found in the critical exigency as well as the (forgive the expression) deconstructive exigency *of* reason?[59]

For Derrida, the deconstruction of sovereign force requires maintaining the unconditionality of sovereignty. For one risks beyond sovereignty that all subjects become nothing more than machines that act automatically and are hence subject to control: "one *knows* what path to take, one no longer hesitates; the decision then no longer decides anything but simply gets deployed with the automatism attributed to machines. There is no longer any place for justice or responsibility."[60] This is ultimately a problem with two sides: on one side, the sovereignty of the sovereign, and on the other, the sovereignty of the subject. The challenge is then to deconstruct, or at least nullify, the former, while maintaining the subject as a force that could decide both in favor of justice and against the violence of sovereignty and cyberwar. Derrida sees as the only possible path forward the need to maintain an impossible separation between sovereignty and the unconditionality, or the "uncalculable," as he also names it, that defines it. For him, this unconditionality is most notably the openness to what arrives under the name of deconstruction. He sees this openness toward the event as marking "the end of the horizon, of teleology, the calculable program, foresight, and providence."[61] The structure here is tripartite, with both sovereignty and responsibility in opposition to the deterministic program. In short, Derrida would like to wrest apart the subject that awaits its own responsibility unconditionally and the subject that turns this unconditionality into the ability to suspend the law in the name of sovereign power, an operation that ultimately insists upon maintaining its distance from the calculability of the program.[62]

Caputo explains that this unconditionality for Derrida is not a "force but the unconditionality of a promise that has not compromised with the conditions of being."[63] Even as this explanation attempts to differentiate this unconditionality from sovereignty by placing it in relation to a promise, it betrays the sovereignty that haunts it. In this explanation, we can detect the same difficulty that confronts Derrida: the unconditional is denied, as a force, but still must maintain its ability to negate the conditions of being. We quickly end up again at the sovereign who is vested with the power of the exception and the ability to destroy, explicitly for Caputo as the negation of the conditions of being.[64] Moreover, as Hägglund notes, Derrida refuses to align himself either with sovereignty or with antisovereignty: the impossibility of complete sovereign knowledge requires that one maintain the possibility of sovereignty and a sovereign decision.[65] In sum, despite everything that threatens to finally do away with the sovereignty of the sovereign, from the impossible aporia of the mass and the individual to the incalculability of calculation, for Derrida, some remnant of sovereignty is to be maintained to allow the possibility of unconditionality and a decision.

Such a path, by insisting on the machinic nature of the program and the separation of its logic from the text, always risks simply reinscribing the force of sovereignty. At the same time, the insistence on the calculability of the program leaves open the possibility that any sovereign force could predict and control any subject that is unable to exercise its unconditionality. Against such a theoretical tactic, it is paramount to insist that the insecurity and entropic openness of all programs guarantee that even as the "autopositioning of sovereignty" falls and disintegrates into the networked subject of control, it maintains an incalculability and unconditionality directly born of calculation itself. There is thus no need to maintain a gap between the sovereign and the program, for the program of sovereignty is its impossibility and its uncalculable force. The exposure of the program to its potential deconstruction produces a trace, which resists all totalizing calculation and direct translation. The machinic force of deconstruction operates upon a machinic trace in the programs it confronts, denying the coherence of sovereign control, while maintaining the possibility of the unconditional.

It is the movement between topography and topology and the deferred time of the program that maintains both the insecurity of any place in the network and the ultimate incalculability of calculation itself. The spacing of networks and flows of text undermines any mastery that would presume to have calculated all of the factors or prepared for all possible outside forces that could destroy the coherence of a system. Computation always requires energy, and so it is immanently bound to the space and time of its inscription, threatening it with its own vulnerability. While in certain cases the outcome may be more or less predictable, the only way to discover the result of the program at a given moment and place is to run it. The calculable program's folding and its exposure to the network around it guarantee that it is always incalculable in its totality. Abandoning any insistence on the determinism of the program and its separation from writing and the unconditional, we are confronted with the impossibility of a sovereign force reigning over a claustrophobic system of control.

CONCLUSION: THE CYBERNETIC TRAGEDY OF SOVEREIGNTY

We can in this light point to what is at stake in cyberwar, especially as it is turned against the population. Ultimately, cyberwar explicates a cybernetic problematic that affects all attempts to extend power and sovereignty over space. Foucault states,

The sovereign is no longer someone who exercises his power over a territory on the basis of a geographical localization of his political sovereignty. The sovereign deals with a nature, or rather with the perpetual conjunction, the perpetual intrication of a geographical, climatic, and physical milieu with the human species insofar as it has a body and a soul, a physical and moral existence; and the sovereign will be someone who will have to exercise power at that point of connection where nature, in the sense of physical elements, interferes with nature in the sense of the nature of human species, at that point of articulation where the milieu becomes the determining factor of nature.[66]

Sovereignty as it attempts to exercise power over space (not just a territory but also the space of the body politic, the Hertzian space of electromagnetic signals, etc.) confronts a topological and topographical intrication of multiple spaces, each with its insecure writings and abstract machines that transform and determine the possible outcomes of these interactions. What Foucault names the milieu is an intersection of a whole host of abstract machines, spaces, connections, disconnections, and entropic processes. Sovereignty as it attempts to control both subjects and their milieus is drawn increasingly toward its exteriors, regardless of whether they are across seas or in the microscopic gaps and wires that constitute our digital technologies. In this process, sovereign systems confront other systems, whose machinic dimensions and cybernetic organization are only available in translation. We can thus place cyberwar as the most recent in a long series of attempts by sovereign power to control what it does not and cannot know completely. Sovereignty is drawn in fits and starts toward the various spaces and connections that challenge the milieu over which it asserts its power. It is in this current historical moment, marked by cyberwar, that sovereignty now attempts to control a vast global machine of connection and disconnection that it begins to fully unravel itself.

In this move toward its exterior, sovereignty confronts a constantly shifting space that is always connecting and disconnecting, but it is never a pure space that is amenable to all manipulations. Rather, the space resists; abstract machines control connections and flows; the logic of systems of writing and programing are turned against themselves; war machines turn against the state. Moreover, the programs and modes of knowing of sovereignty are inscribed in this very space and subjected to the destabilizations of cyberwar. Noise and entropy resist both the sovereignty of the state and the sovereignty of the individual subject. As Stiegler says, drawing on Heidegger, the subject (using the Heideggerian term *Dasein*)

> Dasein is outside itself, in ec-stasis, temporal: its past lies outside it, yet it is nothing but this past, in the form of *not yet*. By being actually its past, it can do nothing but put itself outside itself, "eksist." But *how* does Dasein eksist in this way? Prosthetically, through pro-posing and projecting itself outside itself, in front of itself. And this means that it *can only test its improbability pro-grammatically.*[67]

The cybernetic subject, alongside the sovereignty that attempts to control it, exists in temporal and spatial ec-stasis.[68] It is always outside itself and always confronts a world that disrupts even the most stringent program. Cyberwar reveals that even as the state builds war machines to infiltrate the most minute and intimate networks of daily existence, these systems always reassert the chaotic nonpresent outside they have folded inside themselves. Every system reveals itself as the construction of an uncontrollable chaos as much if not more than as an object of control.

As we witness the technologies and theories that grew out of cybernetics become the grounds upon which cyberwar is fought, we must vehemently disagree with those contemporary thinkers who have put forward the hypothesis that cybernetics is the secret science of contemporary control and power.[69] Likewise, we must dispute Heidegger's claim that

> no prophecy is necessary to recognize that the sciences now establishing themselves will soon be determined and steered by the new fundamental science which is called cybernetics. This science corresponds to the determination of man as an acting social being. For it is the theory of the steering of the possible planning and arrangement of human labor. Cybernetics transforms language into an exchange of news.[70]

With the benefit of hindsight, it is now clear how historically incorrect Heidegger was, along with many of the advocates of cybernetics, who believed it would develop into a metascience that would oversee and make connections between all other sciences. With the same speed at which cybernetics excited a whole class of scientists in the second half of the twentieth century, the field has nearly been forgotten. Despite providing the basis for so many of our contemporary technologies, sciences, and theories, today few even remember what cybernetics attempted to study.

It is not merely the failure to predict the historical development of cybernetics but also the philosophical sentiments that underlie this statement that we must take issue with. Despite the desire of individuals, such as Norbert Wiener, to see cybernetics develop into a science of control and a road map for scientific inquiry, it appears that at its very heart it was fated never to succeed in that regard. Even while cybernetics, in Heidegger's view, was attempting to reduce all language to the exchange of news, it was also discovering that no such reduction could ever be possible. Even when all communication has turned into news, there still lies within any system the entropic possibility of a message that is not merely new but completely unexpected and impossible for the system to handle. Thus, contrary to determining the human as a predictably acting social being, cybernetics, even if its original aim was the exact opposite, determines the human and all systems as ecological and entropic beings. It explicates our ultimate inability to control and the impossibility of being controlled, and it denies the possibility of a sovereign force that can ever step outside a system. Rather, it determines the human as completely embedded in cybernetic systems and reveals that our only contingent outside is in fact that which is most close to us; it is an outside that exists in the microscopic gaps of our networks and the textual gaps of programs and translations. In short, if cybernetics determined anything, it is both our and our milieu's indeterminacy.

Whereas cybernetics set out to define a theory of communication and control, in the end, it succeeded in the exact opposite. It ultimately effaced the possibility of control, especially over communication. Cybernetics attempted to describe systems in such a way that they could ultimately be organized and controlled. Its proponents and detractors failed in many ways to realize that while creating, designing, programming, and utilizing computational machines and models, they were at the same time helping to build the very machines that control so clearly struggles with today. Cybernetics helped to create a globally networked system so complex that no known model could ever describe it, let alone regulate it. With no transcendent space outside of the system, every explanatory, predicative, or controlling mechanism continually produces additional entropy at all levels.[71]

Thus cyberwar marks the end point of cybernetics, its inevitable theoretical and historical development and collapse in upon itself. Cyberwar names a development in military–governmental logic, which creates an entire strategy around the impossibility of control. As waves of cybernetics have replaced each other and their discoveries have been distributed to various technologies and other fields, it has been discovered that it is impossible to ever fully account for the heterogeneity of system spaces and translations between them. Cyberwar has, out of this early science, grown as a theory and means of waging war. Rather than insist on the possibility of controlling, regulating, and understanding systems, cyberwarfare attempts to militarize the inevitable movement between control and its dissolution. This is at once a terrifying development and a potentially liberating one. At the same time that the creation of global networks and microscopic means of fighting war seem to condemn us to an increasingly claustrophobic closure, the advent of cyberwar makes it clear that there exists an unpredictable contingency and a heterogeneity of all spaces and systems that can disrupt even the most insidious forms of control and the most ossified systems of sovereignty.

As states, global capitalism, and war machines develop technologies that attempt to fight wars in the space and time of complex global networks and to develop new prosthetic means of fighting in these unknowable spaces, the chaotic entropy of even the most claustrophobic enclosure appears to open to an internal chaos that guarantees at least the possibility of a future, or a whole set of possible futures. Every writing, plastic rearrangement of networks, or attempts at constructing or controlling abstract machines, no matter how programmatic or how insidious, breaks on the rocks of an entropic fold of an always immanent and nonpresent contingency, an "unlimited finity," to quote Deleuze.[72] Derrida says against an attempt to codify his theoretical edifice, "The grammar of his theologic program, will not have been able to recognize, name, foresee, produce, predict, *unpredictable things* to survive him, and if something should yet happen, nothing is less certain, it must be *unpredictable,* the salvation of a backfire."[73] The global investment by major world powers in cyberwar should be read as an admission of an endemic backfire, the impossibility of removing this possibility. It must be stressed once again that this irrepressible entropic outside does not guarantee any necessary liberation or even respite. It bears within it the possibility of even worse catastrophes and geotopological arrangements, but at the very least, it promises the possibility of other arrangements and other futures and guards against every possible closure.

4

Spear Phishing:
Nodal Subjects

At the same time that states are utilizing the logic and complexities of cyberwar against their own populations, these strategies and technologies simultaneously oppose state power as new forms of digitally enabled subjects turn against the state and other structures of power. Thus we must turn to the question of what cyberwar does to the relations not simply between the state and its citizens but between the state, the war machine, and those who would oppose or resist the injustices of power. It becomes vital to theorize the positive possibilities of the cybernetic subjects we have become.

The exploitation of contingency, heterogeneity, and nonmastery in networks provides the ground for politics but no reassurance of the ultimate efficacy of any given politics. In light of the machinic force of deconstruction and destruction we face today, it becomes challenging, even in light of the autoimmune threat that confronts the state and war machine, to outline a subject that could be anything beyond a mere index of the constant failure of control against contingency. We appear stuck somewhere between a sovereign subject and the random fluctuations of insecure programs. It becomes, in this light, imperative to attempt to find in this subject of control the possibility of something like a decision that would neither merely repeat the sovereignty that increasingly seems impossible nor act as a synecdoche for the cruel randomness of a world always on the verge of falling apart.

In a certain sense, both the subject and state become mere network effects. Such a recognition precludes sovereignty in its essence, but we are then faced with the impossibility of ever deciding or acting in such a network. When one can no longer trust the machinery and networks by which a subject knows the world, the possibility of deciding or acting—the possibility of any efficacious politics—becomes increasingly unlikely. In short, the subject who seeks to act in these complex networks is faced with a double threat: on one hand, the threat of a cyberwar aimed against the subject as an object of control and, on the other hand, the danger that one's own actions inside these complex spatialities and temporalities are doomed to failure. The peril of a deconstruction that would outpace deconstruction threatens to preclude the possibility of politics and replace it with an unstoppable, contingent, and disastrous program.

ANONYMOUS AND THE POLITICS OF RESISTANCE

Recent attacks carried out by Anonymous, a loosely organized group of hackers and pranksters who have engaged in actions ranging from protesting the Church of Scientology to aiding protesters in Tunisia, offer a fruitful place to start such an investigation into the possibility of a politics and a subject that would seize on the entropy at the heart of control without sovereignty. The methods of those who have acted and written under the banner of Anonymous, as well as the difficulty of describing these events in terms of traditional understandings of protest, resistance, or war, offer a prime example of the destabilizing forces at play. Even their name, and their willingness to let diverse groups act under it, purposefully effacing their individuality, suggests that the group may be symptomatic of a new subject position produced in these networks. While more exhaustive anthropological and journalistic sources on the efforts of Anonymous are available, it is helpful to briefly review the history of the group.[1]

The loosely organized group originated in 2003 and dedicated itself to mischief, insults, and provocations. In 2008, Anonymous began their first fully politicized campaign aimed at the Church of Scientology. The operation, which went by the name Project Chanology, began in response to a cease-and-desist letter demanding that *Gawker,* an online gossip blog, remove a video of Tom Cruise discussing the religion. Anonymous responded by prank calling the Church's hotlines, ordering unpaid pizzas, sending black faxes to waste ink, and DDoSing its websites. They also organized street protests against the Church in several cities. The actions against the Church of Scientology ultimately brought to light a number of abusive practices and helped shield former members who have criticized the Church.

Following the Scientology operation, Anonymous became involved in other actions, such as supporting antigovernment demonstrations in Tunisia, attacking Sony for its management of the PlayStation gaming network, and participating in Occupy Wall Street. Throughout these various operations, Anonymous insisted on acting as a nonhierarchal group that openly allowed anyone to take up their mantle and highly discouraged anyone who tried to publicly take credit for a given action. Though multiple subgroups, splinter groups, and alliances formed and dissolved throughout the course of the early 2000s, Anonymous largely acted as a polyvocal and constantly changing group of individuals organized around a general belief in an open Internet. Aside from this core position, individuals of different backgrounds and political beliefs worked together (and sometimes at odds with each other) to carry out actions against states, companies, individuals, and organizations.[2]

One of the more telling events in the history of Anonymous's actions was not a successful attack but rather the FBI's arrest of Sabu, a key member of the organization. Hector Xavier Monsegur, or Sabu, as he was known online, was arrested on June 7, 2011, and pled guilty in a secret hearing on August 15 to charges that carried a combined prison sentence of more than one hundred years. Along with his guilty plea, Sabu agreed to work with the FBI to catch and build cases against other hackers. His cooperation allowed the United States to bring charges against five other hackers, three in the United States and two in the United Kingdom.[3] He also provided information on scores of network vulnerabilities that were then fixed to mitigate the damage of forthcoming attacks. Within the two months between his arrest and his plea, he helped patch 150 such vulnerabilities in networks other hackers were targeting.[4] As part of this assistance, he also helped facilitate attacks on servers to catch other hackers. During the course of his collaboration with the FBI, hackers working closely with Sabu, but unaware of his cooperation with the FBI, targeted and compromised unsecure systems across industries and countries. Jeremy Hammond, one of the hackers that Sabu helped the FBI catch, stated in his defense hearing that "I broke into numerous websites he supplied, uploaded the stolen email accounts and databases onto Sabu's FBI server, and handed over passwords and backdoors that enabled Sabu (and, by extension, his FBI handlers) to control these targets. These intrusions, all of which were suggested by Sabu while cooperating with the FBI, affected thousands of domain names and consisted largely of foreign government websites, including Brazil, Turkey, Syria."[5]

One of Hammond's most notorious attacks was against Stratfor, a U.S. security company. Sabu, possibly at the FBI's direction, provided Hammond with the main vulnerability that let him access their network. In early December 2011, Hammond successfully accessed a small portion of the Stratfor network, at which point the FBI supposedly informed Stratfor of the intrusion. Despite the FBI's and Stratfor's likely awareness of Hammond's actions, over the course of three weeks, he managed to break into the rest of the network, steal credit card and subscriber information, extract Stratfor's e-mails (which were then passed on to WikiLeaks for public dissemination), and finally delete all of the data on Stratfor's servers. Neither Stratfor nor the FBI moved to stop Hammond during this period, ultimately allowing the theft of sixty thousand credit card numbers and the exposure of nearly ten years of employee e-mails.[6] While the exact motives behind the FBI's and Stratfor's inaction may never be completely known, it seems likely that they allowed Hammond to take down a large private security firm solely to build a case against Hammond, who, after pleading guilty, was sentenced to ten years in prison.

It was not only the attacks on various systems that were carried out under the full purview of the FBI but also Sabu's public pronouncements, which were often directly critical of the organization and government with which he was cooperating. Right up to the time he was publicly declared an informant, he was making announcements on Twitter declaring that he would never cooperate with the government and that the government was illegitimately overreaching its bounds, making statements such as "the feds at this moment are scouring our lives without warrants. Without judges [sic] approval. This needs to change. Asap."[7] It is as though the FBI were dealing with a war machine that could not be completely appropriated by the state; or perhaps the FBI itself has become a partially appropriated war machine that threatens the binaries of the state system.

While he claims his writings were his alone, as Coleman recounts, there has been some suggestion that even those were orchestrated by his FBI handlers:

> About 90 percent of what you see online is bullsh—," said the handler, in reference both to posts from Sabu's Twitter account and also "interviews" he gave to the press. Whether this is the truth or an even more elaborate, recursive disinformation campaign, the implication is that Sabu parroted whatever the FBI wanted him to say.[8]

It seems here, like so much of what we have seen of cyberwar, that sides appear nearly undecidable. After Sabu flipped, it became impossible to separate his pronouncements and actions from what the FBI wanted him to do and say. As Kittler suggests, in war, under the conditions of high technology, each side comes to model itself after the other, ultimately undermining the ability to differentiate the two: "Turing's game of imitation became a reality."[9] It quickly becomes unclear where one could demarcate the inside and the outside of this arrangement, producing, as Derrida states, an autoimmunitary process: "that strange behavior where a living being, in quasi-suicidal fashion, 'itself' works to destroy its own protection, to immunize itself against its 'own' immunity."[10] Has Anonymous infected the state, causing it in its self-defense to allow three weeks of such actions and months of Sabu's public vitriol? Or on the contrary, has the state infected Anonymous but, in doing so, initiated an autoimmune response wherein it attacks itself.

While our notions of autoimmune responses tend toward images of an active system reacting against itself or to a largely passive body (e.g., a human and an allergen or a human and his own blood cells), Derrida's notion of autoimmunitary risk points instead toward an entanglement of equally active systems. He says, "This is another necessary consequence of the same autoimmunitary process. In all wars, all civil wars, all partisan wars or wars for liberation, the inevitable escalation leads one to go after one's rival partners no less than one's so-called principal adversary."[11] Autoimmunitary processes are not processes that occur inside a single isolated system. Instead, they, like the logic of the supplement, create folds between the inside and the outside of the system and call into question the very stability of the system that produces an autoimmune response.

Thus we should speak not of an infiltration of Anonymous nor of the FBI possibly using Anonymous; rather, after Sabu's collaboration, we should see a coupling of the systems to create a single system engaged in a self-destructive autoimmune process. Derrida states, "It is not some particular thing that is affected in autoimmunity but the self, the *ipse*, the *autos* that finds itself infected."[12] It is the sovereign functioning of the system that finds itself infected with its own logic. If the state is so quick to turn against itself and its allies, appropriating political resistance to a variety of still unclear ends, it becomes increasingly complicated to resist such a system, let alone to evaluate the efficacy of any resistance.

In the darkness of these networks, where a person can only see her immediate interlocutors and the messages they send, it becomes nearly impossible to know whose side anyone is on. Even if one has access to a plethora of information sources, it is almost impossible to verify or trust any single source. We only have access to our immediate part of the network, a microtopology embedded in a complex global topology that can never be grasped, where complex and shifting texts purport to be messages from the far reaches of the network. In the vertigo of these shifting spatialities and temporalities, it becomes difficult even to imagine where any position beyond sovereign power and the state could begin, or where such sovereignty begins itself.

The intention here is not to condemn or praise the actions or the efficacy of either Anonymous or the FBI. Rather, the formation of the Anonymous–FBI system enabled by cyberwar highlights the difficulty of theorizing the stakes (let alone the strategy) for any entity that would seek to resist sovereign power today. It further suggests the difficulty of even disentangling something that could be called an individual or a subject. These entanglements of power with resistance; the multiplicity of forces, organizations, and systems; and the epistemic challenges of tracing effects through multiple dark networks all conspire to challenge any theory of the political subject.

TRANSPARENCY AND THE POLITICS OF KNOWLEDGE

Before turning directly to theorizing the possibility of politics in the network given the epistemic and ontological challenges provided by cyberwar and the autoimmune backfire it announces, we must first address another modality of resistance to state power that we have already hinted at, namely, resistance through information and transparency. The politics of transparency speak directly to the relationship between subjects and their milieus, for it is through information, especially as cybernetics understands the world, that autopoietic systems interact with their wider networks. Although Julian Assange's theorization of the power of leaks, explored in depth earlier, is based directly on the effects of these leaks on governmental efficiency, others have acted more directly under the belief that leaks and the exposure of information will force the state to reform due to calls from its population and the international community.

Edward Snowden, the NSA contractor who leaked a massive number of documents detailing domestic and international spying in 2013, has stated that what is "sometimes misunderstood is that I didn't stand up to overthrow the system. What I wanted to do was give society the information it needed to decide if it wanted to change the system."[13] Likewise, Chelsea Manning, who leaked secret military information and diplomatic cables to WikiLeaks, stated in a personal statement to the court during her court-martial hearing that she believed "the detailed analysis of the data over a long period of time by different sectors of society might cause society to reevaluate the need or even the desire to even to engage in counterterrorism and counterinsurgency operations that ignore the complex dynamics of the people living in the effected environment everyday [sic]."[14]

While there are several political ideologies and agendas behind these various calls for transparency, Andy Greenberg, a cybersecurity journalist, sums up at least some of the revolutionary potential describing this commitment to radical transparency as "a revolutionary protest movement bent not on stealing information, but on building a tool that inexorably coaxes it out, a technology that slips inside of institutions and levels their defenses against the free flow of data like a Trojan horse of cryptographic software and silicon."[15] Greenberg's statement crystalizes many of the issues confronting cyberwar: a technological maieutic that reshapes the terrain and the state not by some calculation or mastery but instead by inserting an abstract machine into the system, forcing it to reconfigure itself, ultimately creating an unmanageable ambiguity between inside and exterior.

But what could this mean as a politics, let alone a revolutionary movement, to coax out all institutional secrets, to obliterate the secret completely, especially through the use of cryptographic and secret systems to protect those who leak information? In his 1993 "Cypherpunk Manifesto," a document laying out a proposed ideology for a movement advocating strong cryptography, Eric Hughes attempts to differentiate between privacy and secrecy, stating, "Privacy is not secrecy. A private matter is something one doesn't want the whole world to know, but a secret matter is something one doesn't want anybody to know. Privacy is the power to selectively reveal oneself to the world."[16] Such a distinction appears difficult to maintain. Institutional secrecy, as we saw in Assange's writings, requires that those in the institution, or in his terms "the governing conspiracy," are able to share the information. For the institution to function as a conspiracy, it must know information that is not known by those outside of the organization. At the same time, it must share that information internally, otherwise it is of no use to the institution. Institutional secrecy in a certain sense appears closer to Hughes's definition of privacy, in that an institution desires to reveal certain information only to its internal world. Similarly, it seems that one of the best examples of something that one does not want anyone to know would be a cryptographic key—that string of information that allows one to encrypt and decrypt information and that only serves its function so much as no one else comes to possess it. The very thing that would allow a person to maintain what he calls privacy is precisely a secret. The multiple levels of individual and organizational secrecy are in practice difficult to keep separate.

This difficulty is clear in regard to Manning. She succeeded in downloading hundreds of thousands of classified documents from a U.S. military network and providing the documents to WikiLeaks. WikiLeaks published some of the documents as the "Iraq War Logs" and the "Afghanistan War Logs" in 2010. She also downloaded and released through WikiLeaks hundreds of thousands of diplomatic cables the same year. Manning, largely through the use of cryptographic techniques set up by WikiLeaks and her own care in extracting the information secretly—such as using a rewritable CD-ROM with the words "Lady Gaga" written on them and lip-syncing the words to Lady Gaga songs while copying the documents to the CD-ROM—was able to avoid being discovered. But she was ultimately caught when she confided in Adrian Lamo, a former hacker who provided their chat logs to authorities.

Comparing Daniel Ellberg's Vietnam-era leak of the Pentagon Papers to Manning's leaks, Greenberg suggests, "While the technical play-by-play of each leak shows the evolution of leaking technology and methods, the outcome of those cases is a counterintuitive fluke. If not for [her] ill-fated conversation with Adrian Lamo, Manning's high-tech leak would likely have gone unpunished."[17] It seems problematic to write off this "ill-fated conversation" as a mere fluke. If these technologies are capable of coaxing out the secrets of institutions, how could it ever be guaranteed that individuals would be immune to the process? It is as though she, as an individual, had to pay the same "secrecy tax" that Assange says besets governing conspiracies. It is the fluke itself that is now essential and that draws individuals and organizations into their exteriors.

Secrecy and its possible destruction move, like security and cryptography, from the guarantees of an abstract mathematical machine toward a complex world of folded topographies and topologies that threaten anyone or any institution that would claim to have mastered the game. Against Greenberg's claim that Manning was discovered as the result of a "fluke," we should see instead the operation of the untranslatability and heterogeneity of all systems. The contingency at the heart of all systems and the insecurity of their multiple foldings guarantee that secrecy moves easily through networks, unsettling and revealing the secrets of those who would reveal others' secrets; all the while, other folds hide and reveal the secrets of dark networks that run all over the globe. Within these complexities, an abstract machine of secrecy or anonymous leaking offers no teleos, no guarantee of any certain future. Rather, like we saw with cryptography, but perhaps in an even more uncertain manner, these abstract machines may limit and support a certain set of possibilities, but none are guaranteed.

TRUTH IN THE NETWORK

Leaking information, anonymity, and privacy are not only issues of secrecy or its lack but are intimately tied to the subject's relation to truth. Faced with the contingent and vulnerable nature of these networks and information, any political subject always exists in a complex relation to truth or, at the very least, the veracity of her information. Any political efficacy from leaking information and destroying institutional secrecy requires the production of truth or some sort of truth-effect in the network that would engender a political response. Given the risks that false information could be leaked for the purposes of deception, or produced for other ends, as we saw in the case of Sabu, it becomes difficult to determine the veracity of any individual bit of information. More fundamentally, cyberwar in its very functioning is an attack on truth and its material and epistemic underpinnings. Under the threat of cyberwar, and the possibility that any information may have already been compromised, epistemology and truth become not only philosophical concerns but military–strategic problems as well.

In this light, it becomes difficult to separate any truth from its political and military investment. Derrida in "Plato's Pharmacy" suggests that "the opposition between the true and the untrue is entirely comprehended, *inscribed*, within this structure or this generalized writing. The true and the untrue are both species of repetition. And there is no repetition possible without the *graphics of supplementarity*."[18] Here, for Derrida, the true does not transcend the structure of writing in general. There is no unity but only a relation among units of inscription. The true and the untrue are movements of repetition within and between systems, a movement defined by text and network. Truth and its opposite become emergent effects of networks and texts rather than transcendental or global attributes of systems. Like certificate authorities for verifying identity on open networks, the guarantee of any information is merely deferred to a different level. Truth emerges as a result of the structure and folds of a given system.

This is not to suggest that truth is relative; it is intimately tied to the real and material movement of texts, programs, bits, capital, and so on, through the various global networks and systems at stake.[19] Still, what makes information true is precisely its inscription within a given network and its repetition throughout rather than through some preexisting global phenomenon. Lacan's insights in this regard are especially helpful. He suggests that truth is a function of language.[20] Truth is produced by the entire network of signifiers and subjects and always points to the truth of the structure rather than the veracity of an individual statement.[21] Thus truth for Lacan is always a question of the symbolic and is never synonymous with the real. The real can never be falsified, for it is always exactly where it is; it is "always in its place."[22] A bit is never on its own true or false; the signifier in the real is, as Kittler suggests, merely a voltage difference.[23] It is only through language, interpretation, and software that the bit comes to produce an effect; through the networks of signification, the networks of voltage difference become capable of producing a truth-effect. It is on these grounds that cyberwar becomes so insidious, by threatening to flip bits at the level of the real; underneath language, it demonstrates both the symbolic threat possessed by this real and the inability for the symbolic ever to achieve a full unity or mastery.

Truth becomes an effect of its movements through space and the programs that operate upon it. Any politics that commits itself to truth alone as the grounds for a politics risks merely partaking of the auto-immune violence of undecidability. The end of secrecy cannot in itself be a panacea for political injustice. In August 2010, Reporters without Borders sent an open letter to Assange suggesting precisely that his politics (insomuch as they were a politics of truth rather than of mere destruction) were shortsighted and paid little attention to the chain of effects that followed the dissemination of the "Afghanistan War Logs":

> You have unintentionally provided supposedly democratic govern-ments with good grounds for putting the Internet under closer surveillance.... Indiscriminately publishing 92,000 classified re-ports reflects a real problem of methodology and, therefore, of credibility. Journalistic work involves the selection of information.

Reporters without Borders insists that journalistic work is not simply about providing information but rather about filtering, selecting, and assessing information, in short, about the program that is brought to bear upon information. Even though they may take issue with Assange's choices of selecting information, his attempts at sharing leaks were also founded on a commitment to selecting information. Still, his selection was significantly more programmatic and consisted largely of sharing all information, except for information about sources (or even know-ing, as the technological infrastructure behind WikiLeaks was designed to completely protect leakers); this still constitutes a decision to share only certain information.

Either way, this decision amounts to a political and strategic com-mitment. Terranova explains the stakes well when she describes the circulation of images as a type of warfare:

> The hyperreal does not really involve a metaphysics of being and appearance so much as a kind of information ecology which also includes a dimension of warfare—a warfare to determine the differential power and dominance of some types of images over others.[24]

Alongside images, all texts and information are subjected to this dimension of warfare that differentiates their efficacy and ability to reformulate flows and networks. It is not merely the bits of information that determine their efficacy but their selection and differential relation.

The specific politics and strategy of pure transparency ultimately turn against themselves on two levels. On the level of truth, such a commitment can never guarantee the secrecy of the leaker while producing technologies that coax information from organizations. The same secrecy tax that burdens corporations and governments also causes individuals to reveal their secrets. On the level of effect, then, any technological and social system for supporting leaks is forced to engage in these complex networks and texts, in short, to decide what individuals' secrecy matters and what secrecy does not matter. The problem then becomes an undecidable political question. This is not to say that it is a priori negative but that such an act constitutes an opening rather than a necessarily efficacious politics.

With the belief in an abstract machine that moves unwaveringly toward the end of secrecy or the belief that this decision can be avoided through technology, we risk that information becomes its own truth. Leaks become, as raw data, an objectification of the sociopolitical relations that produce, use, and manipulate information and thus mark and measure truth itself. Information thus becomes what Foucault describes as a regime of *veridiction,* which "in fact, is not a law of truth, but the set of rules enabling one to establish which statements in a given discourse can be described as true or false."[25] Information and the technologies of antisecrecy establish both the truth and the very rules enabling one to ascertain the truth. The regime of transparency in an informational economy becomes not about the quality or effect of information but about its mere possession, existence, and exposure. This is not to downplay the importance of these leaks or to minimize the great risks and costs individuals have taken on to bring this information to the public but rather to insist that this information alone does not guarantee an effective politics.

RESISTANCE AFTER THEORY

In this light, we can understand the media as "tactical" insomuch as all sides of these conflicts seize upon media, their reuse, and their reconfiguration for the purposes of war and conflict. Raley, commenting on the Critical Art Ensemble and Lovink's, among others', conception of tactical media, states, "Tactical media comes so close to its core informational and technological apparatuses that protest in a sense becomes the mirror image of its object, its aesthetic replicatory and reiterative rather than strictly oppositional."[26] While the focus of tactical media is largely on art and protest practices, with cyberwar, media become tactical to all involved, including states and armies. Despite these different forces who are now involved in using media tactically, all of them appear caught in this system that Raley outlines, where the use of these media requires that one mirror the object of intervention. When media become objects of war and tactics, it becomes impossible to step outside these processes of mediatization and its disfiguration in the face of this violence.[27]

To understand the media as tactical under the constant siege of cyberwar requires taking the McLuhanesque insight that "the media is the message" in the most deconstructed sense possible. There is no longer any meaningful way to separate the two. Perhaps before the rise of computers, when command functioned on the level of a physical machine and data could not touch it (e.g., no message could be sent over the radio that would turn it off—or worse yet, turn a car off while one is driving), a separation could be made between media and message. The rise of reprogrammable media that combine data and command requires abandoning any distinction between media and message. Subjects and truth are produced through the topologies and texts that send various messages through a multiplicity of media. Tactics in relation to media can then truly no longer be oppositional, for there can be no transcendental space from which a stable space of opposition could be constructed. Rather, the only tactical movement that remains is to discover the outsides that are folded inside texts, networks, and the unstable interface between them. But, the translation of local information to global networks always risks perversions, corruptions, and interventions.

Despite, or perhaps even because of, the difficulty of acting or deciding within these complex global networks, there is a great appeal to the possibility of controlling situations through instantaneously knowable surfaces. Data appear as a vast field of computable truth. But the coherence of these surfaces is always belied by the vulnerability and contingency they contain within and the instability of the subjects whose traces exist in these vast fields of data. Still, many discourses, including those of information transparency, continually claim the efficacy of managing surface effects. Rather than recognizing those forces, which resist control, a host of actors increasingly seek out finer-grained modes of analysis, holding on to the fallacy that everything today is flowing and visible.

Chris Andersen, a prominent technology journalist, has stated the belief in these analytic modes of knowing in its most radical and succinct form. In an argument analogous to Greenberg's claims of a coming transparency, Andersen states that the age of huge data sets means that we no longer need models or theories of the world and instead can "run the data" in real time:

> Out with every theory of human behavior, from linguistics to sociology. Forget taxonomy, ontology, and psychology. Who knows why people do what they do? The point is they do it, and we can track and measure it with unprecedented fidelity. With enough data, the numbers speak for themselves. The big target here isn't advertising, though. It's science. The scientific method is built around testable hypotheses. These models, for the most part, are systems visualized in the minds of scientists.... But faced with massive data, this approach to science—hypothesize, model, test— is becoming obsolete.[28]

For Andersen, we do not need to know why things happen but merely be able to predict them in real time: no theories, no models, no interpretation, just a pure flow of data. In many ways, it is the scientific version of Bill Gates's fantasy of frictionless capitalism, but for Andersen, the signifier of capital is gone too. His is a fantasy of an infinite flow of information processed in real time, and the world constantly re-created anew out of predicting algorithms. It is a utopia, a nonplace, with no slowness and no topography that could hold information into a theoretical system. Beyond theory, we no longer need categories, only momentary statistical conglomerations. In this world, one need not know or theorize gender, class, or even individual subjects; everything becomes an individual record in a large-scale database.

It is, in short, the fantasy of a world without cyberwar, a world beyond cyberwar. This utopian vision would only be possible if computation and data were perfectly secure and always represented the world exactly. These descriptions of a pure world of data-driven discovery rest on the fantasy that all being and becoming can be perfectly encoded as data. This utopia requires that all data be perfectly secure and no accident, gap, or military force affect this correspondence. At the same time, it is a fantasy of the utter success of cyberwar, insomuch as it requires that technicians, politicians, scientists, and bankers are able to extract data from every system. In sum, Andersen hopes for a cyberwar that would end all cyberwars, an impossible cyberwar that would defeat all resistances.

Andersen is not alone in this vision of the future. A whole field of "hypothesis-free science" has gained traction in several disciplines.[29] Advertisers, high-frequency stock traders, and security agencies all mine massive stores of data to find customers, profits, and criminals with no interest in theorizing what is being sought. Even Latour's actor network theory appears committed to the tracing and recording of surface-level phenomena that provide no theory aside from the method of following an individual actor's own theory.[30] Here, again, information becomes its own *veridiction*. As long as the variables correlate, it does not matter why or how, and if the correlation is off, the algorithm updates automatically to improve accuracy for the next round.

These attempts to go beyond theory to understand what is readily apparent are not limited to scientific and technical discourses; they are also being developed as methods to read and understand texts. Best and Marcus advocate for what they call "surface reading" as a way of paying attention to the explanations and descriptions provided by authors. They contrast this mode of reading with what they call "symptomatic reading," which attempts to identify deep structures of truth behind texts; they identify the long history of Marxist and Freudian readings of texts as especially exemplary of this symptomatic type of reading. Thus they provide the literary equivalent, or even application, of Andersen's claim that we are at the end of theory. Their attempts to read only the surfaces of texts frame text as something directly given that can be counted without being theorized. They explicitly link this type of reading to computation, stating, "Digital modes of reading may be the inspiration for the hope that we could bypass the selectivity and evaluative energy that have been considered the hallmarks of good criticism."[31] These attempts at erasing depth and that which is non-present provide a tautological truth: the surface speaks to truth because it affirms the truth of the surface.

We can see this vision of the world in the desire to discover secret documents, and Greenberg's earlier statement that systems for leaking secrets would slip "inside of institutions and level their defenses against the free flow of data." State and military power may function in secret depths, but the process of exposing what is hidden does not require interpretation, selection, or nuanced theories of state power. Rather, one must expose a surface from within the walls of the state archive. From this perspective, secrets are best understood when documents, which can be run through algorithmic analysis without theory, are released into vast communication networks. The walls of institutions are no defense against the free flow of data that hollows them out from inside.

Taken to its extreme, this world without theory, secrets, or friction is a world without form or concept. We risk here, under the threat of the end of theory, the most complete incarnation of autoimmunity. Derrida describes the stakes well:

> For what I call the autoimmune consists not only in harming or ruining oneself, indeed in destroying one's own protections, and in doing so oneself, committing suicide or threatening to do so, but, more seriously still, and through this, in the threatening the I or the self, the *ego* or the *autos,* ipseity itself, comprising the immunity of the *autos* itself.[32]

The end of theory is in short the end of all selves and of all concepts that might hold together for even the shortest period of time. This would not be merely the end of the *autos* in its deconstructed impossibility but rather the final victory of this end. It is the fantasy not of the closure of metaphysics but rather of its completion—an end without end. The *ipseity,* the self, of every subject is for Andersen deconstructed and sent racing through information networks, and simultaneously the computable surface is declared to be the ultimate truth—a total *ipseity* without trace. This, too, is the threat of cyberwar in its most totalizing dimensions. Cyberwar announces the threat that all systems may be compromised and that no theory, no concept, and no self could ever hold together.

Despite this risk that everything will be flattened and coerced to leak its innermost secrets, we continually witness that systems, theories, and secrets, no matter how vulnerable and compromised, continue to be produced and to function for at least a period of time. Despite the constant arrival of the deconstructive threat, even in its most militarized and catastrophic form, systems persist and are reconstructed. The ends of theory, cyberwar, and militarized deconstruction all threaten the complete success of this total deconstruction, the final catastrophe of all systems, the end of deconstruction brought about by its own success. This deconstructive force that threatens every system is simultaneously the grounds of its possibility, the guarantee of the contingent trace and the impossibility of its total end, but still the task remains to outline the contours of a subject that could be more than the name of this openness and at the same time resist the fantasy of an independent sovereignty.

THE CALCULABLE SUBJECT

Under the threat of cyberwar, the sovereignty of the state alongside the sovereignty of the subject now appears not only impossible but truly foreclosed. Especially given our ecological existence, outside of ourselves in the insecure data, technology and texts that flow through various global networks, any guarantee of self-sameness becomes unthinkable. The subject becomes different than itself on two levels. On one level, the subject never can grasp the totality of the data and networks that constitute its existence. On another level, even if the subject were to survey all at once its divestment into these networks, the threat of an attack on any database means there can never be any guarantee that the database in fact contains the information one believes is there. In short, the subject's sovereignty is frustrated by the impossibility of a program that would always run correctly.[33]

Returning to Derrida's attempt to separate unconditionality from sovereign force, it is possible to explicate a form of decision that would not be opposed to the program or fall back into positing the power of the sovereign exception. When Derrida speaks critically of "sovereign self-determination, of the autonomy of the self, of the *ipse*, namely, of the one-self that vies itself its own law, of autofinality, autotely, self-relation as being in view of the self, beginning by the self with the end of self in view,"[34] it is as though he would like to, but cannot, say "automatic." It is as though he would like to name the subject as that *auto-matos,* that self-thinking machine that overdetermines the *autos* for us. The *autos* marks both the self of the sovereign subject but also the automatic machine that merely follows a fixed set of rules, a program. Derrida, while opposed to a simple form of this sovereign self-determination, still seems to resist, despite the autotelic nature of this subject, labeling it "automatic."[35] Even if he rejects this self-determination, for him, neither the subject nor the sovereign can collapse into the automatic or the programmatic. Were the subject to be merely a form of automatism, all texts and traces would be programs written by and for machines.[36] In thinking *(matos)* for itself *(autos),* the automatic machine inserts itself within and directly problematizes this sovereign self-determination. The automatic machine becomes autonomous, but in a way that calls into question every sovereignty.

For Derrida, were sovereignty to collapse into the automatic, two complications would instantly arise. First, the unconditional and the incalculable would be immediately foreclosed. Everything would risk becoming calculable and hence conditional. Second, and as a direct result, there could never be any responsibility or justice as Derrida conceives of them, for he sees as their very definition that they cannot be the implementation of a set of rules and hence a program. Derrida's fear, which necessitates the maintenance of a gap between the subject and automaticity, is that everything would collapse into the program and, with it, there could be no trace, no alterity, and no deconstruction.

This gap between the subject and the automatic serves as a space from which Derrida hopes to be able to rescue the incalculable exception from its sovereign foundations. He sees in this incalculable an unconditional exception, the possibility of waiting for an event that would be completely other; for "without the absolute singularity of the incalculable and the exceptional, no thing and no one, nothing *other* and thus *nothing,* arrives or happens."[37] Only beyond calculation can the other arrive "as other, as the absolute exception or singularity of an alterity that is not reappropriable by the ipseity of a sovereign power and a calculable knowledge."[38] But what arrives, under the name of cyberwar, upsets this entire system and suggests a radically different relation between the calculable program and alterity.

Cyberwar announces the collapse of the gap between the *autos* of the subject and the *auto-matos* of the machine, but not by way of reducing the self to a complete determinism. Rather, the programmatic nature of the automatic gives rise to the incalculable by way of both complexity and insecurity. Derrida says of the exposure to what arrives, "What must be thought here, then is this inconceivable and unknowable thing, a freedom that would no longer be the power of a subject, a freedom without autonomy, a heteronomy without servitude, in short, something like a passive decision. We would thus have to rethink the philosophemes of the decision, of that foundational couple activity and passivity."[39] This freedom without autonomy marked by a passive decision is precisely the force of the subject that maintains no distance from the automatic. The program does not name infinite knowledge but rather the inscription of a passive decision. In short, it is a subject, if such a term still applies, that travels down similar philosophical paths as the subject of control outlined earlier. It is a subject who is not autonomous and whose truths exist outside in the networks and texts through which it moves. It is a subject that acts automatically on the incomplete knowledge of its position in its local network and the messages that flow through that position. It thus has access to an unconditional incalculability, but not by way of anything that could properly be called sovereignty nor be separated from the incalculability of calculation.

We have perhaps not strayed far from Derrida's position, except insomuch as to insist that any unconditionality or incalculability that may oversee a subject's decision arises not from something that can be recuperated or separated from sovereignty but rather from the trace inherent in the program itself. In doing so, it becomes possible to conceptualize the subject in its positive relation to the program, in its exposure to alterity and what arrives as the deconstructability of the automatic itself, an autodeconstruction, rather than on the remnants of the sovereignty of the sovereign. It is here, on the grounds of this automatic decision by what remains of the subject, that a theory of resistance and politics must be thought.

THE NETWORKED SUBJECT

This subject that exists as a fold of the networks and texts that surround it shares important similarities with the Lacanian subject. For Lacan, the subject names a place in a topological field of language more than it names a sovereign individual. A number of aspects of this subject are immediately relevant for our purposes in understanding a subject who both collapses into an untranslatable automaticity and exists outside itself. Lacan says of the subject, "I am thinking where I am not, therefore I am where I am not thinking. These words render palpable to an attentive ear with what elusive ambiguity the ring of meaning flees from our grasp along the verbal string."[40] Likewise, the subject of control thinks and is controlled outside of itself, where it is not. Thought is not an internal sovereignty but rather the fold of the outside. It is the location of an autopoietic system in a network. The meaning of the subject, its very thinking, escapes along the woven strings of signifiers, texts, and programs that constitute the subject and its environs. What in the subject resists control is simultaneously that which divests the subject of its own self.

Moreover, the Lacanian subject's unconscious is defined by the topology and topography of signification. The subject is a result of its relation to a signifier that represents the subject to another signifier. The subject is founded on the void and impossibility of the production of a signified. We can understand this relation as topographical, as Lacan states, because the system operates on a signifier, an inscription that is spaced from the place of the impossible signified. The subject is placed in relation to language, but a language that operates algorithmically and automatically. We will return to this in more depth, but it is worth noting here that Lacan, who had some interest in cybernetics, is much more willing to recognize the subject's automaticity than Derrida.[41]

The structure of the unconscious for Lacan, like language, is not merely this topographic relation to a signifier but also a topological relation to a string of signifiers. In *Seminar XX,* Lacan states, "The subject is nothing other than what slides in a chain of signifiers, whether he knows which signifier he is the effect of or not. That effect—the subject—is the intermediary effect between what characterizes a signifier and another signifier, namely, the fact that each of them is an element."[42] The subject is thus the name of the place of the topographical signifier and the topological string of these signifiers. The subject therefore is "a being whose being is always elsewhere, as the predicate shows. The subject is never more than fleeting and vanishing, for it is a subject only by a signifier and to another signifier."[43] The thought of the subject happens in its environment, where it is not. This subject, outside of itself, leaves its traces in the networks and texts it writes and reads and is thus always exposed to a networked subversion.

In *Seminar XX,* Lacan explicitly places topology, in the form of the science of knots, in relation to writing and the signifier.[44] Topology and topography always border on becoming the other, and both ultimately, as Lacan develops in this seminar, are always produced by the real. If Derrida insists on a single space of deconstruction, Lacan's analysis is beset by the opposite problem: the proliferation of spatialities seems never to cease; topologies and topographies grow nearly infinitely, producing a cacophony of strings, foldings, systems, and entwinements. Simultaneously, everything becomes automatic. There is, for Lacan, no gap between sovereignty and automaticity.

Furthermore, Lacan explicitly links this place of the subject to contemporary technology and its development: "You are now, infinitely more than you think, subjects of instruments that, from the microscope right down to the radiotelevision, are becoming the elements of your existence."[45] The contemporary subject is a product of both the history of technologies and the discourses that shape it. What is explicated through cyberwar is a subject that is historical but also revealed in its very essence by this technological progression. Both Lacan's insistence that the symbolic is the site of truth and Malabou's claim that form and essence cannot be thought separately suggest that the truth of the subject is its historically variable form, its exposure to the temporal and spatial shifts of its topology and topography.[46]

Whereas Derrida resists the automaticity of such a subject, Lacan embraces it nearly completely, stressing its historical development and even mocking "ordinary man" with the possible success of machines outsmarting humans at children's games of chance:

> It is not unthinkable that a modern calculating machine, by detecting the sentence that, unbeknown to him and in the long term, modulates a subject's choices, could manage to win beyond any

usual proportions in the game of even and odd. This is a pure paradox, no doubt, but in it is expressed the fact that it is not because it lacks the supposed virtue of human consciousness that we refuse to call the machine to which we would attribute such fabulous performances a "thinking machine," but simply because it would think no more than the ordinary man does, without that making him any less prey to the summonses of the signifier.[47]

Even more than in games, systems are developed in the heart of algorithmic control that categorize and predict the subject's habits and desires. Though these systems tend to operate through the mass collection and analysis of entire corpora of textual and other data rather than by discerning the single sentence that predicts everything, Lacan draws close to the contemporary usage of such calculating machines and their predictive capabilities. It is precisely because the subject is prey to the summonses of the signifier that it is predictable.

The importance of this is clear for Lacan in his translation of Freud's *Wiederholungswang* as repetition automatism *(automatisme de répétition)* rather than as the more common repetition compulsion *(compulsion de répétition),* explicitly linking the subject to automaticity and hence predictability.[48] Especially as it becomes easier to extract the data of our everyday lives, our most intimate decisions appear predictable. The paradox that is so disconcerting for the contemporary subject is not that the machine can fool a human into believing it is a human, as in the famous Turing test, but exactly the opposite: the human subject, given over to its automaticity and exteriorization, is incapable of fooling the machine into believing it is not another machine.[49]

Tegmark, a contemporary physicist, puts forth a telling proposition in this regard, stating, "Consciousness is the way information feels when being processed in certain complex ways, i.e., that it corresponds to certain complex patterns in spacetime."[50] If we replace information with the stream of signifiers, we essentially have Lacan's position. Lacan's and Tegmark's interpretation of consciousness, and hence the subject, suggests that the subject names this place of information processing. In short, the *auto-matos* of the machine becomes inseparable from the *auto-matos* and self-thinking of the subject. This is not to say that Lacan in some way predicted our current networked predicament; still, the theories of the subject being developed by technologies of control and cyberwar share much in common with the Lacanian subject.

Although this description appears to accurately describe the situation that confronts the subject of control, it is also strikingly dire. In this way, Manning's confession to Lamo, and the secrecy tax that weighs on us all, can be interpreted as an effect of the intertwinement of networks of communication and the subjects they produce. This is not at all to minimize Manning's bravery in exposing the abuses of power documented in the files she leaked but rather to suggest the ways in which all subjects are given over to the summonses of the networks and texts within which they exist. This subject we are confronted with today appears to power as a mere surface effect that is completely exposed to modulation and control. This subject is in Lacan's terms "docile": "It is not only the subject, but the subjects, caught in their intersubjectivity, who line up—in other words, they are our ostriches, to whom we thus return here, and who, more docile than sheep, model their very being on the moment of the signifying chain that runs through them."[51] The docility of this subject is exactly what frightens so many about digital modes of surveillance and control, and also likely why Derrida attempts to maintain a gap between deconstructed sovereignty and the automatic program. The Lacanian account thus describes the problematic of this subject and also represents the most dangerous fate this subject is exposed to: a subject completely mastered by exterior forces.[52] It is a subject that could be controlled by an analyst or machine who could successfully detect the patterns of its automatic decision making. In its most frightening incarnation, it is the subject of control and the Derridean program, a subject merely reacting programmatically to information.

THE PURLOINED PROGRAM

Continuing down this path of the Lacanian subject and the Derridean program brings us close to a number of interwoven historical cyberwars. In 1956, Lacan delivered his seminar on Poe's short story "The Purloined Letter," a story that on its own already has much to tell us about information warfare. Almost two decades later, in 1975, Derrida wrote one of his few early comments on Lacan's work, titled "The Purveyor of Truth," a critical reading of the seminar that amounts in a sense to a cyberwar waged by Derrida against the system Lacan constructs. While questions of literature, truth, and the indivisibility of the signifier are all at play in this cyberwar, one of the central issues that shapes

Derrida's criticism is the question of the automaticity of the subject and its relation to the spaces within which it is embedded.

Lacan begins his seminar immediately by stating, "My research has led me to the realization that repetition automatism *(Wiederholung-swang)* has its basis in what I have called the *insistence* of the signifying chain. I have isolated this notion as a correlate of the *ex-sistence* (that is, of the eccentric place) in which we must necessarily locate the subject of the unconscious."[53] The subject, like the subject of control, is here in ex-stasis—outside itself—and lacking self-sameness. Moreover, the networks that connect the subject to other subjects and the signifiers that flow through them insist upon a subject who responds by repeating them automatically. Following this logic, Lacan concludes the seminar by famously stating, "A letter always arrives at its destination."[54] To be clear, he does not mean that chance events in the world arrange themselves such that the signifier always arrives where it is supposed to but rather that subjects "line up" so that they become the place where the signifier is supposed to arrive at the moment of arrival. The subject for Lacan automatically repeats the insistence of the signifier and thus becomes the necessary and hence correct destination.

Even before Lacan's intervention into Poe's story, we are faced with an intense, if relatively local, cyberwar. The Queen receives a letter from an unknown source. The King enters the room; the Queen flips the letter over to conceal it, and the nefarious Minister steals the letter and replaces it with another note. The Queen, who notices, is unable to respond as a result of the King's presence, thus allowing the Minister to blackmail the Queen. The scene is then repeated (at least for Lacan) when Dupin, the detective working on behalf of the Queen, successfully finds and steals the letter from the Minister, once again placing a fake letter in its place. The whole story is set in motion by the Queen and her secret correspondent's poor operational security. Though we never find out the text of the message or its source, given the events that follow, it seems unlikely the message was encrypted. At the very least, even if the message itself were obfuscated, then it appears that the metadata alone (e.g., who sent the letter) is enough to allow the Minister to blackmail the Queen.

The Minister's security is slightly more elaborate, as he refolds the letter to write a new address on it and affixes his own seal in place of the one that originally decorated the letter. The police are unable to find the letter after months of rigorous searching, as they assume that the letter will look as it is supposed to and that it must be in some elaborate hiding place. The Minister's strategy is reminiscent of what is now called security through obscurity, where a system is protected by being located somewhere that is unlikely to draw attention rather than by a complex and often noticeable security system.

Lacan spends a considerable portion of his seminar discussing this strategy of hiding the letter, the police's failure to discover it, and Dupin's ultimate success. He says explicitly about the spatial aspects of the whole affair,

> We were to understand this—regarding the field in which the police, not without reason, assumed the letter must be found—in the sense of an exhaustion of space, which is no doubt theoretical but which we are expected to take literally if the story is to have its piquancy. The division of the entire surface into numbered "compartments," which was the principle governing the operation, is presented to us as so accurate that "the fiftieth part of a line," it is said, could not escape the probing of the investigators.[55]

Lacan reads in this failure of the letter to be in space, despite ultimately being discovered by Dupin in the space of the apartment, an allegory for the signifier. He says of the signifier that it is the symbol of an absence and so it "will be *and* will not be where it is wherever it goes."[56] The signifier is an absence, which cannot be found by those looking for it as a positive entity that matches its own description. The signifier is never itself.

Beyond Lacan's reading of the letter as signifier, this description also stresses the heterogeneity of space. The letter disappears from space as a result of its folding. The space of the police search is a striated space. The entire surface of the apartment is methodically gridded, allowing a completely exhaustive search of the space. A microscope is even employed so that a single grain of dust that was out of place would be discovered. Still the letter is able to escape this exhaustive search as a result of becoming, by way of a fold and modification of its exterior text, different from itself. Hence the letter exits the striated space of the police search toward a smooth space heterogeneous from the first. The apparatus of the police gaze is vulnerable to such a trick precisely because of the inevitable inability to account for all spatialities.[57] At the same time, the folding of the letter is not foolproof, and Dupin is able ultimately to discover the letter. The heterogeneity of space forecloses either an exhaustive search or a foolproof security mechanism. Furthermore, all of these complex machinations demonstrate the impossibility of complete sovereign control. Lacan notes, "Neither the King nor the police who replaced Him in that position [the place of the law] were capable of reading the letter because that *place entailed blindness.*"[58]

We can see here, in the failure of the police and the King to detect the letter, the inevitable failure of modes of analysis that insist that truth is a surface phenomenon. The reduction of the space of Dupin's apartment to a surface that could be exhausted is also a transformation of space into data, but one that fails to detect the letter. Arguments, such as Andersen's, that the world can be understood through its apparent surface-level givenness as data rather than as mediated through theories fall prey to the same blind spot that afflicts the police and the King. These attempts at striating and exhausting an entire system end up missing what is hiding there in plain sight but folded beyond easy recognition, as they ignore the theoretical assumptions they make about the nature of space and text.

In this regard, Lacan offers strong words for those who would insist that a surface can be divided into a grid and computed to understand what truly lies there. He states,

> It is the imbecility of the realist who does not pause to observe that nothing, however deep into the bowels of the world a hand may shove it, will ever be hidden there, since another hand can retrieve it, and that what is hidden is never but what is *not in its place.* . . . For it can *literally* [*à la lettre*] be said that something is not in its place only of what can change places—that is, of the symbolic. For the real, whatever upheaval we subject it to, is always and in every case in its place.[59]

It is along these lines that those who insist on the importance of surfaces or analysis without theory confuse the real and truth. There is, for Lacan, no truth to the real, as everything is exactly where it is supposed to be. Truth, conversely, is an effect of the networks of signifiers that constitute the symbolic. The symbolic network, by tying together disparate signifiers and giving names to locations, provides the possibility for something not being in its place. Invariably, attempts to operate directly on the real as though it could be true end up achieving nothing other than becoming prey to the blind spot that troubles the police in Poe's story, who end unable to find the letter but still following it all the same.

Best and Marcus, in their article on surface reading, explicitly reference this story, stating, "What lies in plain sight is worthy of attention but often eludes observation—especially by deeply suspicious detectives who look past the surface in order to root out what is underneath it."[60] They draw the opposite conclusion from Lacan and insist on a form of the realist position that the letter is somehow there, exposed in the real. Contrary to their reading, it is the police who treat the apartment as an immense surface, even if it occasionally finds its way inside table legs, and are thus unable to find anything hidden. If one addresses interpretation, reading, science, and so on, to the real, there is nothing there to be learned, as no truth can be produced out of this entropic chaos. In these attempts to understand only surface effects, we can see a version of both the societies of control and how the state would like to treat cyberwar and networks: as spaces of pure information flow that can be counted and managed. But cyberwar and, with it, the depths of symbolic insecurity announce the impossibility of this surface and the inevitable complications that arise for those who would attempt to operate within these networks without getting caught within their depths and multiple spatialities.

It is the letter's movements through the fold of topology and topography, where neither can be properly or determinably identified, that define its efficacy: "For we have learned to conceive of the signifier as sustaining itself only in a displacement comparable to that found in electronic news strips or in the rotating memories of our machines-that-think-like-men, this because of the alternating operation at its core that requires it to leave its place, if only to return to it by a circular path."[61] Both the Queen's letter and our contemporary digital writing take on their import by leaving their place and moving through complex networks of cables and discourse. This movement that the subject—as its signifiers—is subjected to causes it to automatically act in the intersubjective networks that define it. Today, the wars that are fought over information and messages increasingly determine the subject and its automaticity.

DERRIDA AT WAR

Lacan's reading of "The Purloined Letter" suggests a number of conflicts over information and the way in which they determine the subject's actions and knowledge. Against this reading, Derrida attacks Lacan on a number of fronts, accusing him of, among other things, sexism, erasing literature, failing to acknowledge prior readings (Derrida claims Marie Bonaparte had already provided a more nuanced and complete version of the analysis Lacan attempts), phallocentricism, a belief in the possibility of mastery, and an overreliance on determinism. In her reading of their respective writings on "The Purloined Letter," Johnson cites a number of prior affronts between the two, such as Derrida's claim to intentionally have ignored Lacan since *Of Grammatology* as a result of Lacan's supposed antipathy to and reappropriation of his work. She says, "If it thus becomes impossible to determine 'who started it' (or even whether 'it' was started by either one of them), it is also impossible to know who is ahead, or even whose 'turn' it is."[62]

Among the number of attack vectors that Derrida attempts to exploit to disaggregate and deconstruct the system Lacan articulates in his reading, two are especially telling. Derrida attacks the Lacanian system once focusing on its outside, by insisting that part of the story and its context have been ignored, and again from its inside, by arguing that a letter can always fail to arrive at its destination, thus negating the coherence of the system. In the first instance, Derrida pushes the Lacanian system into its exteriors to destabilize it. He insists that Lacan frames the story, ignoring the narrator and additional texts of Poe. Derrida states, "Bonaparte does what Lacan does not do: she establishes the connection between 'The Purloined Letter' and other texts of Poe,"[63] and that even within the text of "The Purloined Letter," the framing of the narrator's position is ignored: "The seminar pays no specific attention to that extra text."[64]

By insisting on the larger context of literature, criticism, and narration, Derrida attempts to demonstrate the insecurity of the Lacanian system. He recognizes that a nominally secure piece of software has been installed on an insecure system and from here the interior system of the psychoanalytic software begins to unravel as well. Derrida begins adding additional inputs to the system. He says,

The narrator's place is excluded by analytical decipherment, neutralized, or more accurately, by a process we hope to follow, this decipherment acquiesces to the narrator's dictation of an effect of neutralizing exclusion ("narrator" as "commentary") which transforms the entire Seminar into an analytical fascination with a content. In this way a scene is lacking. Where Lacan sees two ("There are two scenes"), there are at least three. And where he sees one or two "triads," there is always a supplementary square whose opening complicates the computation.[65]

A third scene supplements the two scenes, and a fourth subject, the narrator, supplements the three. Each of these additions functions by appropriating a remainder that is left outside of the system and destabilizing it by reintroducing the remainder. The supplementary term adds an additional dimension that the system cannot account for and thus introduces a contagion. Any security system can be undermined by the engagement of the exterior spaces it exists within: secure software can be undermined by attacking hardware, hardware can be undermined by breaking into the office it sits in, physical security can be compromised by coercing employees, and so on.

Despite these attacks, as Johnson observes, Derrida ends up repeating the same erasures and exclusions of which he accuses Lacan, ultimately ignoring critical portions of Lacan's own text.[66] Johnson notes that this does not invalidate his claims but rather suggests that Derrida repeats the same position taken by Lacan. Such a maneuver is of a certain structural necessity; for a system to be enclosed such that its security and coherence can even begin to be considered, it must be separated from its exteriors. The only way in which all exteriors could be confronted would be to map and compute a single global, or even cosmological, system, but such attempts always reach the same limit: the map or the computer network can never exist in a transcendental space outside of the territory and hence always produces effects that can never be accounted for. Thus it is always possible to approach a text or a system from a dimension that was excluded in its creation and turn the system against itself, activating its autoimmune potential.

Derrida makes a second move against Lacan, from a more directly internal place within the Lacanian system. Within the network of signifiers that Lacan insists upon, Derrida asserts that a letter can always be divided and hence not arrive at its destination. Derrida states of the letter that

> its "materiality" and its "topology" result from its divisibility, its ever-possible partition. It can always be broken up irrevocably and this is what the system of the symbolic, of castration, of the signifier, of truth, of the contract, and so forth, try to shield it from: the point of view of the King and that of the Queen are here the same, bound together by contract in order to reappropriate the bit.[67]

For Derrida the letter is always given over to a dissemination that the symbolic order attempts but fails to reappropriate. The signifier breaks into bits and precludes its arrival in full. Networked communication is subjected to all sorts of deferrals, failures, and corruptions. Derrida states, "Here dissemination threatens the law of the signifier and of castration as a contract of truth. Dissemination mutilates the unity of the signifier, that is, of the phallus."[68] The King and Queen, on the side of law, are both engaged in an impossible attempt to regain the entirety of the letter against its inevitable dissemination.

Against this dissemination of the letter, Derrida claims that both the Queen and Lacan hope to reappropriate it to the law of the unified signifier that can make demands upon the subject: "Lacan leads us back to the truth, but this truth does not get lost. He returns the letter and shows that it returns itself to its proper place by way of a proper trajectory, and, as he expressly mentions, this destination is what interests him. Destiny as destination. The signifier has its place in the letter which rediscovers proper meaning in its proper place."[69] For Lacan, in order for the signifier to invoke its automatic response in the subject, to hold the subject under its summonses, the destination of the signifying chain must be its predetermined destiny. Derrida then cites his own work in *Of Grammatology* as deconstructing this unity of the signifier. According to Derrida's reading, for the letter to arrive at its proper destination, the signifier must be whole. Conversely, if the signifier is not whole, if it disseminates itself, then the letter cannot arrive and the whole system of the seminar collapses.

Derrida, suggesting that we are dealing here with cyberwar and information security, declares that the divisibility of the letter is the "key or safetybolt of the Seminar."[70] He offers an attack vector, a singular element in the system on which the security of the entire system depends. Both of Derrida's arguments outlined here, that the seminar cuts out part of the frame and that it fails to account for dissemination, are direct attacks against the information security of the Lacanian system. His attacks work in concert, from within and without, to undermine our belief in the security and coherence of the system. Readers of Derrida's essay, as in the case of Eligible Receiver, are confronted with the possibility that they should not believe anything from the analyst on down.

Derrida, not because he necessarily wins this cyberwar but because he is on the side of the insecurity in Lacan's program, suggests the lesson cyberwar offers us:

> The letter would have no fixed place, not even that of a definable gap or void. The letter would not be found; it might always not be found; it would in any case be found less in the sealed writing whose "story" is told by the narrator and "deciphered" by the Seminar, less in the context of the story, than "in" the text escaping on a fourth side the eyes of both Dupin and the psychoanalyst.[71]

Even for the subject—who as subject of the signifier is given over to automaticity—a network of signification can never be secured or completely mastered. Some insecurity or vulnerability always escapes notice. The scene of Poe's story does not merely repeat twice but rather repeats infinitely, with the letter always escaping and its security always self-deconstructing.

Even if one accepts Derrida's insistence on the importance of dissemination and the danger of ignoring parts of texts and systems, as Johnson points out, his overall argument requires a reductionist reading of the seminar to conclude that Lacan is unaware of the threats of dissemination and the wayward path a signifier can take. Derrida assumes that the destination for Lacan is a fixed place and, in doing so, refuses the possibility that the Lacanian system accounts for or at least allows dissemination.[72] Johnson surmises in the face of these difficulties that "what Derrida is in fact arguing against is therefore not Lacan's *text* but Lacan's *power.*"[73] In Derrida's attack against the Lacanian system, it is not a text alone, or even a series of texts, that is at issue but rather a system that consists of texts, individuals, and their relations. The autopoietic and self-organizing system of "Lacan" is what is at stake, not the seminar in isolation.

It is for this reason that we should not be surprised that Derrida repeats exactly that of which he accuses Lacan. The maneuver and strategy are successful; they tend to undermine any system. There is, though, as we have seen in the history of cyberwar, always a risk in employing such techniques against systems, because one can never be in a position of mastery when tracing the insecurity of complex systems. Johnson notes, "Whatever Derrida actually thinks he is doing here, his contradictory way of explaining it obeys the paradoxes of parergonal logic so perfectly that this self-subversion may have even been deliberate."[74] What Derrida terms parergonal is the fold, the unavoidable entwinement between form and essence, as he suggests the ultimate aim of his criticism is "to prove that the structure of the framing effects is such that no totalization of the border is even possible. The frames are always framed: thus by some of their content."[75] The logic Derrida both detects in Lacan and is entrapped by himself is that of the fold, where frames are always enframed by their content. The parergon, like the supplement, is added from the content to stabilize the frame but in the same movement guarantees its possible deconstruction.

In tracing this parergonal logic in Lacan's reading, Derrida cannot help but get caught in these threads. We are left with the same attribution problem that plagues cyberwar: as Derrida repeats that of which he criticizes Lacan, Johnson is unable to determine whether Derrida's "self-subversion" is deliberate. All of the involved actors attempt to reappropriate the bit, to master the story and the letter, but everywhere the systems of information security and the programs that run on these literary networks are exposed to their own insecurity. In short, cyberwar, and with it these palimpsests of analyses of Poe's story, becomes stuck on exactly the impossible logic that Lacan recognizes when Dupin "starts with the story of the child prodigy who takes in all his classmates at the game of even or odd with his trick of identifying with his opponent, concerning which I have shown that he cannot reach the first level of its mental elaboration—namely, the notion of intersubjective alternation— without immediately being tripped up by the stop of its recurrence."[76] Those embroiled in conflict are always assuming that their opponent is one step ahead and so pretending to be one step behind, but these preemptive moves oscillate infinitely, and one is inevitably "tripped up" by the need to stop them at some point. When one attempts to destroy a system by subtly tracing its inner logic, one invariably becomes entwined with the system, negating one's own self-sameness.

In this light, perhaps we should not be surprised when Derrida says without saying, years later, after writing on Lacan's seminar and after Lacan's death, that they loved each other: "And if I said now: 'You see, I believe that we loved each other a great deal, Lacan and I...' I am almost sure that many here could not bear it. This is why I don't know yet whether I am going to say it."[77] In his attempt to subvert the Lacanian system from inside and from without, Derrida ends in a way by identifying with it, by saying without saying under the erasure of an "if I said" that he loved Lacan. It is as though Derrida here found himself in a similar situation to Sabu and the FBI, by the twists and turns of various symbolic networks identifying with and working for those against which they set out.[78]

Johnson suggests, "If the face-off between two opponents or polar opposites always simultaneously backfires *and* misfires, it can only be because 2 is an extremely odd number."[79] Even more, any number can be made an extremely odd number, especially today, when so many numbers are represented, transmitted, and computed in binary. When the message is given over to the logic of dissemination, even if it is between two authors or computer code, it can always be made to be more or less and hence to be subverted and turned against itself. It becomes evident, with each new letter that is added, that while each subject is prey to the summonses of the signifier, it is always under the law of dissemination. If the subject automatically repeats its place in the signifying chain, what is repeated is dissemination itself. One repeats the insecurity of the signifier. While Derrida perhaps neither wins nor intends to, he accurately captures the stakes of all these cyberwars and his own position when he says of all people involved that they are "all more insightful and more foolish than the others, more powerful and more powerless."[80]

THE AUTOMATIC SOVEREIGN

Despite Derrida's careful and thorough deconstruction of Lacan's system, Derrida completely ignores Lacan's long exposition on the relationship between determination and randomness.[81] It is only by ignoring and excluding Lacan's theory of the relationship between randomness and symbolic determination that Derrida can assert that Lacan refuses the possibility of a letter disseminating. The relationship between determination and randomness carefully explicated by Lacan underwrites the possibility of a destination as well as the chance occurrence of a letter failing to arrive.

In an extensive introduction that follows the main seminar in *Ecrits*, Lacan demonstrates how a random binary series can create structurally regular series. He suggests a number of ways in which one can create sliding windows of, for instance, three consecutive binary values and how these sets of three will have certain regular aspects. For example, if one codes three similar values as 1 (+ + + or − − −), alternating values as 2 (+ − + or − + −), and two similar values preceded or followed by the opposite as 3 (+ + −, − − +, + − −, or − + +), such that the random sequence + − − − + − would be coded as 3132, it then becomes impossible for a 2 to follow or precede a 1. This is simply because if one takes the last two values of a 1 (+ + + or − − −), neither a + or a − will create an alternating sequence as required for a 2. The same is true if one takes the opposing set of two values that conclude a 2; it is then impossible to add anything that would make the three values all the same. Lacan expands upon this coding schema further, and one can follow it in the seminar, but the important point is that he explicitly provides this complex example to relate the determination of the signifying chain (the coding) to a completely random series.[82]

Through this demonstration, Lacan shows how dissemination, as the random chain of binary values, can still produce a destination. The destination arises out of randomness. The bit itself is never reappropriated; rather, it is the long chain of random noise that, through its gathering up into these sliding windows, produces a structure, which can then produce a signifier and, ultimately, a place for a subject. It is the combination and the difference between the topographic space of the signifier and the topological space of intersubjective communication that produces signification and an automatic subject. Likewise, it is the insecurity, the divisibility, and the vulnerability of the signifier that threatens to return it to this random noise. Lacan develops the relationship between random chance and the law of the signifier significantly in his later work, but he hints at the importance of the question toward the end of the seminar, stating,

> What remains of a signifier when it no longer has any signification? This is the very question asked of it by the person Dupin now finds in the place marked by blindness. For this is clearly the question that has led the Minister there, assuming he is the gambler we are

told he is, as his act suffices to indicate. For the gambler's passion is no other than the question asked of the signifier, which is figured by the automaton of chance. "What are you, figure of the dice I roll in your chance encounter [*tuchē*] with my fortune? Nothing, if not the presence of death that makes human life into a reprieve obtained from morning to morning in the name of significations of which your sign is the shepherd's crook. Thus did Scheherazade for a thousand and one nights, and thus have I done for eighteen months, experiencing the ascendancy of this sign at the cost of a dizzying series of loaded tosses in the game of even or odd."[83]

When the events of the story have played out and the letter has been returned, it ceases to hold any signifying power; the letter is destroyed, disseminated, and returned to bits. Life becomes the moment when chance is held together into a signifying system, but this system is always watched over by its inevitable dissolution into chance and entropy at the end. It is precisely because the letter cannot arrive at its destination that for a moment it does arrive before it again, inevitably, fails to arrive.

In making the reference explicit in a footnote to the preceding quote, Lacan directly draws on the relationship between *tuchē* and *automaton,* two terms he refigures from Aristotle's *Physics.*[84] For Lacan, especially in his later development of the relationship between *automaton* and *tuchē,* these terms come to mean something quite different from Aristotle's original meaning. *Automaton* names the subject's relationship to the signifier, specifically the way in which the subject automatically repeats the signifier and is pulled along the signifying chain. Opposed to this, *tuchē,* the chance encounter, is the random, undetermined nature of the real that always threatens signification and life itself.

At the end of the seminar, it is the *automaton* of chance, built of *tuchē* itself, that threatens the signifier with the end of signification. *Tuchē* is here the figure of death, the possibility that the signifier will not arrive at its destination and hence cease to signify. In many ways, it is in this part of the seminar where the entire system holds together by theorizing the possibility of its own dissolution, its inevitable dissemination. Lacan, speaking from the place of the Minister, attributes the ability to maintain a signifying system, as the Minister has done for eighteen months by possessing the letter, to repeatedly winning at a game of chance, a feat that will eventually and inevitably fail.

In his seminar of 1964, these concepts are further developed, and there *tuchē* translates *"the encounter with the real. The real is beyond the automaton,* the return, the coming-back, the insistence of the signs, by which we see ourselves governed by the pleasure-principle. The real is that which always lies behind the automaton."[85] Chance and *tuchē,* which are both behind and beyond the automaton, threaten to undermine, while at the same time founding, the subject's automatic processes of repeating the demands of the signifier. In Verhaeghe's reading, this chance that undermines the signifying automaticity founds the subject's ability to choose: "The subject is fundamentally undetermined, and that is why it has a possibility of choice, beyond the determination of the *automaton.* This aspect of choice was already implicit in Freud's idea of *Neurosenwahl* (choice of neurosis) and it is made explicit with Lacan's idea of *la position du sujet*: the subject has to take a position."[86]

We must be careful not to fall back into a subject that chooses against automaticity as a selfsame sovereign; this subject chooses not despite but as a result of its automaticity. Lacan hints at a direction by the last question he raises in the seminar, namely, what happens to a signifier when it ceases to signify, or we could say in regard to cyberwar, what happens to a system when it ceases to function? The signifier and the system are both returned by way of chance to death. *Tuchē* is both the past and the future of all signifying systems, and this conclusion, under the name of dissemination, is exactly what Derrida allows us to read into Lacan's seminar while he insists that it is not there. Not only does random chance threaten any signifying system but a signifying network risks becoming pure entropy itself, ultimately constituting the tychic—the adjectival form Lacan makes out of *tuchē*—nature of the symbolic on another level. This is exactly what has happened with our global networks of computation: in their growing complexity, they have ceased to function as a symbolic store of knowledge and instead have been constituted as a vulnerable real that threatens every symbolic exchange. At any given moment, part of these networks may be understood symbolically; we can read the programs that run our machines. But, they always threaten, when we look away, to unleash a rogue piece of code that would destroy the entire network.

In this sense, we can situate Lacan's statement that the real is that which "doesn't stop not being written."[87] The tychic encounter with the real continually produces signifiers that are never able to represent it.

It could be stated less cryptically that the real continually tries and fails to be written in its total complexity. The process of attempting to write and produce programs that would successfully write and predict the developments of the real never fully succeeds and ultimately reproduces contingency. Despite this failure, the real continually elicits new attempts to describe and predict it, further unleashing the unpredictable and undeterminable tychic forces that lay within.

Johnson explains, "The 'undeterminable' is not *opposed* to the determinable; 'dissemination' is not *opposed* to repetition. If we could be sure of the difference between the determinable and the undeterminable, the undeterminable would be comprehended within the determinable. What is undecidable is precisely whether a thing is decidable or not."[88] In short, it becomes impossible to separate the automatic from the tychic; the two define and structure each other. Derrida, in a later lecture from 1982, arrives at a similar conclusion when he attempts to integrate a reading of chance into his reading of dissemination in Lacan. In the lecture, Derrida makes explicit reference to *tuchē* and *automaton* as well as Lacan's reading of Poe. He states,

> Language, however, is only one among those systems of *marks* that claim this curious tendency as their property: they *simultaneously* incline toward increasing the reserves of random indetermination *as well as* the capacity for coding and overcoding or, in other words, for control and self-regulation. Such competition between randomness and code disrupts the very systematicity of the system while it also, however, regulates the restless, unstable interplay of the system.[89]

Derrida, in these two sentences, condenses much of what is at stake and what is produced by the conflict between him and Lacan. Language—and a whole host of other systems of marks of which language is but one example—has a tendency simultaneously to produce control and randomness.[90] Moreover, though Derrida may mean that this play between control and randomness disrupts the systematization of a system in its ability to control, we should read this as broadly as possible to mean that the simultaneity of these contradictory tendencies disrupts the very possibility of delimiting the system itself. What is at stake is not only the boundary between control and randomness but the possibility of the system itself as an identifiable and signifying entity. Thus even the differentiation between any system, such as the program and literature, becomes impossible, but at the same time, this impossibility creates the condition for the possibility of each.

The conflict that arises between Derrida and Lacan structures the system but also infuses it with a random core that undermines the distinction between sides and even the boundary and meaning of the system. It is not only mastery and destination that slip away between Lacan and Derrida but even the possibility of their distinction.[91] Still, at the same time that they slip away and become indeterminate, we arrive at the possibility of a functioning system. The real continues to produce signifying systems, and as these systems grow in complexity, they simultaneously reconstitute the real by producing random effects and oscillations that can never be accounted for, undermining any sovereignty. In this way, the program and the machine are not opposed to deconstruction; deconstruction functions as a program and, as such, programs the force of deconstruction. Program and text slide into the others, pulled along by the force of the signifier and its dissemination, but at the same time, something in these networks of signifiers and noise can always catch, getting hung up in a repetition that offers the briefest of reprieves from one morning to the next, allowing a system to signify and function.

Thus it is too with the subject: in its automatic exposure to *tuchē,* which is both symbolic and real, it becomes undeterminable, unpredictable, and vulnerable. The subject is able, from the place of this vulnerability, ultimately to act and create itself. This vulnerability is decidedly not a flatness nor a pure surface that can be read simply as truth. On the contrary, the subject's automaticity and its inherent insecurity guarantee that no surface and no force of control can ever fully account for what it is. Exposed to cyberwar and the vulnerability of programs, there is no guarantee of any outcome, but at the same time, the possibility of the subject and any politics is founded on rather than opposed to the program. Any complex system as subject experiences a collapse of itself into the automatic; its ability to decide becomes synonymous with its automatic self-thinking, but both become possible and productive only as a result of their inevitable contingency and nonpresence. It is insomuch as the subject is positioned in the fold between topography and topology, the determinate and the indeterminate, text and code, repetition and dissemination, essence and accident, *automaton* and *tuchē*, that the subject comes to name a depth without sovereignty that is able to decide in the instant of executing its program.

CONCLUSION: THE RESISTANCE OF THE SUBJECT

In the initial game of the match in which Deep Blue beat Kasparov to become the first computer to officially defeat a reigning world chess champion, a small bug in the code caused the computer on the forty-fourth move to move a rook to absolutely no effect. If it could not find an optimal move, the computer was programmed to select a risk-free move at random, hence the seemingly pointless maneuver. Kasparov won that first game, and the bug was fixed before the second. Still Kasparov, without knowing about the glitch or its remedy, became convinced that the Deep Blue team was cheating and that the machine was receiving help from a grand master. He figured that such a senseless and random move would never be made by a machine designed to calculate every possible advantage. Kasparov believed that such a counterintuitive move signified a higher intelligence behind the machinic program.[92]

While the ability of the machine to consider 200 million moves per second was likely responsible for its success in beating Kasparov, what produced the uncanny sense that it possessed the intelligence of a human was an error in its program. It was the inability of those engineers who designed the system to master the programmatic language in which they wrote that appeared to produce a thinking subject. There is no ghost in the machine, only a bug. The accidental bit of unaccounted code undermined the strict automaticity of the program and produced the slight mistake that allowed the system to produce novel forms and appeared to Kasparov as thought. The accident did not arrive from elsewhere to destroy the machine's proper functioning; rather, its programmatic logic grew to a level of complexity that frustrated the mastery of its creators. The bug appeared at once to be both a direct development of the logic of the program and some outside force that would attest to the presence of a subject.

Kasparov, in expecting the smooth surface of computational cunning and unerring calculation, failed to see the possibility of a bug and instead assumed, like Poe's police, that some deep intelligence perpetually frustrated him. Neither the subject nor the machine has a transcendental depth that assures a secret interiority; instead, the vulnerability of every automaticity and programmatic logic produces folds that belie the stability of the system's surface. This lack of transcendental depth coupled with a multiplication of temporalities and spatialities resists every attempt at mastery or accounting only for surfaces. The program will always produce traces that instantiate its deconstructive vulnerability. The only function this surface can provide is to offer up the subject to systems of control. Still, simply to refuse the coherence of these surface effects does not guarantee the end of attempts to control them.

These bugs arise out of the tychic instability of language subjected to dissemination. While granting the subject a depth that is unpredictable to control, it simultaneously demonstrates the program and the subject's dependence on the larger network within which they exist. This dependence and openness to its network makes the automatic subject capable of an unconditional waiting, but it is not a mere choice of the subject to unconditionally await the unpredictable event that would come from the other. Rather, this unconditional waiting constitutes the structure of the automatic and programmed subject. It is the automaticity of the exposed program and the subject that produces the possibility of what Derrida calls an event, which

> must touch an exposed vulnerability, one without absolute immunity, without indemnity; it must touch this vulnerability in its finitude and in a nonhorizontal fashion, there where it is not yet or is already no longer possible to face or face up to the unforeseeability of the other. In this regard, autoimmunity is not an absolute ill or evil. It enables an exposure to the other, to *what* and *who* comes—which means that it must remain incalculable.[93]

This vulnerable awaiting of an unforeseeable other turns out to be, under the threat of cyberwar, not that which forever remains incalculable but rather the essence of calculation. As calculation and computation are exposed as a kind of writing, the function of a program becomes precisely to await an unforeseeable other, to repeat constantly its symbolic program, but always awaiting some unforeseen input. From the core of the calculable, we arrive at a waiting and an exposure that found the chance of a politics that opens itself to the event of the other's arrival.

The possibility of a subject capable of resisting the control of the state, along with the violence and disruption of our modern war machines, requires that we confront their calculability and automaticity. If such a politics is today possible under the conditions of cyberwar, it must arise from a subject that in executing its program, beholden to the signifiers its environment produces, embraces this condition as its openness to the world. The conditions of control are, at the same time, the foundations of a subject endowed, or perhaps more accurately, programmed, with an unconditional openness toward the other and an ability to await the event of politics. We can see in this light what is at stake in the politics of Anonymous, Manning, Snowden, and so on, and those who utilize the methods of cyberwar against forces of control, disrupting the normal functioning of networks and exploiting the tactical nature of media. They function not as some political program that could stand outside of the networks in which they operate and grasp at once what must be done; rather, they create and are themselves the errors in the program that free our networks from the constant repetition of war and capital exchange. There is no command center, just the program turned against itself and exposed to the tychic fold of the real, the same real that continually fails to write itself into a program that could ever master the situation—the real that writes failure into every program it produces.

It is in this sense that it becomes clear what is risked and gained by the politics of freedom of information. To release all information into the network is impossible on its face, as we saw with the struggles over the selection of information that WikiLeaks and Assange have faced. More important, even if one were able to ally oneself completely with the free flow of information, it would turn into a politics of the surface and the dictates of the signifier. This is not to say that such actions cannot produce political results but rather that, to do so, they cannot achieve their effects directly through the production of surface-level truths. Instead, if they are to succeed, it will be as a result of complex network effects and selections that trace the folds and gaps of untranslatable programs and subjects.

Serres says of the parasite, "He pays in information, in energy on the microscopic level. He offers words for the force—yes, his voice, air, for a solid substance. Worse yet, he takes control and governs. The parasite invents something new. He obtains energy and pays for it in information."[94] Politics is now a politics of the bug, enmeshed within the environment and networks of energy and information. For a moment, perhaps, it appears that the parasite controls the host and its networks, but once the price has been paid in information, the parasite, like Poe's Minister, has used up the letter and ends with nothing. But, still, it is possible something has changed, a letter has disseminated or a system has been corrupted. Everything advances like clockwork, but only by following the exploited code that turns the system against itself. The accident and the computer virus control the host for a moment, but it soon becomes impossible to differentiate the host and the parasite.

When one accepts the program as a formal logic lacking all depth, this writing without trace haunts every politics and philosophy, always threatening to reduce the subject to an automatic future of mere control. Those who supposedly write this text without trace then appear as absolute sovereigns controlling all flows of information, and the subject appears everywhere constructed by forces from without, subjected always to the effects of cyberwar, given over to the whims of the war machine and the state. On the contrary, when the program is understood as writing, which gives rise to dissemination and exposure to the real, the subject is capable from its programmatic repetition of affirming its own finitude and simultaneously awaiting the unforeseeable other. Mastery everywhere is dissipated at the same time the subject is left to decide, not on the grounds of a sovereign decision, but rather, as Derrida suggests, as a passive decision. This subject without autonomy is a subject bound to no transcendent law or nomos. It is not in spite of cyberwar and its program but because of them, and because of the inevitable mistake in the code, that the subject is capable of deciding on its openness to the other and to its environment. The cybernetic subject decides automatically without autonomy, making a decision that gives itself to thinking without sovereignty: a program rather than a law.

CONCLUSION

Firmware Vulnerabilities

The growing connection of our global life support systems to networks that extend their reach along with their vulnerability threatens to turn local vulnerabilities and attacks into systemwide catastrophes. As war spills outside the time and space of declared war and these technological networks open new attack vectors, war begins to atomize and move fully into our everyday lives and the technologies that are part of them. Our relationship to war is no longer limited to the military–industrial complex or the outbreak of traditional wars in specific parts of the world. Rather, war moves into our electric grids, banking systems, phones, and personal computers.

This new mode of war directly seizes upon the networked and textual vulnerabilities of our technologies and the systems that constitute life in the twenty-first century. The rise of cyberwar as a military strategy marks an explicit apperception of our dependency on fundamentally insecure global networks. It directly calls into question our ability to control the technologies, programs, and infrastructures that we build and rely upon. Regardless of the efficacy or impact of a single attack, this marks an important historical and philosophical realization.

Cyberwar, as it moves through our unstable spatialities, writings, and systems, carries with it a digital argument and force that suggest, directly on the level of the bits it affects, that all systems are necessarily insecure, heterogeneous, and unstable. It is precisely the interwoven nature of space and text that always undermine the stability of any system. As the vast complexity of global networks and programming languages are folded into the devices that are being brought into our homes and provide the basis for our daily existence, this war, outside of the time and place of war, is transformed into the background noise and chaos of the everyday. In this light, cyberwar comes to name the insecurity and fragility of our existing in ecologically connected systems.

EQUATION GROUP

In early 2015, Kaspersky Lab reported the discovery of "a threat actor that surpasses anything known in terms of complexity and sophistication of techniques, and that has been active for almost two decades— The Equation Group."[1] The group was named for their affinity for using advanced encryption algorithms and obfuscation. The Equation Group appears especially advanced owing to their use of two pieces of malware, now known as EquationDrug and GrayFish, which are implanted into a target hard drive's firmware, the first known instance of an attack utilizing hard drive firmware.[2] Because the firmware runs the hard drive and is not located in actual hard drive memory, placing malware here is extraordinarily insidious; it is able to persist even if the hard drive is completely wiped and the operating system reinstalled. Once in the firmware, malicious code can be loaded into the operating system every time the computer is turned on, giving an attacker essentially unfettered access to the machine. Moreover, an infection is almost impossible to detect after the fact, as Raiu, director of the Global Research and Analysis Team at Kaspersky Lab, explains: "For most hard drives there are functions to write into the hardware firmware area, but there are no functions to read it back. It means that we are practically blind, and cannot detect hard drives that have been infected by this malware."[3] Computation is unable to detect its own conditions: a program can only assume it will be executed as expected. In the case of EquationDrug, the subversion runs so deep that there is no way for the computer to ask itself if it is infected; only an external instrument can determine if a machine is infected. The malware can easily subvert any process and even capture cryptographic keys, exposing any data on the targeted machine.[4]

While Kaspersky Lab has not publicly identified the organization behind Equation Group, they have connected a number of exploits and parts of the code to both Stuxnet and Flame, two pieces of malware that have been linked clearly to the U.S. government.[5] F-secure, another security research lab, directly tied the attack to the National Security Agency (NSA), claiming that the firmware attack was the same as a tool named IrateMonk that was listed in a secret internal NSA technology catalog published by *Der Spiegel* in 2013.[6] The evidence seems to point toward the NSA, including time stamps in the code that suggest the programmers were working nine to five in an Eastern U.S. time zone.[7] Since its release in 2001, the malware has infected thousands of machines in more than thirty countries used in fields ranging from nuclear research to mass media.[8] The tool kit used by Equation Group even contains modules to first evaluate whether an infected computer is an intended high-value target.[9]

Stuxnet marked a major milestone in the history of cyberwar, as it was one of the first confirmed attacks to cross the barrier into physical destruction. In some ways, EquationDrug and the other technological advancements achieved by Equation Group represent an even more important development in the history of cyberwar. By infecting the firmware of hard drives in a nearly undetectable fashion, the theoretical vulnerability of all computation has become not only a reality but, at least for states that can afford the initial development, economically viable. The internal NSA technology catalog revealed by *Der Spiegel* lists the unit cost for the use of IrateMonk at zero U.S. dollars (suggesting that the NSA had covered the upfront development costs and would allow internal reuse of the software for free).[10] With this technology, it is now possible for the NSA to intervene directly between computation and computers. Computing has become from this moment on radically and completely ungrounded. Before, a bug or a virus may have disrupted one part or another of a machine or network, inserting a gap between program and output, but now the possibility of this radical alterity between all computation and itself is instantiated in a piece of code that has made its way into thousands of machines.[11] In an infected machine, every piece of data or instruction that is read or written to the hard drive can be observed or manipulated by whoever controls the malware.

In one of the most extreme cases reported by Kaspersky Lab, Equation Group was supposedly able to implant malware onto CDs containing conference proceedings from a scientific conference in Houston, Texas, which were sent to participants afterward. Once the CDs were used in a conference participant's machine, Equation Group's advanced malware was installed.[12] The group seems to target high-value machines, so it is unlikely this was an accidental spread of the malicious software. Rather, it is likely that some of the attendees were explicitly targeted for surveillance or even to control their computers. While there is no way to know if the aims were the former or the latter, we have reached a point where it would be possible for the NSA to manipulate experimental results that were either produced or stored on an infected machine. One could easily imagine the appeal of such an intervention either to maintain national competitiveness in a highly valuable industry or to derail another country's nuclear research program. With this attack, the NSA can now directly intervene in scientific research.

The machines that today manage scientific inquiry and discovery have been infected and subverted, calling into question the repeatability of any computational operation. This is not to say that the machines ran perfectly before, that coding errors or even other viruses could not affect experimental outputs. Rather, the efficacy and danger of EquationDrug is due precisely to it being injected into a gap that predates it and exists immanently in the systems of computation and writing it exploits. Scientific research, law, economics, the state, and even the coherence of the subject rely on algorithmic systems, whose provenance, functioning, code, and connections always come from elsewhere. Thus the Houston attack both comes from outside the scientific machinery it exploits and simultaneously seizes upon an autoimmune violence that always already threatened the system.

We can then grasp, under the conditions of this threat to the computational substratum of the systems and discourses we are enmeshed within, that what determines computation and its social, economic, political, and military effects is not primarily what is commonly understood as mathematics but rather the insecure act of inscription. In the writing down and recording of the inputs, instructions, and outputs of computation, we are constantly exposed to the nonpresence of writing. It is a writing whose networks of nonpresence matter as much as the text itself. Insecure networks connect insecure programs, always deferring the moment of collapse that would arrive from elsewhere to exploit that which lies in the program's deepest depths. The arche-violence of writing moves increasingly deeper into the machines that control more and more of our physical world. As computation and digital communication networks increasingly form the substrate of industries, disciplines, states, communities, and even the conditions of life, this auto-alterity wrought in the trenches of cyberwar risks infecting every discourse and media through which we come to know the world and ourselves. Cyberwar seizes upon the vulnerability of these networks, and in doing so, militarizes writing itself.

THE FORCE OF DECONSTRUCTION

The Houston attack demonstrates the full deconstructive force of cyberwar; all digital logic and reason now arise from a demonstrably insecure origin. As the networks though which these inscriptions travel have grown and the speed with which they move has increased exponentially, the danger of this ineffaceable nonpresence only grows. War becomes increasingly nodal, no longer aimed exclusively at holding territory but instead at controlling and manipulating certain nodes in vast networks of technology, politics, media, and information. The danger that cyberwar discovers in these networks is not new. It is both the danger and promise of writing and language: they always come from the other, from elsewhere, every message arriving from an insecure origin across mutable spaces and times. But cyberwar militarizes this logic and exploits the growing linkages between the vulnerability of writing and massive networks that manage our global systems.

We must be clear: it is not the military, the NSA, or lone hackers who engage in deconstruction. The deconstruction of these systems of discourse, sovereignty, computation, and so on, is as nonpresent as the trace and *différance* that is exploited. The deconstruction that is at stake here is exploited, utilized, instrumentalized, and given over to a certain readability, but its force exists outside of any specific attack. In Lacanian terms, the deconstruction we witness here proceeds along the vector of the real's not writing itself. Every symbolic system, whether it is the symbolic logic of computation or the production of meaning in so-called natural language, precludes mastery, always failing to account for the infinitely complex times and spaces of the real. Deconstruction, then, names the eruption of this real, a tychic moment that overwhelms a symbolic surface, turning it against its own system.

Deconstruction names the auto-matic and autoimmune movement by which a system collapses under the weight of its self-difference. This deconstruction is then an exposure, a vulnerability, to the violence of a destruction that would exploit the inability for the signifier or the program ever to account for the complex networks and environments that produce it. The fact that computation cannot interrogate its own conditions, that programmers include code they did not write or that machines are connected by networks ranging from supply chains to power grids, was never planned by Equation Group. While organizations, such as the NSA, have discovered in this complex ecology means of exploiting these vulnerabilities, the deconstructive force we witness in their actions exists in the very logic of these systems as an arche-violence and arche-writing. The forces of cyberwar, like any text that takes up issues of deconstruction, do not write deconstruction or even perform it; rather, they attest to the deconstructive forces and nonpresence that haunt any inscription.

Even the supposed actors in these attacks risk being swept away by the deconstructive forces they discover, exposed to, as Derrida says, "the fragility of nation-state-sovereignty, to its precariousness, to the principle of ruins that is working it over."[13] Every attack carried out by any organization that understands itself as a sovereign force risks a backfire that would continually work it over, exposing it to the same autodeconstructive tendencies it finds in its enemies' systems. Moreover, for Derrida, what is increasingly lost is even "the concept of *war,* and thus of *world war,* of *enemy* and even *terrorism,* along with the distinction between civilian and military or between army, police and militia."[14] The notion of enmity, of sides, is swept away by this principle of ruins. There is no subject of deconstruction, just a principle of ruins that continually works on the position of any subject. Perhaps, as Kittler suggests, we are witnessing the rise of warfare carried out not between opposing sides but between and within media. War, if we can even maintain the name, now appears as a series of texts, writings, and counterwritings. This does not guarantee that it will become any less violent or traumatic, but still, it fundamentally reshapes its logic. When we cease to know what war is, as it spreads unrestricted into every domain, our only hope is to understand its logic or lack thereof, which today appears as a form of deconstruction.

The Houston attack, in situating itself at the closest point to the read/write head of the hard drives that store the raw data for scientific inquiry, is directly an attack on reading–writing, on the inscribability of the world and knowledge. It is, then, not merely a deconstructive threat to sovereign systems but also a deconstructive threat to deconstruction itself. It brings a machine and a program to bear on deconstruction and insists upon the nonpresent textuality of a machine that has haunted deconstruction from its beginning. Even what Derrida calls the program or the machine is fundamentally a form of writing that touches upon the originary nonpresence of writing and all origins. There is no program that would be a full-knowledge, only an exposure to the vulnerability of writing. Cyberwar calls deconstruction, beyond any hope to limit it to an authored and safe theoretical activity, to account for the machine that it is.

This is not a discovery unknown to Derrida; even in *Of Grammatology,* writing is always in relation to technology. In the grammatology, we are told, "a certain sort of question about the meaning and origin of writing precedes, or at least merges with, a certain type of question about the meaning and origin of technics,"[15] but, under the threat of cyberwar, this "or at least" determines everything. If the question of writing precedes technics, the grammatology tells a different story than if the question of writing merges with the question of the meaning of technics. Technics, especially in its automatic and machinic nature, demonstrates itself to be inseparable from the meaning of writing. As the line between writing that instructs machines and writing that instructs humans blurs, under the conditions of an increasingly noticeable insecurity, the origin and meaning of both merge. Derrida further clarifies what is at stake:

> It is therefore as if what we call language could have been in its origin and in its end only a moment, an essential but determined mode, a phenomenon, an aspect, a species of writing. And as if it had succeeded in making us forget this, and *in willfully misleading us,* only in the course of an adventure: as that adventure itself. All in all a short enough adventure. It merges with the history that has associated technics and logocentric metaphysics for nearly three millennia. And it now seems to be approaching what is really its own *exhaustion.*[16]

What exhausts itself, in the advent of cyberwar, is precisely this association of technics and logocentricism. The affinity between technics and a fully present word slips away with the fantasy of full security. Even reason itself appears vulnerable to the attacks of cyberwar. This short adventure ends with language, the logos, speech returning not as orginary but as a species of writing, a writing that does not precede technics but instead merges with it. In the final analysis, what we call language, and even what we call writing, appears under the threat of cyberwar as a moment in a longer history of the program and the machine. Even so-called natural language appears, especially since Lacan, to elicit the subject's automatic repetition. So, what exhausts itself in cyberwar is precisely the history—or perhaps even history itself, insomuch as history names the logocentric myth of language as a full and present speech that could make a past present—of an alliance between technics and a metaphysics that understands writing as both the fall and remembrance of a once full speech.

In exhausting this alliance between technics and logocentricism, cyberwar threatens, not that programming languages will become analogous to natural language, but the direct opposite: natural language and writing must be understood as species of machinic and technical inscription that simultaneously define the human and point beyond it. This is at once what most threatens deconstruction and simultaneously what guarantees its importance to the future. Derrida reminds us that even deconstruction and the differences and deferments it puts into play are never static and always subjected to the same forces he identifies: "The thematic of *différance* may very well, indeed must, one day be superseded, lending itself if not to its own replacement, at least to enmeshing itself in a chain that in truth it never will have governed."[17] Deconstruction will never have had a security mechanism, something that could guarantee its theoretical fixity and safety. Deconstruction itself is exposed to militarization and mechanization, especially now as it is daily worked over by that principle of ruins that both risks and promises exhausting the primacy of the *logos*.

FUTURE SYSTEMS

The systems we have traced here (writing, geography, cryptography, sovereignty, even Derrida, Malabou, Lacan, etc.) are themselves vulnerable and contingent. What has been termed topology and topography or writing and language are systems that may already be compromised. They have been constructed out of so many unstable digital and physical traces in a method analogous to that used by researchers who may attribute an attack to a purported group by assembling a theory from so many bits of digital forensics. The purpose is not to maintain some stable point for analysis going forward. Still, in utilizing and infiltrating them momentarily, it has hopefully been possible to elucidate the theoretical and political developments unleashed by cyberwar.

These systems of meaning are productive even as they are simultaneously exposed to their own autodeconstruction and the possibility of military subversion. Though these analyses may produce certain results today, it is always possible that at any moment, such systems of analysis will be infected, subverted, accidently broken, or even simply turned off like a server whose proprietor has ceased to pay the electric bill. In tracing the fate of these systems as they are potentially infected by the malicious code of cyberwar, we must always hold open the possibility that their own logic will or already has been turned against them. It is precisely the entropic and contingent fragility of these systems that simultaneously exposes them to their own destruction and holds open the possibility of future systems and future decisions.

Thus, even in the depths of microscopic control and military intervention, there arise entropic possibilities that, while never guaranteeing a happy future, guard against the possibility of complete control and closure. While so often our digital technologies are hailed either as the means of a coming digital utopia or the tools of ever-increasing digital control and destruction, the history of cyberwar suggests, to the contrary, that these technologies, and with them all systems and networks, guarantee that no space can ever become a nonplace of either fixity or closure. Our technologies and networks contain within them a polyvocality of writing, spatiality, temporality, and machinic arrangements within which no subject nor sovereign power can ever completely exert control.

Cybernetics originally intended as a science of control—in both the animal and machine, as Wiener suggested with the subtitle of his famous text—appears at the beginning of the twenty-first century poised to "oust all metaphysical concepts including its own conserving only writing and trace." But it has progressed in such a way, not through its ability to scientifically account for the world, but on the contrary, through the effacement and subversion of science itself. This is the lesson of cyberwar and the growing military attack on our cybernetic systems: the program and the machine were never forces that deconstruction needed to resist or exclude but rather the very force of deconstruction. This machinic deconstruction now appears poised to declare, or continue only to whisper in the most threatening way—like a wind that slowly erodes all that is solid—that the program has never been affiliated with any ontotheology or metaphysics of presence but rather has always threatened to sweep away any belief in security. The necessary insecurity that we continually discover everywhere, and especially in our most rigorous and programmed discourses, repeatedly subverts any and all metaphysics that would claim fixity.

While the real continually fails to write itself in the form of a dangerous deconstruction, the structure of this unceasing failure constitutes the possibility of a system as subject, beyond sovereignty, unconditionally open both to a future and to the creation of new systems. While the real is over and over again inscribed in insecure symbolic systems destined for failure, this very failure is auto-matically repeated. The auto-matic repetition of the program is simultaneously the inscription of a system as meaning and its exposure to the tychic contingency of existence that requires that every system await its always-deferred future. If science holds a future for humanity, it is not in spite of its vulnerability and openness but because of it. This is not to say that these risks or the contingency they promise are not potentially catastrophic. Cyberwar still threatens the destruction of our global life support systems, especially as it is carried out by nuclear-armed powers.

Still, this contingency in the heart of all programs founds a thought beyond all sovereignty, a thought that, as Deleuze says, is always an exposure to the future and the outside of chance; it always upsets systems by "making the past active and present to the outside so that something new will finally come about, so that thinking, always, may reach thought."[18] Likewise for Derrida, "the concept of play keeps itself beyond this opposition, announcing, on the eve of philosophy and beyond it, the unity of chance and necessity in calculations without end."[19] Calculation, always exposed to its chance vulnerability, constantly puts the subject and every system into play. The program and calculation are not opposed to the spontaneity and chance of human language or deconstruction. All language and all writing program the automatic repetitions of systems, including humans and machines. They drone on for centuries following the trail of signifiers, machines, and programs laid down by unknown subjects and machines that went before, but in the midst of this automatic repetition, subjected to dissemination, accident, and vulnerability, these systems think themselves.

Notes

FOREWORD

1   Sigmund Freud, *Introductory Lectures,* trans. James Strachey (New York: W. W. Norton, 1989): 25–26.
2   Sigmund Freud, *The Interpretation of Dreams: The Complete and Definitive Text,* trans. James Strachey (New York: Basic Books, 2010), 78, emphasis added.

INTRODUCTION

1   Thomas Rid, *Cyberwar Will Not Take Place* (Oxford: Oxford University Press, 2013).
2   Eric H. Arnett, "Welcome to Hyperwar," *Bulletin of Atomic Scientists* 48 (1992): 14.
3   James Der Derian, *Anti-diplomacy: Spies, Terror, Speed, and War* (Cambridge: Blackwell, 1992), 175.
4   John Arquilla and David Ronfeldt, *Networks and Netwars: The Future of Terror, Crime, and Militancy* (Santa Monica, Calif.: RAND Corporation, 2001), 14.
5   John Arquilla and David Ronfeldt, "Cyberwar Is Coming!," *Comparative Strategy* 12, no. 2 (1993): 146.
6   Steve Lohr, in a September 30, 1996, *New York Times* article titled "National Security Experts Plan for Wars Whose Targets and Weapons Are All Digital," references a role-playing game carried out the year prior at the Government's National Defense University and begins, "A huge refinery near Dhahran was destroyed by an explosion and fire because of a mysterious malfunction in its computerized controls. A software 'logic bomb' caused a 'new Metro-Superliner' to slam into a misrouted

freight train near Laurel, Md., killing 60 people and critically injuring another 120. The Bank of England found 'sniffer' programs running amok in its electronic funds transfer system. And a 'computer worm' started corrupting files in the Pentagon's top-secret force-deployment data base." Clarke likewise suggests one "imagine a day in the near future" when communications systems fail, air traffic control breaks down, trains derail, and so on. Richard Clarke and Robert Knake, *Cyber War: The Next Threat to National Security and What to Do about It* (New York: Ecco, 2010), 64. Carr, early in his book, imagines a cyberattack in the year "20**" on nuclear infrastructure, which he describes in the form of an imaginary letter written from the director of the National Nuclear Security Agency to the House Permanent Select Committee on Intelligence. Jeffery Carr, *Inside Cyber Warfare*, 2nd ed. (Sebastapol, Calif.: O'Reilly, 2012), 8–9.

7   For example, a July 1, 2010, article in the *Economist* titled "War in the 5th Domain," on cyberwar, begins with this early "logic bomb." Clarke and Knake, *Cyber War,* 92, refer to this event as "one of the first logic bombs, and possibly the first incidence of cyber war."

8   Thomas Reed, *At the Abyss: An Insider's History of the Cold War* (New York: Presidio Press, 2004).

9   Paul Virilio and Sylvère Lotringer, *Pure War* (New York: Semiotext(e), 2008), 68.

10 For example, see Martin Libicki's book *Cyberdeterrence and Cyberwar* (Santa Monica, Calif.: RAND Corporation, 2009), which was written for RAND and attempts to describe how older concepts of war, such as deterrence, can be rethought to make sense of this new form of war.

11 Anatoly Medetsky, "KGB Veteran Denies CIA Caused '82 Blast," *Moscow Times,* March 18, 2004.

12 Thomas Rid, "Think Again: Cyberwar," *Foreign Policy* 192 (2012): 80–84.

13 Peter Elkind, "Sony Pictures: Inside the Hack of a Century," *Fortune,* July 1, 2015.

14 Mark Seal, "An Exclusive Look at Sony's Hacking Saga," *Vanity Fair,* February 28, 2015.

15 Ibid.

16 Reuters, "Sony Probes North Korea Link to Cyber Attack after Threats over Seth Rogen and James Franco Movie," November 30, 2014.

17 Reuters, "North Korea Complains to UN about Film Starring Rogen, Franco," July 9, 2014.

18 Seal, "An Exclusive Look at Sony's Hacking Saga."

19 Barack Obama, "Year-End Press Conference," December 2014, https://www.whitehouse.gov/.

20   Elkind, "Sony Pictures."

21   Kim Zetter, "Experts Are Still Divided over Whether North Korea Is Behind Sony Attack," *Wired,* December 23, 2014; Krypt3ia, "Fauxtribution," December 20, 2014, https://krypt3ia.wordpress.com/. Also, prior to the official announcement attributing the attack to North Korea, most of the evidence had already been leaked to the press by anonymous U.S. intelligence sources. An article in *Wired* responded to the evidence point by point. Kim Zetter, "The Evidence That North Korea Hacked Sony Is Flimsy," *Wired,* December 17, 2014.

22   David Sanger and Martin Fackler, "N.S.A. Breached Networks before Sony Attacks, Experts Say," *New York Times,* January 18, 2015.

23   Issie Lapowsky, "What We Know about the New U.S. Sanctions against North Korea in Response to Sony Hack," *Wired,* January 2, 2015.

24   Jack Kim, "North Korea Blames U.S. for Internet Outages, Calls Obama 'Monkey,'" Reuters, December 28, 2014.

25   Obama, "Year-End Press Conference."

26   Bruce Bennet, quoted in William Boot, "Exclusive: Sony Emails Say State Department Blessed Kim Jong-Un Assassination in 'The Interview,'" *The Daily Beast,* December 17, 2014.

27   Friedrich Kittler, *Gramophone, Film, Typewriter,* trans. Geoffrey Winthrop-Young and Michael Wutz (Stanford, Calif.: Stanford University Press, 1999), xli.

28   Aaron Sorkin, "The Sony Hack and the Yellow Press," *New York Times,* December 14, 2014.

29   Jason Koebler, "Sony Threatens to Sue Twitter Unless It Removes Tweets Containing Hacked Emails," *Vice,* December 22, 2014.

30   Dawn Chmielewski and Arik Hesseldahl, "Sony Pictures Tries to Disrupt Downloads of Its Stolen Files," *Recode,* December 10, 2014.

31   Sanger and Fackler, "N.S.A. Breached Networks before Sony Attacks."

32   Jordan defines social engineering as follows: "Social engineering is the term for techniques that seek to crack open a system by tricking a human into giving out information." Tim Jordan, *Hacking: Digital Media and Technological Determinism,* Kindle ed. (Hoboken, N.J.: John Wiley, 2013), "Cracks in Electronic Walls."

33   Jean Baudrillard, *The Gulf War Did Not Take Place,* trans. Paul Patton (Bloomington: Indiana University Press, 1995), 56.

34   Chris Gray, *Postmodern War: The New Politics of Conflict* (New York: Routledge, 2013), 2.

35   Carr, *Inside Cyber Warfare,* 1, recounts the events of Magomed Yevloev's death in August 2008 as an example of a death in a cyberwar. Yevloev

ran an anti-Kremlin website that was the target of Russian cyberattacks beginning in 2002. Yevloev was apprehended for questioning by police, and one of the officers "accidently" discharged his weapon, killing Yevloev and suggesting both the stakes involved in cyberwar and the possibility of undermining digital infrastructure by attacking its physical and vital components.

36   Clarke, *Cyber War,* 178, states that the Obama doctrine on cyberwar is "one of cyber equivalency, in which cyber attacks are to be judged by their effects, not their means. They would be judged as if they were kinetic attacks, and may be responded to by kinetic attacks, or other means." Such a policy likely discourages attacks but at the price of easing the escalation of such conflicts to kinetic warfare.

37   Alexander Galloway and Eugene Thacker, *The Exploit: A Theory of Networks* (Minneapolis: University of Minnesota Press, 2007), 9.

38   Kittler, *Gramophone, Film, Telephone,* 18–19.

39   Hayles sees in Kittler's statement a risk of reducing everything to a single causal component. N. Katherine Hayles, *My Mother Was a Computer: Digital Subjects and Literary Texts* (Chicago: University of Chicago Press, 2005), 31. However, Kittler's claim is more complicated than a simple reduction if it is read in the context of his claim that we are witnessing wars between media.

40   Jay David Bolter and Richard Grusin, *Remediation: Understanding New Media* (Cambridge, Mass.: MIT Press, 1999); Lev Manovich, *The Language of New Media* (Cambridge, Mass.: MIT Press, 2001).

41   Baudrillard, *The Gulf War Did Not Take Place.*

42   Michael Riley, "We Assume the Bad Thing Has Already Happened," *Bloomberg Business,* June 19, 2015.

43   Bruce Schneier, *On Security* (Indianapolis, Ind.: John Wiley, 2008), vii–viii.

44   Ibid., viii.

45   Jussi Parikka, *Digital Contagions: A Media Archaeology of Computer Viruses* (New York: Peter Lang, 2007), esp. 292–94.

46   Alexander Galloway, "Language Wants to Be Overlooked: On Software and Ideology," *Journal of Visual Culture* 5, no. 3 (2006): 325.

47   Alexander Galloway, "The Poverty of Philosophy: Realism and Post-Fordism," *Critical Inquiry* 39, no. 2 (2013): 358.

48   David Golumbia, *The Cultural Logic of Computation* (Cambridge, Mass.: Harvard University Press, 2009).

49   Manovich, *Language of New Media,* 21–30, insightfully claims that com-

puters are not merely computational devices but also mediatic machines that produce images and other forms of engagement. Still he suggests that what defines digital media is its numerical representation. The advent of cyberwar and its insistence on the inevitability of insecure computation require us to recognize that this numerical representation is simultaneously an insecure inscription.

50   Jacques Derrida, *Of Grammatology,* trans. Gayatri Spivak (Baltimore: Johns Hopkins University Press, 1998), 43.

51   Parikka, *Digital Contagions,* 7.

52   One of the central questions that arises around cyberwar is whether what we are witnessing is fundamentally "new" or merely the digital version of what have long been the conditions of war, namely, the peripheral inclusion of sabotage, deceit, and propaganda. Cyberwar exploits the always vulnerable nature of writing as a technical externalization. Sloterdijk provides a fruitful framework to theorize such historical shifts when he says of gas warfare, "The fact of the living organism's immersion in a breathable milieu arrives at the level of formal representation, bringing the climatic and atmospheric conditions pertaining to human life to a new level of explication. In this movement of explication the principle of design is implicated from the start, since to enable the operational manipulation of gas milieus in open terrain, requires making certain 'atmotechnic' innovations." Peter Sloterdijk, *Terror from the Air,* trans. Amy Patton and Steve Corcoran (Los Angeles: Semiotext(e), 2009), 23. This structure of *explication* suggests that what is brought to light and militarized is simultaneously historical and essential. We have always lived in the air, but the technical innovations involved in this form of warfare make this fact both more directly representable and immediately important. Thus a historical development while providing no fixed origin uncovers and simultaneously changes metaphysics. In this way, while human existence has always been within-writing, cyberwar has, by way of certain "cybertechnic" innovations, militarized and *explicated* this fact, simultaneously altering its underlying metaphysical structure.

53   Alexander Galloway, *Protocol: How Control Exists after Decentralization* (Cambridge, Mass.: MIT Press, 2004), xxliv. Despite this commitment, in the same text, he later claims that the unique nature of computer code "lies not in the fact that code is sublinguistic, but rather in the fact that it is hyperlinguistic. Code is a language, but a very special kind of language. Code is the only language that is executable" (165).

54   Ibid., 165–66.

55 Hayles, *My Mother Was a Computer,* 48.

56 For example, "numpy" is a commonly used library that performs advanced mathematical functions in Python, an extensively used programming language, but parts of the library are written in Fortran, a language originally designed in the 1950s. Though Fortran is still used for many applications, there are likely many users of numpy (myself included) who have never used Fortran nor would have any idea how to understand the Fortran code.

57 Joseph Steinberg, "Massive Internet Security Vulnerability—Here's What You Need to Do," *Forbes,* April 10, 2014, http://www.forbes.com/sites /josephsteinberg/2014/04/10/massive-internet-security-vulnerability -you-are-at-risk-what-you-need-to-do/.

58 Dan Goodin, "Critical Crypto Bug in OpenSSL Opens Two-Thirds of the Web to Eavesdropping," *Ars Technica,* April 17, 2014.

59 Hayles, *My Mother Was a Computer,* 52–53.

60 Kittler, "There Is No Software," *CTheory* 10, no. 18 (1995): 147–55.

61 Cox makes a similar argument, drawing on Judith Butler's work, in claiming that code is analogous to speech and, like speech, is "out of control." Geoff Cox, *Speaking Code: Coding as Aesthetic and Political Expression* (Cambridge, Mass.: MIT Press, 2013), 15.

62 Wendy Hui Kyong Chun, "Crisis, Crisis, Crisis, or Sovereignty and Networks," *Theory, Culture, and Society* 28, no. 6 (2011): 91–112.

63 Some of the earliest programming languages were assembly languages, which used mnemonics both for storage locations and commands. Salomon provides a technical history of these early languages. David Salomon, *Assemblers and Loaders* (West Sussex, U.K.: Ellis Horwood, 1993).

64 Hayles, *My Mother Was a Computer,* 15.

65 Between 1988 and 2012, buffer errors were the most common type of vulnerability in the National Vulnerability Database. Yves Younan, "25 Years of Vulnerabilities: 1988–2012," *Sourcefire,* 2013, https://info.source fire.com/25yearsof_security_vulnerabilities_preregister.html. For an early technical description of buffer overflow vulnerabilities, see Aleph One, "Exploiting the Stack for Fun and Profit," *Phrack* 49 (n.d.), http:// insecure.org/stf/smashstack.html.

66 Hayles, *My Mother Was a Computer,* 47. Moreover, some programming languages are designed to support late-binding (a technique that she discusses later in her book), in which even variable types are dynamically set during execution rather than during compiling.

67 Cox, *Speaking Code.*

68 N. Katherine Hayles, "Print Is Flat, Code Is Deep: The Importance of Media-Specific Analysis," *Poetics Today* 25, no. 1 (2004): 67–90.

69 Hayles's statements about code not being citational may appear initially at odds with her claim that code is deep, but for her this depth is always a local depth (e.g., when the code is running, one is rarely looking at it) and hence not citational in the way "natural language" is. This notion of depth is critical for understanding computer programming, but we must add that, especially given the growth of computer networks, this depth is never exclusively local and always points elsewhere by way of citation.

70 Friedrich Kittler, "There Is No Software," 147–48.

71 Kittler claims at the end of *Gramophone, Film, Typewriter,* 263, that the computer age is bringing about the end of history.

72 Galloway, "Language Wants to Be Overlooked," 321.

73 Kittler, *Gramophone, Film, Typewriter,* xxxix.

74 Gilles Deleuze, *Foucault,* trans. Seán Hand (Minneapolis: University of Minnesota Press, 1988), 132.

75 Gilles Deleuze and Félix Guattari, *A Thousand Plateaus: Capitalism and Schizophrenia,* trans. Brian Massumi (Minneapolis: University of Minnesota Press, 1987), 76.

76 Ibid., 87.

77 See Deleuze and Guattari, "On Several Regimes of Sign," in *A Thousand Plateaus,* 111–48.

78 Rita Raley, "Reveal Codes: Hypertext and Performance," *Postmodern Culture* 12, no. 1 (2001). Raley further argues that despite the impossibility of locating metaphysical difference, we cannot downplay emergent differences. The point is not to overlook these emergent differences; rather, as Raley argues, only through abandoning this quest for metaphysical differences between text and program can we hope to understand the complexities and emergent differences.

79 Bernard Stiegler, *Technics and Time,* vol. 1, *The Fault of Epimetheus,* trans. Richard Beardsworth and George Collins (Stanford, Calif.: Stanford University Press, 1998), 137.

80 Jacques Derrida, "Force of Law: 'The Mystical Foundation of Authority,'" in *Acts of Religion,* ed. Gil Anidjar (New York: Routledge, 2002), 252.

81 Alan Turing, "On Computable Numbers, with an Application to the Entscheidungsproblem," *Proceedings of the London Mathematical Society, Series 2* 42 (1937): 230–65, doi:10.1112/plms/s2-42.1.230.

82   Jacques Derrida, *Rogues,* trans. Pascale-Anne Brault and Michael Naas (Stanford, Calif.: Stanford University Press, 2005), 157.

83   These vulnerable systems are given over to what Derrida calls "hetero-affection," the condition of always being other than oneself. It is our, and all systems', exteriorization in technologies and writing that subjects us to this experience of heteroaffection. Hägglund explains: "autoaffection is always already heteroaffection. If the subject can constitute itself only through inscription, it is dependent on that which is exterior to itself." Martin Hägglund, *Radical Atheism: Derrida and the Time of Life* (Stanford, Calif.: Stanford University Press, 2008), 71.

84   Kittler, *Gramophone, Film, Typewriter,* 17.

85   Alexander Galloway, *The Interface Effect* (Cambridge: Polity, 2012), 20.

86   Jacques Derrida, *Margins of Philosophy,* trans. Alan Bass (Chicago: University of Chicago Press, 1982), 23.

87   Ronell demonstrates how this logic is operative with the telephone, showing that prior to the Internet, communication technology is an implement of both survival and risk. Avital Ronell, *The Telephone Book: Technology—Schizophrenia—Electric Speech* (Lincoln: University of Nebraska Press, 1989), 350–51.

88   Wendy Hui Kyong Chun, "On Software, or the Persistence of Visual Knowledge," *Grey Room* 18 (2004): 26–51.

89   Galloway, "Language Wants to Be Overlooked," 327.

1. BUFFER OVERFLOW

1   Manuel Castells, *The Rise of the Network Society,* 2nd ed. (Chichester, U.K.: Wiley-Blackwell, 2010).

2   Gregory Vistica, "We're in the Middle of a Cyberwar," *Newsweek,* September 20, 1999.

3   This does not seem ever to have been the prevailing theory, but Drogin suggests in his article for the *LA Times* on Moonlight Maze that some unnamed experts believed it to be the case. Bob Drogin, "Yearlong Hacker Attack Nets Sensitive U.S. Data," *Los Angeles Times,* October 7, 1999.

4   For a schematic overview of state-based actions, see Kim Zetter, "We're at Cyberwar: A Global Guide to Nation-State Digital Attacks," *Wired,* September 1, 2015.

5   Drogin, "Yearlong Hacker Attack."

6   For instance, within days of Kaspersky Lab revealing an advanced espio-

nage program, named "Red October," aimed at diplomatic, governmental, and scientific information, which had been operating for five years undetected, the entire operation was shut down. Lorenzo Franceschi-Bicchierai, "Mystery Online Theft Operation 'Red October' Is Winding Down, *Mashable,* January 17, 2013.

7   Paul Boutin, "Slammed!," *Wired,* July 1, 2003.

8   Microsoft's security bulletin announcing the patch is available online at http://technet.microsoft.com/en-us/security/bulletin/ms02-039.

9   Paul Virilio, *The Information Bomb,* trans. Chris Turner (New York: Verso, 2000), 9.

10 Often the instantaneity of these networks and texts is stressed. For example, Poster suggests that to understand the relationship between "computer writing" and deconstruction, it is imperative to stress that this writing, "instantaneously available over globe, inserts itself in a nonlinear temporality that unsettles the relation to the writing subject." Mark Poster, *The Mode of Information: Poststructuralism and Social Context* (Chicago: University of Chicago Press, 1990), 128. Or geography is made secondary to temporality; Der Derian, following Virilio's insistence on the rise of chronopolitics over geopolitics, argues that within the frame of cyberwar, "the construction and destruction of the enemy other would be measured in time not territory." Der Derian, *Anti-diplomacy,* 182. It is critical to recognize the multiple speeds and spatialities that constitute even networked digital spaces, especially in relation to deconstruction and the spacing and deferment of writing.

11 Castells, *Rise of the Network Society.*

12 Ibid., 417.

13 Paul Virilio, *Strategy of Deception,* trans. Chris Turner (London: Verso, 2000), 31.

14 Bruno Latour, "On Actor-Network Theory: A Few Clarifications," *Soziale Welt* 47, no. 4 (1996): 371.

15 Both Galloway's book *Protocol* and his book with Thacker, *The Exploit,* are books about the ascendancy of network forms of organization. For a general description of the logic of networks by a proponent of theorizing a wide variety of phenomena as networks, see Albert-László Barabási, *Linked: The New Science of Networks* (New York: Basic Books, 2014). Moreover, even Latour's actor network theory speaks to the allure of networks as a contemporary mode of analysis. Bruno Latour, *Reassembling the Social: An Introduction to Actor-Network-Theory* (Oxford: Oxford University Press, 2005).

16   John Hamre, as quoted in "Newsweek Exclusive: 'We're in the Middle of a Cyberwar,'" *Newsweek,* September 12, 1999.

17   The *New York Times* and the BBC first used the term *cyberwar* to describe the events in Estonia (the BBC had used the term but never in relation to a real conflict). Likewise, *Wired* referred to the conflict as "Web War One." Cyrus Farivar, "A Brief Examination of Media Coverage of Cyber Attacks: 2007–Present," in *The Virtual Battlefield: Perspectives on Cyber Warfare—Proceedings 2009* (Tallinn: NATO Cooperative Cyber Defence Centre of Excellence, 2009), https://ccdcoe.org/.

18   BBC, "Tallinn Tense after Deadly Riots," April 28, 2007.

19   Michael Lesk, "The New Front Line: Estonia under Cyberassault," *IEEE Security and Privacy* 5, no. 4 (2007): 76–79; *Daily Mail,* "Russia 'Launches Cyberwar' on Estonia," May 17, 2007.

20   Lesk, "New Front Line"; Joshua Davis, "Hackers Take Down the Most Wired Country in Europe," *Wired,* August 21, 2007.

21   Clarke and Knake, *Cyber War,* 14–16.

22   Ibid.

23   Davis, "Hackers Take Down the Most Wired."

24   Scheherazade Rehman, "Estonia's Lessons in Cyberwarfare," *US News and World Report,* January 14, 2013.

25   John Markoff, "Before the Gunfire, Cyberattacks," *New York Times,* August 12, 2008; Clarke and Knake, *Cyber War,* 17–21.

26   Erich Follath and Holger Stark, "The Story of Operation Orchard," *Der Spiegel,* November 2, 2009.

27   Sally Adee, "The Hunt for the Kill Switch," *IEEE Spectrum,* May 1, 2008.

28   Ibid.

29   While it is unclear the full extent to which there was malicious intent involved, a recent report has suggested that Chinese-made military chips contain a possible back door. Bruce Schneier, "Backdoor Found (Maybe) in Chinese-Made Military Silicon Chips," *Schneier on Security* (blog), May 2015, https://www.schneier.com/.

30   Clarke and Knake, *Cyber War,* 5.

31   In his May 9, 1950, declaration, Robert Schuman, French foreign minister, proposed a unified coal and steel market, suggesting, "The solidarity in production thus established will make it plain that any war between France and Germany becomes not merely unthinkable, but materially impossible." Schuman, "The Schuman Declaration," May 9, 1950, http://europa.eu/.

32   It is along these lines that Galloway and Thacker, *Exploit,* 5, suggest "that

the juncture between sovereignty and networks is the place where the apparent contradictions in which we live can best be understood." It is precisely at these nodal sites that sovereign force intervenes in networks and is simultaneously shaped by these network structures.

33 Virilio, *Strategy of Deception,* 37.

34 Brian Krebs, "Experts Warn of New Windows Shortcut," *Krebs on Security,* July 2010, http://krebsonsecurity.com/. The initial reports claimed that the target was a Siemens SCADA (supervisory control and data acquisition), but later analysis suggested that the ultimate targets were two different Siemens PLCs (Programmable Logic Controllers).

35 David Albright, Paul Brannan, and Christina Walrond, "Did Stuxnet Take Out 1,000 Centrifuges at the Natanz Enrichment Plant?," *ISIS Report,* December 22, 2010, http://isis-online.org/.

36 Kim Zetter, "Blockbuster Worm Aimed for Infrastructure, but No Proof Iran Nukes Were Target," *Wired,* September 23, 2010. A person-month is the amount of work one programmer can do in a month.

37 David Sanger, "Obama Order Sped Up Wave of Cyberattacks against Iran," *New York Times,* June 1, 2012.

38 Joseph Menn, "Exclusive: U.S. Tried Stuxnet-Style Campaign against North Korea but Failed," Reuters, May 29, 2015.

39 Joseph F. Nye, "Cyber War and Peace," *Project Syndicate,* April 10, 2012, http://www.project-syndicate.org/.

40 Derek Gregory, "The Everywhere War," *The Geographical Journal* 177, no. 3 (2011): 238–50.

41 Castells, *Rise of the Network Society,* along with Boltanski and Chiapello, provides an excellent framework for understanding the geography and ideology of networked global capitalism as it vacillates between and exploits the difference between connected and disconnected spaces and individuals. Luc Boltanski and Eve Chiapello, *The New Spirit of Capitalism,* trans. Gregory Elliott (London: Verso, 2007).

42 BBC, "US 'Launched Flame Cyber Attack on Sarkozy's Office,'" November 21, 2012.

43 Chamayou contends that drone warfare does away with the territorial enclosure of sovereignty and instead is founded on a "hunter state" with the right to pursue "dangerous prey" on others' land. Moreover, the addition of this "aeropolitical" domain to territorial sovereignty means that the rules of engagement become three-dimensional and vary neighborhood to neighborhood. Grégoire Chamayou, *Drone Theory* (London: Penguin, 2015), 52–59. These forms of power and military violence thus

operate and reshape these networks of geography, territory, law, and so on, as they seek out nodes in various networks.

44 Virilio, *Strategy of Deception,* 24.

45 For example, see the Electronic Frontier Foundation's article about the ramifications for intellectual property law as a result of the proposed Trans-Pacific Partnership Agreement. Electronic Frontier Foundation, "Trans Pacific Partnership Agreement," https://www.eff.org/issues/tpp.

46 Reuters, "Cyber Attack Appears to Target Iran-Tech Firms," September 24, 2010.

47 Deleuze and Guattari, *A Thousand Plateaus,* 381.

48 Katharina Ziolkowski, "Stuxnet—Legal Considerations," *NATO CCD COE Publications* (2012), 25.

49 Mandiant, "APT1: Exposing One of China's Cyber Espionage Units," *Mandiant Reports,* February 2013, 2.

50 Jeffrey Carr, "More on Mandiant's APT1 Report: Guilt by Proximity and Wright Patterson AFB," *Digital Dao* (blog), February 22, 2013, http://jeffreycarr.blogspot.com/.

51 While Galloway's argument focuses more on power than geography per se, this is essentially the central thesis of *Protocol*: networks are not completely horizontal, immediate fluid structures but rather combine hierarchical and diffuse forms of control. Networks function by distributing power to local authorities, not by eliminating organization altogether. Likewise, in spatial terms, networks tend not to be structures of complete connection but rather produce clustered, preferential, and robust connection patterns.

52 Bruno Latour, "Some Experiments in Art and Politics," *e-flux,* 2011.

53 Adam Jourdan, "China–U.S. Cyber Spying Now Turns Spotlight Back on Shadowy Unit 61398," Reuters, May 20, 2014.

54 Galloway and Thacker, *Exploit,* 11.

55 Galloway, *Interface Effect,* 99.

56 For instance, Jason Healey, "The Spectrum of National Responsibility for Cyberattacks," *Brown Journal of World Affairs* 18 (2011): 57: "To rein in attacks raging across the Internet, the international security community must focus on the needs of policy makers, which is best served by looking to the responsibility of nations. Too much time has been wasted obsessing over which particular villain pressed the ENTER key."

57 Despite Healey's support for such an idea, he admits, "The United States in particular will find itself in a difficult position: it is the country targeted by 65 percent of all denial-of-service attacks (floods of traffic that

disrupt normal operations of computers or networks)—the most of any country. The United States is also the top source for attacks, accounting for 22 percent of the global total." Ibid., 67.

58 Jeremy Rabkin and Ariel Rabkin, "To Confront Cyber Threats, We Must Rethink the Law of Armed Conflict," 10, http://www.hoover.org /research/emerging-threatsto-confront-cyber-threats-we-must-rethink -law-armed-conflict.

59 Deleuze and Guattari, *A Thousand Plateaus,* 387.

60 See *The Economist,* "War in the 5th Domain," July 1, 2010.

61 BBC, "US Military Train in Cyber-City to Prepare Hack Defence," November 28, 2012, http://www.bbc.com/news/technology-20525545.

62 Robert O'Harrow Jr., "CyberCity Allows Government Hackers to Train for Attacks," *Washington Post,* November 26, 2012.

63 Deleuze and Guattari, *A Thousand Plateaus,* 467.

64 *Information Week,* "Anti-U.S. Hackers Infiltrate Army Servers," May 28, 2009.

65 Younan, "25 Years of Vulnerabilities," 2013.

66 For more on injection attacks, see Ponemon Institute, "The SQL Injection Threat Study," April 2014, http://www.dbnetworks.com/.

67 This is rarely how such a program would be structured and is highly insecure, but it illustrates how an injection attack functions.

68 Richard Szafranski, "Neocortical Warfare? The Acme of Skill," *Military Review,* November 1994, 43.

69 Qiao Liang and Wang Xiangsui, *Unrestricted Warfare,* trans. Foreign Broadcast Information Service (Beijing: PLA Literature and Arts, 1999), 41.

70 This inversion is the same one that Foucault explores at length and traces the history of in his *Society Must Be Defended: Lectures at the Collège de France, 1975–76,* ed. Mauro Bertani, Alessandro Fontana, and David Macey (New York: Picador, 2003). R. L. DiNardo and D. J. Hughes, "Some Cautionary Thoughts on Information Warfare," *Airpower Journal* 9, no. 4 (1995).

71 Chun, "On Software."

72 Charles Dunlap, "Law and Military Interventions: Preserving Humanitarian Values in 21st Conflicts," paper presented at the Humanitarian Challenges in Military Intervention Conference, Washington, D.C., November 29, 2001.

73 Virilio, *Strategy of Deception,* 76.

74 Ibid., 15.

75   Virilio and Lotringer, *Pure War,* 227.
76   Boltanski and Chiapello, *New Spirit of Capitalism.*

2. INJECTION ATTACK

1   James Adams, "Virtual Defense," *Foreign Affairs,* May/June 2001.
2   For example, John Hamre, deputy secretary of defense from 1997 to 1999, referenced the exercise multiple times in a 2003 PBS interview. Hamre, "Interview," PBS, April 24, 2003, http://www.pbs.org/.
3   John Arquilla, "Interview John Arquilla," PBS, March 4, 2003, http://www.pbs.org/.
4   For an overview of the CIA triad as a model for security, see Mark Merkow and Jim Breithaupt, *Information Security: Principles and Practices,* 2nd ed. (Indianapolis, Ind.: Pearson, 2014).
5   Riley, "We Assume the Bad Thing."
6   Parikka, *Digital Contagions,* 1.
7   Paul K. Saint-Amour, "Bombing and the Symptom: Traumatic Earliness and the Nuclear Uncanny," *Diacritics* 30, no. 4 (2000): 64.
8   Parikka, *Digital Contagions,* 294.
9   Hägglund, *Radical Atheism,* 75.
10   Jacques Derrida, "No Apocalypse, Not Now: Full Speed Ahead, Seven Missiles, Seven Missives," *Diacritics* 14, no. 2 (1984): 27.
11   Hägglund, *Radical Atheism,* 45, suggests that Derrida's comments on nuclear catastrophe are not limited to the historical epoch of the Cold War but rather invoke the radical finitude of all life and hence the deconstructability of all symbolic systems.
12   Derrida, *Of Grammatology,* 24.
13   Kamuf suggests, "Deconstruction inhabits, in a certain way. It is within structures that it shakes up and deconstructs from inside, a certain inside, which nevertheless opens to some outside. Deconstruction is a way of inhabiting structures that turns them inside out or upside down." Peggy Kamuf, "A Certain Way of Inhabiting," in *Reading Derrida's "Of Grammatology,"* ed. Sean Gaston and Ian Maclachlan (New York: Continuum, 2011), 36.
14   Derrida, *Of Grammatology,* 158.
15   Raley, in regard to the Web, states, "Without a complete systems crash, hypertext by its very nature cannot come to rest." Raley, "Reveal Codes," para. 31. Programs and hypertext always defer their meaning. It is only

in catastrophe, after the complete destruction of these dynamic systems, that we could ever say conclusively what they were.

16   "A History of Windows," http://windows.microsoft.com/.

17   For a more detailed historical account of Maturana and Varela's theories, see N. Katherine Hayles, *How We Became Posthuman: Virtual Bodies in Cybernetics and Literature* (Chicago: University of Chicago Press, 1999), 131–59.

18   Humberto Maturana and Francisco Varela, *Autopoiesis and Cognition: The Realization of the Living* (Dordrecht, Netherlands: D. Reidel, 1980), 89–90.

19   Jacques Derrida, "Plato's Pharmacy," in *Dissemination,* trans. Barbara Johnson (Chicago: University of Chicago Press, 1981), 63.

20   Derrida, *Of Grammatology,* 288.

21   Jacques Derrida, "Letter to a Japanese Friend," in *Derrida and Différance,* ed. David Wood and Robert Bernasconi (Evanston, Ill.: Northwestern University Press, 1988), 3.

22   Gasché states that deconstruction "cannot be mistaken for anything resembling scientific procedural rules." Rodolphe Gasché, *The Tain of the Mirror: Derrida and the Philosophy of Reflection* (Cambridge, Mass.: Harvard University Press, 1986), 123. Although, in another essay, he is much more willing to describe it as a method: "Deconstruction which for many has come to designate the content and style of Derrida's thinking, reveals to even a superficial examination, a well-ordered procedure, a step-by-step type of argumentation." Gasché, "Infrastructures and Systematicity," in *Deconstruction and Philosophy,* ed. John Sallis (Chicago: University of Chicago Press, 1987), 3. In this later essay, Gasché responds to the suggestion that deconstruction provides free license for any interpretation of a text. Thus we can see in these two statements how carefully deconstruction is shielded from discourses that would, on one hand, make it too programmatic and, on the other, make it too pliable. Although of course it is important to maintain the philosophical rigor of terms, one can see how, between these two sentiments, deconstruction is carefully secured from spiraling out of control.

   Marrati, in speaking of "the risk of turning deconstruction into a formal and empty structure," even attempts to excise Derrida's own programmatic uses of deconstruction, stating, "Although it is true that an impulse toward just such a formalism, far from being simply the product of a certain 'Derrida-ism,' can also be found in the work of Derrida himself, who also falls prey on occasion to the allure of method, this is far from being of a piece with Derrida's project as a whole or from corresponding to his most fundamental insights (at least insofar as one can speak in such terms regarding a thinking of contamination)." Paola Marrati, *Genesis and Trace: Derrida Reading Husserl and Heidegger* (Stanford, Calif.: Stanford University Press, 2005), 181.

23   Derrida, *Of Grammatology,* 14.

24   Poster argues that Derrida's descriptions of "electronic writing" and its relationship to deconstruction are "general, contradictory, hesitant and unclear," but he goes on to suggest that this troubled relationship with electronic writing mirrors Derrida's concern for the danger inherent in deconstruction itself. Poster, *Mode of Information,* 104–5. Strathausen similarly notes that for Derrida, electronic media serve "as a generic and conceptually underdeveloped counterfoil for an ever more refined understanding of writing and (linguistic) performativity." Carsten Strathausen, "The Philosopher's Body: Derrida and Teletechnology," *CR: The New Centennial Review* 9, no. 2 (2009): 142.

25   Both Stiegler and Christopher Johnson have stressed this technical and machinic nature of writing in their readings of Derrida, especially Derrida's reading of Leroi-Gourhan. Stiegler, *Technics and Time,* vol. 1; Christopher Johnson, "Derrida: The Machine and the Animal," *Paragraph* 28, no. 3 (2005): 102–20.

26   Jacques Derrida, "Ulysses Gramophone: Hear Say Yes in Joyce," trans. François Raffoul, in *Derrida and Joyce: Texts and Contexts,* ed. Andrew Mitchell and Sam Slote (Albany: State University of New York Press, 2013), 70.

27   Ibid., 80.

28   Jacques Derrida, "The Time of a Thesis: Punctuations," trans. Kathleen McLaughlin, in *Philosophy in France Today,* ed. Alan Montefiore (Cambridge: Cambridge University Press, 1983), 40. Derrida here does not specifically name deconstruction but rather refers to what he was trying to "work out" in the three texts published in 1967.

29   Jacques Derrida, *Writing and Difference,* trans. Alan Bass (Chicago: University of Chicago Press, 1978), 226.

30   Maratti, *Genesis and Trace,* argues that Derrida's thought is fundamentally a question of different contaminations, the transcendental and the empirical, the finite and the infinite, life and death, and so on. And Derrida, in speaking of animals, hints that the contamination of writing by animals and machines has always been central to his work: "This animal-machine has a family resemblance with the virus that obsesses, not to say invades

everything I write. Neither animal nor nonanimal, organic or inorganic, living or dead, this potential invader is *like* a computer virus. It is lodged in a processor of writing, reading and interpretation." Jacques Derrida, "The Animal That Therefore I Am (More to Follow)," trans. David Wills, *Critical Inquiry* 28, no. 2 (2002): 407. Christopher Johnson, "Derrida," 104, says of this "italicized *like*, . . . that the virus is a metaphor but also perhaps more than a metaphor." Perhaps, then, all of deconstruction has been a question of this contamination between "natural" languages and programs, of the machine and the human (and the animal somewhere between them). Thus programmatic writing has never been ignored in deconstruction, but rather its very centrality means that the futures of cyberwar, viruses, computer writing, and deconstruction are intimately tied together.

31 Derrida, "Ulysses Gramophone," 61.

32 Ibid., 79.

33 Stiegler, *Technics and Time,* 1:257.

34 Derrida, *Of Grammatology,* 218. The French reads: "On ne pourra distinguer la question de classification morphologique des langues, qui tient compte des effets du besoin sur la forme de la langue, et la question du lieu d'origine de la langue, la typologie et la topologie."

35 Topology can define a space as having a metric for measuring distance, but it is not necessary for topological space.

36 Ibid., 251. The French reads: "On ne peut donc décrire la structure ou l'essence générale de la langue sans tenir compte de la topographie."

37 Ibid.

38 Hägglund, *Radical Atheism,* 75.

39 Catherine Malabou, *Plasticity at the Dusk of Writing: Dialectic, Destruction, Deconstruction,* trans. Carolyn Shread (New York: Columbia University Press, 2010), 53–54.

40 Ibid., 47.

41 Derrida, *Of Grammatology,* 314.

42 Ibid., 99.

43 Critchley provides an excellent overview of the question of closure in two parts. Simon Critchley, "The Problem of Closure in Derrida [Part One]," *Journal of the British Society for Phenomenology* 23, no. 1 (1992): 3–19; Critchley, "The Problem of Closure in Derrida [Part Two]," *Journal of the British Society for Phenomenology* 23, no. 2 (1992): 127–45. He stresses the double meaning of this term, first explicating its spatial meaning as enclosure (part I) and then explaining its temporal meaning as the

process of bringing an epoch to an end (part II). In regard to the spatial sense, Critchley demonstrates that this closure is not the encircling of a homogenous field but is rather, in Derrida's words, a "twisted [*retorse*] structure" (I:14). As a result, the space of the metaphysical closure both permits transgressions and recuperates them within metaphysics, a double gesture that makes of transgression a restoration of metaphysics (I:13). It is then the trace that shows the gap in the closure of the logocentric space (I:14–15) or, as Derrida says in *Of Grammatology*, "designate[s] the crevice through which the yet unnameable glimmer beyond the closure [*l'outre-clôture*] can be glimpsed" (14). Thus Derrida does not mean simply a completely closed-off and inescapable space. Still, this concept of closure, especially one that recuperates transgressions, even if a cracked and contorted closure, suggests a monolithic space that is the singular place of a unifying metaphysics rather than a heterogeneous field of multiple spatialities and multiple metaphysics. Thus to speak of "the language of metaphysics" as that which must be used to critique metaphysics (I:12) undervalues the importance of topology, as the connection between words and texts, in language. If one approaches language from the space of topology, it is the combination of words and their colocation that are important rather than exclusively the reuse of a given word or concept. It is the specific spacing and inscription of a text that comes to matter rather than a unified space of metaphysics.

The temporal nature of closure provides an even stronger case for understanding this closure as an attempted homogenization. Critchley argues that the temporal notion of the closure of metaphysics should not be understood as a critique of Heidegger's claims of the end of philosophy but rather as a corrective to those who would read in Heidegger's terminology a notion of this end as a completion (II:128–29). For Heidegger, this closure does not mark the completion of metaphysics; rather, it marks the exhaustion of metaphysics as philosophy and the commencement of metaphysics as the goal of the sciences. In this way, "metaphysics dissolves into the empirical and technologized sciences," which "continue the metaphysical project and carry it forward to its ultimate and total global domination" (II:128). Thus metaphysics appears as a machine in the grammatology, because the book of metaphysics has been closed, and now an infernal machine carries out what has been written there. We have not reached the end of metaphysics, for we live among its machines, but rather its closure as philosophy. We can detect, then, in such a temporal closure a resistance to the possibility that technoscience, the machine, or the program could rewrite or reconfigure metaphysics. Temporally, the closure of metaphysics unifies even more strongly than spatial closure. The operating system of metaphysics is presented to us as already completely secure and written; it is now merely being executed. No program can threaten its execution; it can only offer to reify its singular and securitized logic. While the trace and deconstruction point to a "glimmer beyond the closure," the securitization of this closure to a singular metaphysics and single contorted space risks overstating the spatial and temporal coherence of the metaphysical system and narrowing deconstruction to a singular meaning, space, and time.

44   It should be noted that in Derrida's later work, this closure begins to open up, even in relationship to the program. Along the lines of this later opening of the program's closure and the computer's hypermnesic interiorization, it is of the utmost importance to stress the impossibility of this closure in relation to Derrida's earlier writings about metaphysical closure.

45   Deleuze and Guattari, *A Thousand Plateaus,* 352.

46   Though Derrida talks at length about oppositions and their deconstruction, he never refers to these oppositions as "binary" in *Of Grammatology.* Derrida does refer occasionally to binary oppositions directly, such as in the afterword to *Limited Inc.,* where he discusses "the conditions of this classical and binary logic." Jacques Derrida, *Limited Inc.,* trans. Samuel Weber (Evanston, Ill.: Northwestern University Press, 1988), 117. And in the preface to *Dissemination,* he refers to "a finite culture of binary oppositions" (25), but it is here for Derrida not a question of deconstructing binaries from within but rather always a process of taking "on the figure of a totally different partition" (25). In his later text "Ulysses Gramophone," this binary relationship becomes in itself impossible: "It is not just binarity, but also and for the same reason totalization, which proves impossible" (80). Though one should take care not to read too much into this impossibility, because Derrida also tells us that deconstruction itself is the impossible. Jacques Derrida, "The Future of the Profession or the University without Condition (Thanks to the 'Humanities,' What Could Take Place Tomorrow)," in *Without Alibi,* trans. Peggy Kamuf (Stanford, Calif.: Stanford University Press, 2002), 54. This complex relation to binarity suggests that deconstruction is not so far from the war machine, but still the language of the war machine is helpful as it allows us to draw out the machinic and bellicose elements that are latent in deconstruction.

47   Smith suggests the major difference between Deleuze and Derrida in their relation to metaphysics: "Put crudely, then, if Derrida sets out to undo metaphysics, Deleuze sets out simply to *do* metaphysics." Daniel Smith, "Deleuze and Derrida: Immanence and Transcendence," in *Between Deleuze and Derrida,* ed. Paul Patton and John Protevi (London: Continuum, 2003), 50. For Deleuze, metaphysics is significantly more open and pliable. Thus the possible forces that can overcome binaries are more substantial and numerous in Deleuze than in Derrida. Smith further says, "This is why one does not find, in Deleuze, any general pronouncements concerning the 'nature' of 'Western metaphysics' (as 'logocentric,' or as a 'metaphysics of presence'), since, as Derrida notes, the only position from which one could make such a pronouncement is a position of transcendence, which Deleuze rejects. Consequently, there is no concept of closure in Deleuze (since closure likewise depends on transcendence)." Ibid.

48   Though Derrida does not use the term *binary,* this description of deconstruction is largely the one that he offers in *Positions,* where he describes it as a double gesture that first overturns the oppositional hierarchy and then places the distinction between the two terms under erasure. Jacques Derrida, Alan Bass, and Henri Ronse, *Positions* (Chicago: University of Chicago Press, 1981), 41–42.

49   Deleuze and Guattari, *A Thousand Plateaus,* 421.

50   See Tor Project, "Tor: Overview," https://www.torproject.org/about /overview.

51   Cheney-Lippold describes and explains the ways in which these systems function algorithmically to create and understand identity based on these data. John Cheney-Lippold, "A New Algorithmic Identity: Soft Biopolitics and the Modulation of Control," *Theory, Culture, and Society* 28, no. 6 (2011): 164–81.

52   Whitfield Diffie and Susan Eva Landau, *Privacy on the Line: The Politics of Wiretapping and Encryption* (Cambridge, Mass.: MIT Press, 2007), 273.

53   Andy Greenberg, *This Machine Kills Secrets: How WikiLeakers, Cypherpunks, and Hacktivists Aim to Free the World's Information* (New York: Dutton, 2012), 149.

54   Norbert Wiener, *Cybernetics: or, Control and Communication in the Animal and the Machine,* 2nd ed. (New York: MIT Press, 1961), 5.

55   Galison argues that Wiener's work and the larger project of cybernetics originating in this antiaircraft gun produced an explicitly ontological

conception of both the enemy and the antiaircraft gunner that completely blurred the line between human and machine. Peter Galison, "The Ontology of the Enemy," *Critical Inquiry* 21, no. 1 (1994): 228–66.

56 Galloway and Thacker, *Exploit,* 70.

57 McKenzie Wark, *A Hacker Manifesto* (Cambridge, Mass.: Harvard University Press, 2004), 158. Galloway, in *Protocol,* suggests something similar, arguing that hackers are subjects of historical processes rather than what causes this process: "hacking is an index of protocological transformations taking place in the broader world of techno-culture. Hackers do not forecast the death (or avoidance or ignorance) of protocol, but are instead the very harbingers of its assumption" (157).

58 Barad suggests something similar in her book on quantum mechanics, where she argues that the measuring apparatus produces both the subject and the measured phenomenon or object. Karen Barad, *Meeting the Universe Halfway: Quantum Physics and the Entanglement of Matter and Meaning* (Durham, N.C.: Duke University Press, 2007).

59 Derrida, "Force of Law," 253.

60 Derrida, "Letter to a Japanese Friend."

61 Derrida, *Of Grammatology,* 111–12. Grosz explains the complex relationship between arche-violence, writing, law, and the colloquial concept of war. Elizabeth Grosz, "The Time of Violence: Deconstruction, and War," *Cultural Values* 2, no. 2–3 (1998): 190–205.

62 Derrida, *Of Grammatology,* 71.

63 Deleuze, *Foucault,* 86.

64 Ibid., 118–19.

65 Ibid., 123.

66 Derrida, *Of Grammatology,* 215.

67 Ibid., 46.

68 Derrida, *Positions,* 41–42.

69 Gaston argues that deconstruction tends to operate by adding additional terms: dissemination adds a third term to metaphysical binaries and a fourth to the triangle of dialectic synthesis. Sean Gaston, *The Impossible Mourning of Jacques Derrida* (London: Continuum, 2006), 17–18.

70 Gasché, *Tain of the Mirror,* 277, suggests the relationship between writing-in-general and arche-writing in its full specificity: "Inscription in general is therefore to be considered as the specificity, so to speak, of the clustered synthesis of arche-writing."

71 Derrida, *Of Grammatology,* 44.

72 Ibid., 36.

73 Gasché explains in *Tain of the Mirror* that the system involves three terms—writing, speech, and the structure of their relationship (writing-in-general or arche-writing): "It is not writing itself that is at issue here but the system of relations that link it to speech. It is this system that Derrida names general writing. If Derrida persists in calling this system writing, although writing in the vulgar sense is its dissimulation in the form of a metaphor, it is because, he admits, arche-writing essentially communicates with the vulgar concept of writing, insofar as, historically speaking, writing has signified by its situation 'the most formidable difference' from speech" (275).

74 Derrida, *Of Grammatology*, 112.

75 Hägglund, *Radical Atheism*, 49, says it is "with arche-writing that life itself will have begun." Stiegler likewise argues that this "arche-structure" produces history as technics by the very exteriorization of memory through prostheses. See his *Technics and Time*, esp. 1:183–84.

76 Derrida, *Of Grammatology*, 57.

77 Marrati, *Genesis and Trace*, 77–78, states, "The primordial supplement designates the non-fullness of presence, its being subject, 'from the origin,' to division and to delay; however, it also designates a function of primordial supplementary the structure of an 'in-the-place-of' that, while characterizing the sign in general, is not, as Husserl and an entire philosophical tradition would wish, limited to the field of signification alone." The logic of the supplement creates multiple spatialities through division and deferment, and the structure of this "in-the-place-of" folds these multiple spaces into each other.

78 Derrida, "Plato's Pharmacy," 109.

79 Ibid., 130.

80 Derrida, *Dissemination*, 25.

81 Catherine Malabou, *The New Wounded: From Neurosis to Brain Damage*, trans. Steven Miller (New York: Fordham University Press, 2012), 17.

82 Catherine Malabou, *Ontology of the Accident: An Essay on Destructive Plasticity*, trans. Carolyn Shread (Cambridge: Polity Press, 2012), 17.

83 Malabou, *Plasticity at the Dusk of Writing*, 45.

84 Ibid., 51.

85 Derrida, *Of Grammatology*, 24.

86 Catherine Malabou, *The Future of Hegel: Plasticity, Temporality, and Dialectic*, trans. Lisabeth During (New York: Routledge, 2004), 162.

87 Deleuze, *Foucault*, 117.

88 Malabou, *Plasticity at the Dusk of Writing*, 10.

89 Malabou, *Ontology of the Accident,* 10.

90 Malabou, *Plasticity at the Dusk of Writing,* 59.

91 For a more in-depth history and explanation, see Steven Levy, *Crypto: How the Code Rebels Beat the Government, Saving Privacy in the Digital Age* (London: Penguin, 2001).

92 RSA is one of the main public-key cryptographic systems used today, and it is based on multiplying two very large prime numbers together. Breaking the system requires factoring the result of this multiplication, which is possible but requires such a significant amount of computation time that it is, for the time being, infeasible.

93 Schneier provides an example of a man-in-the-middle attack in nondigital communication and explains the application of this vulnerability to digital systems. Bruce Schneier, "Man-in-the-Middle Attacks," *Schneier on Security* (blog), July 2008, https://www.schneier.com/.

94 Joseph Menn, "Key Internet Operator VeriSign Hit by Hackers," Reuters, February 2, 2012.

95 Friedrich Kittler, "No Such Agency," trans. Paul Feigelfeld, *Theory, Culture, and Society* (blog), February 12, 2014.

96 Gasché, *Tain of the Mirror,* 118.

97 Derrida, *No Apocalypse,* 28.

98 Derrida, *Of Grammatology,* 9.

99 Ibid.

3. DISTRIBUTED DENIAL OF SERVICE

1 Siegfried Zielinski, "The Media Have Become Superfluous," *Continent* 3, no. 1 (2013): 2–6.

2 Galloway, *Protocol,* 17, suggests that even attempts at resisting protocol tend to further its aims as it is designed to recuperate failures and transform accordingly. Thus, he concludes, "it is through protocol that one must guide one's efforts, not against it."

3 David Sanger and Eric Schmitt, "Spy Agency Consensus Grows That Russia Hacked D.N.C.," *New York Times,* July 26, 2016.

4 Diffie and Landau, *Privacy on the Line*; Levy, *Crypto.*

5 Levy, *Crypto,* 146–54.

6 Diffie and Landau, *Privacy on the Line,* 120–24.

7 Ibid., 255–56.

8 Ibid.

9   Ibid., 249–50.

10   Ibid., 254.

11   Julian Assange, Jacob Appelbaum, Andy Müller-Maguhn, and Jérémie Zimmermann, *Cypherpunks: Freedom and the Future of the Internet* (New York: Or Books, 2012), "Introduction: A Call to Cryptographic Arms."

12   Mohit Arora, "How Secure Is AES against Brute Force Attacks?," *EE Times,* May 7, 2012.

13   Stiegler, *Technics and Time,* 1:75.

14   There is a possibility that the invention of quantum computers could alter the balance, "breaking" a whole number of currently used cryptographic systems, but even such a development would likely usher in widespread adoption of new quantum cryptographic methods continuing this maieutic process.

15   Deleuze, *Foucault,* 36–37.

16   Deleuze explicitly links the abstract machine and the diagram in multiple places. In *Foucault,* he says, "The diagram is no longer an auditory or visual archive but a map, a cartography that is coextensive with the whole social field. It is an abstract machine" (34).

17   Ibid.

18   Assange et al., *Cypherpunks,* "Introduction: A Call to Cryptographic Arms."

19   Ibid.

20   Zetter outlines some of the earlier conspiracy theories about NSA back doors in encryption standards (including DES) and also suggests that in relation to Dual_EC_DRBG (see later), there is still an ongoing debate about whether the flaw in the algorithm was intentional or simply a horrible mistake. Kim Zetter, "How a Crypto 'Backdoor' Pitted the Tech World against the NSA," *Wired,* September 24, 2013, http://www.wired .com/2013/09/nsa-backdoor/.

21   James Ball, Julian Borger, and Glenn Greenwald, "Revealed: How US and UK Spy Agencies Defeat Internet Privacy and Security," September 5, 2013, http://www.theguardian.com/world/2013/sep/05/nsa-gchq-encryption -codes-security.

22   Kim Zetter, "RSA Tells Its Developer Customers: Stop Using NSA-Linked Algorithm," *Wired,* September 19, 2013.

23   Bruce Schneier, "The NSA Is Breaking Most Encryption on the Internet," *Schneier on Security* (blog), September 5, 2013, https://www.schneier .com/.

24   Galloway, *Protocol,* 245, notes that the threat of digital media is not pri-

marily the threat of the state or the market but rather the forces unleashed by the diagrammatic shape of society itself. Likewise, for Kittler (and to a lesser extent Zielinski), it is media and mediatic arrangements—the flow of information across technology—rather than the relationship between the state and population that determine how power functions. Despite this, Foucault's insights are critical to understanding digital communication systems and the power of various organizational diagrams for two reasons. First, to understand Deleuze's insights into societies of control, they must be contextualized in relation to Foucault's work. Second, these media and technologies are operationalized both through law and cyberwar to manage the state's relation to its population.

25   Michel Foucault, *Security, Territory, Population: Lectures at the Collège de France, 1977–78,* ed. Michel Senellart, François Ewald, and Alessandro Fontana (Basingstoke, U.K.: Palgrave Macmillan, 2007), 8.

26   Ibid., 20.

27   Ibid., 21.

28   Ibid., 169.

29   Ibid., 185.

30   Ibid., 263.

31   Ibid., 346.

32   Foucault, *Society Must Be Defended,* 253.

33   Ibid., 242.

34   Gilles Deleuze, "Postscript on the Societies of Control," *October* 59 (Winter 1992): 4.

35   Ibid.

36   Ibid., 5.

37   Ibid.

38   Galloway, *Protocol,* 87. Galloway, like Deleuze, drops security out of the historical progression. He offers Foucault's historical periodization as consisting of two parts: sovereignty and discipline. Ibid., 3.

39   Hardt, leaving out apparatuses of security like Deleuze, goes even further than Galloway, writing, "Deleuze claims to be following Foucault in this insight, but I must admit it is difficult to find anywhere in Foucault's opus (the books, essays, or interviews) a clear expression of the passage from disciplinary society to the society of control." Such a claim misses the entire development of security and biopower. In not engaging Foucault's work, there is a risk that one overlooks some of the most incisive writing for theorizing this shift. Moreover, understanding Deleuze's position in relation to Foucault's full development can best elucidate what is unique

in Deleuze's writing about control. Michael Hardt, "The Global Society of Control," *Discourse* 20, no. 3 (1998): 139.

40   See Grégoire Chamayou, *The Theory of the Drone,* esp. "Pattern-of-Life Analysis," 42–51.

41   Cora Currier and Justin Elliott, "The Drone War Doctrine We Still Know Nothing About," *Pro Publica,* February 26, 2013, http://www.propublica .org/article/drone-war-doctrine-we-know-nothing-about.

42   Galloway, *Interface Effect,* 91.

43   Hallward contends that the critical difference between Deleuze and Foucault is one between the singular (Deleuze) and the specific (Foucault). He argues that "a specific individual is one which exists as part of a relationship to a context, to other individuals and to itself, a singular individual is one which like a Creator-god transcends all such relations." Peter Hallward, "The Limits of Individuation, or How to Distinguish Deleuze and Foucault," *Angelaki: Journal of Theoretical Humanities* 5, no. 2 (2000): 93. In this way, we can understand control for Deleuze as an unfortunate reduction of the subject to the specific or to its environment. Thus, to understand the subject of control for Deleuze, it is important to stress, first, the relationship to Foucault's conception of security and, second, Deleuze's concept of the subject vis-à-vis control. The Deleuzian subject thus points to both what is critical and dangerous within the conditions of control, namely, the reduction of a subject, whom Deleuze would like to be singular, to the specific (i.e., its modulation). What ultimately fails in control is the impossibility of the reduction of the singular to the specific, but at the same time, what makes it so violent is the desire for this reduction.

44   Gregory Bateson, "The Cybernetics of 'Self': A Theory of Alcoholism," *Psychiatry* 34, no. 1 (1971): 14–15.

45   Levy, *Crypto,* 109–11.

46   Hardt, "Global Society of Control," 140.

47   Jens Schröter, "The Internet and 'Frictionless Capitalism,'" *Triple C* 10, no. 2 (2012): 302–12.

48   Julian Assange, "The Non Linear Effects of Leaks on Unjust Forms of Governance," December 2006, http://cryptome.org/0002/ja-conspiracies .pdf.

49   Ibid.

50   Julian Assange, "Conspiracy as Governance," December 2006, http:// cryptome.org/0002/ja-conspiracies.pdf.

51   Manuel de Landa, *War in the Age of Intelligent Machines* (New York: Zone Books, 1991), 191.

52   Galloway and Thacker, *Exploit,* 31.

53   Foucault eloquently suggests the impossibility of such a homogenous closed space and the importance of theorizing multiple spatialities in his essay on heterotopias. He states, "The space in which we live, which draws us out of ourselves, in which the erosion of our lives, our time and our history occurs, the space that claws and gnaws at us, is also, in itself, a heterogeneous space." Michel Foucault, "Of Other Spaces: Utopias and Heterotopias," trans. Jay Miskowiec, *Diacritics* 16, no. 1 (1986): 23.

54   Hardt, "Global Society of Control," 143.

55   Brian Massumi, "The Remains of the Day," Histories of Violence, 2012, http://historiesofviolence.com/.

56   Malabou, *Future of Hegel,* 192–93.

57   Justin Joque, "Cyber-Catastrophe: Towards a New Pedagogy of Entropy," in *Pedagogies of Disaster,* ed. Vincent W. J. van Gerven Oei, Adam Staley Groves, and Nico Jenkins (Brooklyn, N.Y.: Punctum Books, 2013).

58   Arora, "How Secure Is AES?"

59   Derrida, *Rogues,* 142.

60   Jacques Derrida and Giovanna Borradori, "Autoimmunity: Real and Symbolic Suicides: A Dialogue with Jacques Derrida," in *Philosophy in a Time of Terror: Dialogues with Jürgen Habermas and Jacques Derrida,* ed. Giovanna Borradori (Chicago: University of Chicago, 2004), 134. Likewise, Chun, in "Crisis," 99, argues that digital media collapse decision-making to the programmed response to crises: "What we experience is arguably not a real decision but rather one already decided in a perhaps unforeseen manner: increasingly, our decisions are like actions in a video game. They are immediately felt, affective, and based on our actions, and yet at the same time programmed."

61   Derrida, *Rogues,* 135.

62   Agamben, reading Schmitt, argues that the entire Western juridical tradition is founded on the function of this sovereign exception. Giorgio Agamben, *State of Exception,* trans. Kevin Attell (Chicago: University of Chicago Press, 2005).

63   John Caputo, "Without Sovereignty, without Being: Unconditionality, the Coming God, and Derrida's Democracy to Come," *Journal for Cultural and Religious Theory* 4, no. 3 (2003): 14.

64   Contrary to this position, Hägglund, *Radical Atheism,* 183, suggests that "the traditional notion of the unconditional as a sovereign instance (which is the foundation of Schmitt's decisionism) is therefore quite incompatible with Derrida's thinking of the unconditional. For Derrida, what is unconditional is the exposure to the undecidable coming of time, which

compromises the sovereignty of every instance a priori . . . the uncondi-
tional coming of time deconstructs the ideal of sovereignty from within." Here Hägglund faces the same difficulty that besets Derrida and Caputo; the sovereign exception (in Schmitt's sense) is precisely a response to the exposure of the undecidable coming of time. The sovereign nullifies the law because the program of the law can never account for the to-come of the event. The impossibility of sovereignty to account for the unde- cidable coming of time is what ties the law or norm to the necessity of the sovereign exception. Between Caputo and Hägglund, sovereignty is asserted to be different from the unconditional, in the first case because the unconditional is more sovereign (e.g., never compromises with being) and in the second case because sovereign power is never confronted with the unknown. In both cases, the desire to maintain a decision makes it increasingly difficult to do away with a notion of sovereignty.

65   Ibid.

66   Foucault, *Security, Territory, Population*, 23.

67   Stiegler, *Technics and Time*, 1:234.

68   This subject is perhaps also what Schirmacher calls Homo Generator, that subject that creates itself through modern technology needing neither Being nor certainty. "Homo Generator—Militant Media and Postmod- ern Technology," in *Culture on the Brink: Ideologies of Technology,* ed. Gretchen Bender and Timothy Duckrey (New York: New Press, 1994), 65–79.

69   See Alexander Galloway, "The Cybernetic Hypothesis," *Differences* 25, no. 1 (2014): 107–31.

70   Martin Heidegger, "The End of Philosophy and the Task of Thinking," in *Basic Writings: From "Being and Time" (1927) to "The Task of Thinking" (1964),* ed. David Krell (New York: Harper and Row, 1977), 434.

71   Already with second-wave cybernetics, there began to be an increasingly strong realization that no system could be objectively observed since the observer always became part of the system. See Hayles, *How We Became Posthuman*, 131–59.

72   Deleuze, *Foucault*, 132.

73   Jacques Derrida, "Circumfessions," in *Jacques Derrida,* by Geoffrey Bennington and Jacques Derrida (Chicago: University of Chicago Press, 1993), 31.

4. SPEAR PHISHING

1   Gabriella Coleman, *Hacker, Hoaxer, Whistleblower, Spy: The Many Faces of Anonymous* (New York: Verso, 2014); Parmy Olson, *We Are Anonymous: Inside the Hacker World of Lulzsec, Anonymous, and the Global Cyber Insurgency* (New York: Little, Brown, 2012).

2   Coleman, *Hacker,* 16.

3   Charles Arthur, Dan Sabbagh, and Sandra Laville, "LulzSec Leader Sabu Was Working for Us, Says FBI," *The Guardian,* March 6, 2012, http://www.theguardian.com/technology/2012/mar/06/lulzsec-sabu-working-for-us-fbi.

4   Olson, *We Are Anonymous,* 392.

5   Jeremy Hammond, "Statement at November 2014 Sentencing," as quoted in Coleman, *Hacker,* 359.

6   Nigel Parry, "Sacrificing Stratfor: How the FBI Waited Three Weeks to Close the Stable Door," Nigelparry.com, March 25, 2012, http://web.archive.org/web/20130414020834/http://nigelparry.com/news/sacrificing-stratfor.shtml.

7   Sabu, as quoted in Arthur et al., "LulzSec Leader Sabu Was Working for Us."

8   Coleman, *Hacker,* 356.

9   Kittler, *Gramophone, Film, Typewriter,* 257.

10   Derrida and Borradori, "Autoimmunity," 94.

11   Ibid., 112.

12   Derrida, *Rogues,* 109.

13   Katrina vanden Heuvel and Stephen F. Cohen, "Edward Snowden: A 'Nation' Interview," *The Nation,* October 28, 2014, http://www.thenation.com/article/186129/snowden-exile-exclusive-interview.

14   The court refused to allow a transcript to be published, so this quote is drawn from Alexa O'Brien's transcript. Chelsea Manning, "Bradley Manning's Personal Statement to Court Martial: Full Text," *The Guardian,* March 1, 2013, http://www.theguardian.com/world/2013/mar/01/bradley-manning-wikileaks-statement-full-text.

15   Greenberg, *This Machine Kills Secrets,* 7–8.

16   Eric Hughes, "A Cypherpunk's Manifesto," March 9, 1993, http://www.activism.net/cypherpunk/manifesto.html.

17   Greenberg, *This Machine Kills Secrets,* 46.

18   Derrida, "Plato's Pharmacy," 168.

way of understanding the real that would suggest that the real as symbolic void and the real as material are not so far apart. First, it is important to note that the symbolic is always a trace, inscribed outside of the body, written into a material support. Thus, in a physical sense, the symbolic is always material. It is inscribed within our mediatic world. Second, what cracks (in a Derridean sense) the symbolic is perhaps its always already being inscribed in insecure media/materiality. Representation, in Zupančič's sense, exceeds itself precisely because it exists outside of itself, in inscription. The real is not, then, material in the simple sense of being beyond representation; rather, the real is material insomuch as the real-materiality of the symbolic precludes the possibility of it totalizing itself and guarantees its vulnerability.

24   Tiziana Terranova, *Network Culture: Politics for the Information Age* (New York: Pluto Press, 2004), 142.

25   Michel Foucault, *The Birth of Biopolitics: Lectures at the Collège de France, 1978–79*, ed. Michel Senellart, trans. Graham Burchell (Basingstoke, U.K.: Palgrave Macmillan, 2008), 35.

26   Raley, *Tactical Media*, 12.

27   Der Derian, in *Anti-diplomacy*, 5, argues that in our post–Cold War world, diplomacy and war "respond better to *interpretation* than *verification*."

28   Chris Anderson, "The End of Theory: The Data Deluge Makes the Scientific Method Obsolete," *Wired,* June 23, 2008.

29   See, e.g., Steve Kelling, Wesley M. Hochachka, Daniel Fink, Mirek Riedewald, Rich Caruana, Grant Ballard, and Giles Hooker, "Data-Intensive Science: A New Paradigm for Biodiversity Studies," *BioScience* 59, no. 7 (2009): 613–20; Sabina Leonelli, "Introduction: Making Sense of Data-Driven Research in the Biological and Biomedical Sciences," *Studies in History and Philosophy of Biological and Biomedical Sciences* 43, no. 1 (2012): 1–3.

30   Bowker makes this connection between Latour's and Anderson's positions eloquently. Geoffrey Bowker, "Big Data, Big Questions| The Theory/Data Thing," *International Journal of Communication* 8 (2014): 5.

31   Stephen Best and Sharon Marcus, "Surface Reading: An Introduction," *Representations* 108, no. 1 (2009): 17.

32   Derrida, *Rogues*, 45.

33   Galloway likewise attempts to theorize a networked subject that would not be a fetishization of sovereign power. He finds inspiration in Agamben's notion of "whatever being." He explicitly opposes this generic subject to the "postfordist economic subject," stating, "It would be a mistake to

think that the whatever is merely the fully unique, customized, qualitatively special postfordist consumer . . . each woman a woman consumer, each black a black consumer, each gay a gay consumer, each chicano a chicano consumer." Galloway, *Interface Effect,* 140. But it is not entirely clear how this generic subject does not merely collapse back into this economic subject; its "being such as it is," in Agamben's words, seems eerily similar to the subject of control, a consumer or a target of state violence whose microidentity is calculated in real time.

34   Derrida, *Rogues,* 10–11.

35   In one of his last seminars, published in two volumes as *The Beast and the Sovereign,* trans. Geoffrey Bennington (Chicago: University of Chicago Press, 2010), Derrida takes up the term *automatic,* especially in his discussion of the marionette. The distinction between text and program haunts the relationship between animal and human he works on there. Here he draws possibly the closest to deconstructing the opposition between program and text, but on the precipice of this deconstruction, he returns to work on the opposition between animal and human. He criticizes Lacan for opposing the animal *reaction* to human *response* but demurs from pushing this opposition beyond the border between human and animal to the one between animal and machine.

36   Cox, *Speaking Code,* 109. Cox likewise concludes that subjects and programs write themselves in analogous ways: "both subjectivity and code recursively write their own instrumentation."

37   Derrida, *Rogues,* 148.

38   Ibid.

39   Ibid., 152.

40   Lacan, "Instance of the Letter," 430.

41   Fink says of Lacan's models of language developed in the afterword to the seminar on the purloined letter that "few attempts have yet been made to outline the ramifications of these models, and indeed, they present a view of the functioning of language that is quite unfamiliar to anyone who is not versed in computer languages." Bruce Fink, *The Lacanian Subject: Between Language and Jouissance* (Princeton, N.J.: Princeton University Press, 1995), 16.

42   Jacques Lacan, *On Feminine Sexuality: The Limits of Love and Knowledge, Seminar XX,* ed. Jacques-Alain Miller, trans. Bruce Fink (New York: W. W. Norton, 1998), 50.

43   Ibid., 142.

44   Ibid., 122.

45   Ibid., 82.

46   There is a certain risk in proceeding this way, of turning what in Lacan is in many ways the structure of the unconscious into a specific historical and technologically mediated subject or inversely suggesting in some way that Lacan predicted the subject of global networked technology. In the light of this risk, it should be pointed out that in many ways the Lacanian subject is a cybernetic subject, given his ties to the field, along with his claims that the subject is produced in relation to technology. Flieger, invoking the multiple networks and spatialities in Lacan's work, explicitly ties it to cybernetics. Jerry Flieger, *Is Oedipus Online? Siting Freud after Freud* (Cambridge, Mass.: MIT Press, 2005), 11. Along these lines, texts, such as Flieger's and others' (e.g., Slavoj Žižek, "Cyberspace, or the Unbearable Closure of Being," *Pretexts: Studies in Writing and Culture* 6, no. 1 [1997]: 53–79), have taken up the issue in much more depth of how technologies, media, and networks have reshaped Freudian and Lacanian dynamics.

47   Lacan, "Seminar on 'The Purloined Letter,'" in *Ecrits,* 45.

48   Laplanche translates *Wiederholungswang* as *compulsion de répétition* in his 2006 translation of *Beyond the Pleasure Principle*. In a slightly different translation, but still suggesting something much closer to Laplanche than Lacan, Jankélévitch's 1927 translation of *Beyond the Pleasure Principle* uses *contrainte de répétition*. Lacan borrows the translation as *automatisme* from French psychiatry, especially Janet and Clérambault. Dylan Evans, *An Introductory Dictionary of Lacanian Psychoanalysis* (London: Routledge, 1996), 167.

49   The aim is not to rehash debates around the Turing test, which suggests that if a computer and human are indistinguishable to a human, then the computer is "intelligent," but rather to ask what happens to the subject when its desires, actions, and habits become predictable by aggregating the information it leaves behind in the environment (French provides a well-documented summary of debates surrounding the Turing test; see Robert French, "The Turing Test: The First 50 Years," *Trends in Cognitive Science* 4, no. 3 [2000]: 115–22).

50   Max Tegmark, "Consciousness as a State of Matter," arXiv preprint arXiv:1401.1219 (2014), 1.

51   Lacan, "Purloined Letter," 21.

52   Lacan does suggest that the subject is capable of resistance, especially in his discussions of Antigone and, as will be explained later, his theory of *tuchē*. Jacques Lacan, *The Ethics of Psychoanalysis, Seminar VII, 1959–1960,*

ed. Jacques-Alain Miller, trans. Dennis Potter (New York: W. W. Norton, 1992). Despite these possible modes of resistance, the Lacanian subject is still an overwhelmingly determined and predictable subject in comparison to the Derridean subject.

53 Lacan, "Purloined Letter," 7.

54 Ibid., 30.

55 Ibid., 15–16.

56 Ibid., 17.

57 Another danger of "surface reading" should be noted here, namely, that this exhaustive exposure of surfaces, especially without the proper context of depth, risks engendering what Der Derian calls "the paranoia of cyberspace." We end up able to "see and hear the other, but imperfectly and partially—below our rising expectations. This can induce paranoid behavior—that is, reasoning correctly but from incorrect premises." Der Derian, *Anti-diplomacy*, 33.

58 Lacan, "Purloined Letter," 27.

59 Ibid., 17.

60 Best and Marcus, "Surface Reading," 18.

61 Lacan, "Purloined Letter," 21.

62 Barbara Johnson, "The Frame of Reference: Poe, Lacan, Derrida," *Yale French Studies* 55/56 (1977): 467.

63 Jacques Derrida, "The Purveyor of Truth," *Yale French Studies*, no. 52 (1975): 67.

64 Ibid., 50.

65 Ibid., 48.

66 Johnson, "Frame of Reference," 465.

67 Derrida, "Purveyor of Truth," 65–66.

68 Ibid., 66.

69 Ibid., 57.

70 Ibid., 107.

71 Ibid., 64.

72 Johnson, "Frame of Reference," 502.

73 Ibid., 477.

74 Ibid., 485.

75 Derrida, "Purveyor of Truth," 99n36.

76 Lacan, "Purloined Letter," 14.

77 Jacques Derrida, "For the Love of Lacan," *Cardozo Law Review* 16 (1994): 702.

78 Derrida suggests this directly in relation to the play of différance: "Contrary to the metaphysical, dialectical, 'Hegelian' interpretation of the

economic movement of *différance,* we must conceive of a play in which whoever loses wins, and in which one loses and wins on every turn." Derrida, *Margins of Philosophy,* 20.

79   Johnson, "Frame of Reference," 469.

80   Derrida, "Purveyor of Truth," 109.

81   Johnson notes this in her reading as one of the main exclusions that Derrida cuts out in his framing of Lacan's seminar. Johnson, "Frame of Reference," 465.

82   Fink provides an extensive description of this system and its implications in two appendices to *The Lacanian Subject,* 153–72.

83   Lacan, "Purloined Letter," 28–29. Greek transliteration has been modified.

84   Aristotle, *Physics,* Book II, Parts 4–6.

85   Lacan, *Seminar XI,* 53–54.

86   Paul Verhaeghe "Causation and Destitution of a Pre-ontological Non-entity: On the Lacanian Subject," in *Key Concepts of Lacanian Psychoanalysis,* ed. Dany Nobus (New York: Other Press, 1998), 172.

87   Lacan, *Seminar XX,* 94.

88   Johnson, "Frame of Reference," 504.

89   Jacques Derrida, "My Chances," in *Taking Chances: Derrida, Psychoanalysis, and Literature,* ed. Joseph H. Smith and William Kerrigan (Baltimore: Johns Hopkins University Press, 1988), 2.

90   Derrida here suggests something along the lines of Hayles's "dialectic of randomness and pattern," wherein the relation between presence and absence is supplemented by a play between pattern and randomness but what Lacan and Derrida, in the moments that we hear the machinic force of deconstruction at work in this writing, suggest is that this dialectic cannot hold and is given over to deconstruction. Hayles, *How We Became Posthuman,* 25–29.

91   Caputo describes Derrida's unconditional with a nearly Lacanian structure (without referring to Lacan): "summoned by their voice. Something, which is not a thing, lays an unconditional *claim* upon us—*uns in Anspruch nehmen,* as Heidegger would say—not as a sovereign power in the order of being that invades and overpowers us but as a summons that provokes us, a call that incites us, a promise that lures us and awakens our desire. Something of unconditional appeal, without the force of sovereignty." After Caputo, "Without Sovereignty," 14.

92   Nate Silver, *The Signal and the Noise: Why So Many Predictions Fail but Some Don't* (New York: Penguin, 2012), 276–79.

93   Derrida, *Rogues,* 152.

94   Michel Serres, *The Parasite*, trans. Lawrence Schehr (Minneapolis: University of Minnesota Press, 2007), 36.

CONCLUSION

1   Kaspersky Lab, "Equation Group: The Crown Creator of Cyber-Espionage," *Virus News*, February 16, 2015, http://www.kaspersky.com/.

2   Ibid.

3   Costin Raiu, quoted ibid.

4   Kaspersky Lab, "Equation Group: Questions and Answers Version 1.5," February 2015, https://securelist.com/.

5   Kaspersky Lab, "Equation Group: The Crown Creator."

6   F-Secure Labs, "The Equation Group Equals NSA/IRATEMONK," February 17, 2015, https://www.f-secure.com/.

7   Dan Goodin, "New Smoking Gun Further Ties NSA to Omnipotent 'Equation Group' Hackers," *Ars Technica*, March 11, 2015, http://ars technica.com/security/2015/03/new-smoking-gun-further-ties-nsa-to -omnipotent-equation-group-hackers/.

8   Kaspersky Lab, "Equation Group: The Crown Creator."

9   The module has been named DoubleFantasy by Kaspersky Lab. See "Equation Group: Questions and Answers."

10   Bruce Schneier, "IRATEMONK: NSA Exploit of the Day," *Schneier on Security* (blog), January 2014, https://www.schneier.com/.

11   Chun, "Crisis," refers to this as the gap between code and action.

12   Kaspersky Lab, "Equation Group: Questions and Answers."

13   Derrida, *Rogues,* 154.

14   Ibid.

15   Derrida, *Of Grammatology,* 8.

16   Ibid.

17   Derrida, *Margins of Philosophy,* 7.

18   Deleuze, *Foucault,* 119.

19   Derrida, *Margins of Philosophy,* 7.

Index

abstract machines: of cryptography, 116–18, 120; and political *technē*, 118–21; power of, 140, 146, 155; and sovereignty, 143–44; uncertainty of, 157, 160; use of term, 117

Adams, James, 70–71

Advanced Encryption Standard (AES), 115, 118, 192

Advanced Persistent Threat 1 (APT1), 50

AES. *See* Advanced Encryption Standard

allopoietic systems, 77

Andersen, Chris, 162–63, 164–65, 174

Anonymous, 32, 150–54, 189

apocalypses, 31, 73, 109

APT1. *See* Advanced Persistent Threat 1

arche-writing, 73–74, 92–93, 96–98, 102, 196, 224n73, 224n75

Aristotle, 183

Arms Export Control Act, 113

Arnett, Eric H., 2–3

Arquilla, John, 3, 28–29, 71

Assange, Julian, 116–19, 135–37, 155–57, 159, 189

attack-vectors, 27, 45, 51, 67, 83, 106, 176, 178, 191

authentication. *See* identity/ authentication

autoimmunity, 26, 135, 149, 153–55, 159, 164, 177, 188, 194, 195

automaticity, 29, 166, 168, 169–70, 175, 184, 186, 187–89

automaton, 166, 183–87

autopoietic systems, 77–79, 124, 155, 168, 179

Ban Ki-moon, 9

Bassel, Eric, 57

Bateson, Gregory, 131

battle space: in cyberwar, 3–4, 42, 46, 48, 53, 57–58, 79, 133; elements of, 133; expansion of, 64–65; high-dimensional, 63–66, 67

Baudrillard, Jean, 12

Best, Stephen, 163, 175

biopower, use of term, 127–28

Boltanski, Luc, 68

buffer overflows, 18, 19–20, 31–32

Bush, George W., 44

calculation: as function of computers, 15; as incalculable, 82, 139–42, 166–67; and perfect knowledge, 138–39; and subject, 165–68; undecidability of, 24–26;

(continued from page ii)

19   As Gasché argues in "Infrastructures and Systematicity," deconstruction is not about completely free play but rigorously traces the inner logic of texts and contexts.

20   Jacques Lacan, "The Instance of the Letter in the Unconscious," in *Ecrits: The First Complete Edition in English,* trans. Bruce Fink (New York: W. W. Norton, 2006), 436.

21   Lacan suggests that even lies and deception speak to the truth of the unconscious: "If I have said that the unconscious is the Other's discourse (with a capital O), it is in order to indicate the beyond in which the recognition of desire is tied to the desire for recognition. In other words, this other is the Other that even my lie invokes as a guarantor of the truth in which my lie subsists." Ibid.

22   Jacques Lacan, *The Four Fundamental Concepts of Psycho-analysis: Seminar XI,* ed. Jacques-Alain Miller, trans. Alan Sheridan (New York: W. W. Norton, 1978). Lacan elaborates this most clearly in the seminar on the purloined letter, as we shall see shortly.

23   One could define the Lacanian real in multiple ways. Zupančič argues (in an article building on and taking issue with Badiou's interpretation of the real), "Here, representation as such is a wandering excess over itself; representation is the infinite tarrying with the excess that springs not simply from what is or is not represented (its 'object'), but from this act of representation itself, from its own inherent 'crack' or inconsistency. The Real is not something outside or beyond representation, but is the very crack of representation," thus explicitly denying that the real is some thing or material that escapes symbolization. Alenka Zupančič, "The Fifth Condition," in *Think Again: Alain Badiou and the Future of Philosophy,* ed. Peter Hallward (London: Continuum, 2004), 199. Likewise, Žižek suggests that this real is a void: "the Real Thing is ultimately another name for the Void." Slavoj Žižek, "Welcome to the Desert of the Real," in *The Universal Exception,* ed. Rex Butler and Scott Stephens (London: Continuum, 2006), 267. All of these descriptions suggest important elements of this real that resist or crack the symbolic. Despite these interpretations, Kittler, in *Gramophone, Film, Typewriter,* 16, suggests in a more media-centric manner, "Machines take over functions of the central nervous system, and no longer, as in times past, merely those of muscles. And with this differentiation—and not with steam engines and railroads—a clear division occurs between matter and information, the real and the symbolic." Despite the differences between Kittler's material description of the real and Zupančič's and Žižek's definitions, there is a

Justin Joque is the data visualization librarian at the University of Michigan. He holds a master's degree of science of information from the University of Michigan, with a focus on information analysis and retrieval, and a PhD in media and communication from the European Graduate School.

Catherine Malabou is a philosopher and professor in the philosophy department at the Centre for Research in Modern European Philosophy at Kingston University, London. She is author of *Before Tomorrow: Epigenesis and Rationality* and, with Judith Butler, *You Be My Body for Me: Body, Shape, and Plasticity in Hegel's* Phenomenology of Spirit.